BREAKING OUT

Other books by the author

Beyond Coming Out

BREAKING
OUT

THE COMPLETE GUIDE TO BUILDING AND ENHANCING A POSITIVE GAY IDENTITY FOR MEN AND WOMEN

KEVIN ALDERSON PHD., C. PSYCH.

INSOMNIAC PRESS

Edited by Richard Almonte
Copy edited by Adrienne Weiss
Designed by Mike O'Connor

National Library of Canada Cataloguing in Publication Data

Alderson, Kevin George
    Breaking out : the complete guide to building a positive gay identity for men and
    women

Includes bibliographical references.
ISBN 1-894663-31-4

    1. Gays—Identity. I. Title.

HQ76.25.A43 2002   305.9'0664   C2002-903810-3

The publisher gratefully acknowledges the support of the Canada Council, the Ontario Arts Council and the Department of Canadian Heritage through the Book Publishing Industry Development Program.

Printed and bound in Canada

Insomniac Press
192 Spadina Avenue, Suite 403
Toronto, Ontario, Canada, M5T 2C2
www.insomniacpress.com

I dedicate this book to the men, women and children who have taught me what it means to have a positive gay identity, and to God who I know loves me with all of my strengths and frailties.

"I am but a flower, still waiting to fully blossom."

CONTENTS

Author Note 7 • *Preface* 11 • *Introduction: How to Use This Book* 14

Part 1 The Inside of Breaking Out

Chapter 1 Putting the Enemy to Sleep 25
Chapter 2 Learning to Like Yourself 35
Chapter 3 Squashing Denial 47
Chapter 4 Reclaiming Your Self 58
Chapter 5 Relinquishing the Lies That Haunt You 69
Chapter 6 Releasing Your Personal Power 80
Chapter 7 Struggling with Spirituality and Religion 90

Part II The Outside of Breaking Out

Section One—Stepping Into the Gay World
Chapter 8 The Joy of Being Gay 105
Chapter 9 Friendships That Count 116
Chapter 10 The Art of Successful Dating 126
Chapter 11 Having Great Sex 138
Chapter 12 Creating Sustainable Relationships 149
Section Two—Reconnecting with the Straight World
Chapter 13 Breaking the Silence 165
Chapter 14 Breaking Out of the Family Closet 175

Part III Special Concerns of Adolescents

Chapter 15 The Inside of Being a Gay Adolescent 189
Chapter 16 The Outside of Being a Gay Adolescent 200

Part IV Today and Tomorrow

Chapter 17 Breaking Out Around the World 213

Epilogue: Final Thoughts and Reflections 216
References 218

Appendix A How Do I Know If I Am Gay? 228 • *Appendix B Choosing a Therapist* 230
Appendix C Internet Resources 232 • *Appendix D Recommended Readings* 233
Appendix E Preventing HIV/AIDS Update 235

AUTHOR NOTE

My Story

If you read my first book, *Beyond Coming Out*, you already know more about me than my mother does. Not that I withhold much from her, but she has to show an interest first.

I was born in Edmonton, Alberta, Canada in 1956. That year also saw the beginning of A & W, and I still feel an allegiance to the burger family as though I belonged to it myself. Family is really important to me now, but it reaches farther than I ever thought it could when I was a younger person. There is far more family out there than you and I ever imagined.

A lot of rednecks traditionally lived in Alberta, and many still do. When I used to gaze at gorgeous young men when I was young, I knew that I would likely lose my small bits if I was found out. The journey into denial and minimizing my feelings was no small undertaking. Neither was the task of coming out at age 36, which meant I had to uncover this denial and my repressed feelings. Sooner or later, you have to clean out the garbage that fills the crevices in your psyche.

My wife and I divorced a few years ago. After the initial shock, she and I have resumed a friendship we have known for years. I am still proud of her, and I still love her. But I also love, and am in love romantically, with my same-sex partner of over six years.

I was an intellectual child, although no one (including myself) knew it at the time. I wasn't nurtured to become an academic, but something inside pushed me toward this. In retrospect, I think I was overcompensating for having terrible self-esteem and a self-concept that I wouldn't wish on anyone. So I attended the University of Calgary right out of high school.

I soon decided to pursue a Bachelor of Arts degree in psychology with a minor in sociology. I love both subjects and many others. Psychology helps you see more deeply into people's behaviour, whereas sociology helps you see the bigger picture—the context in which human behaviour occurs.

After graduating, I worked for a few years before returning for round two—a masters degree in clinical psychology. Those were still the days when they were using aversion therapy, mostly mild electric shocks, to try to convert homosexual desire into heterosexual lust. Still preferable to castration, I suppose. I was never part of this type of therapy. I still wasn't admitting to myself that I was strongly attracted sexually to men.

After that degree, I was fortunate enough to get hired at Mount Royal College (MRC) where I stayed for the next 16 years. I never felt so much at home, yet a part of me was yearning for something greater. In 1995, after securing a sabbatical from work and acceptance into the University of Alberta, I went for round three—this time, a Ph.D. in counselling psychology. I had come out in 1993, and I decided to learn as much as I could about gay men and lesbian women while I attended university once more.

Boy did I learn. I remember when two classmates told me to be careful whom I told in the department about my research interests. When I went looking for a dissertation supervisor, I remember one professor tried to encourage me to drop the idea of gay studies and pursue health psychology instead. What he didn't know is that I had been there many times before. After denying my attractions and minimizing my feelings for 36 years, I wasn't prepared to do it anymore, regardless of the consequence. In fact there was no consequence that I could detect. I sailed through the Ph.D. and finished first in my class. That was an experience I'll never forget. I am forever grateful that MRC gave me two years away from work to follow the beckoning call of my passion, dream and soul.

I returned to MRC in 1997, just in time for my mid-life crisis. I loved the college, but a part of me needed more. So I wrote *Beyond Coming Out*. That changed my life because then I knew I wanted to write more than anything else. In June 2002, the University of Calgary offered me an opportunity to become an assistant professor of counselling psychology. I accepted. My specialty is gay studies and I am keenly interested in all aspects of human sexuality.

Now I have been a licensed psychologist for 16 years. I have worked with clients with nearly every problem you can imagine. I most enjoy working with family—my gay family, that is. With them, I feel the closest affinity. I have worked with hundreds of gay men and lesbian women. Not just for identity concerns, but more often for general human concerns.

My Beliefs About Change

Life experience shapes us. Coming out was a profound experience for me, and it had profound consequences. It helped shape my view of what is helpful to people.

As a therapist, I believe the most important quality is congruence, which means being who I am and being real in all of my dealings with people. In essence, I strive to be a person who changes little while fulfilling various life roles. I like to think that the "Kevin" you come to know through my writing is not markedly different from the "Kevin" that others get to know, whether it be my lover, children, friends, colleagues or clients. To give people a false impression of myself is to deny them the opportunity to see the person I am.

My philosophy of life has been shaped by humanism and feminism. I believe that we are all equal before God and before each other. Without question, we all have distinct traits, characteristics, strengths and weaknesses. Some of us are better at math, and some are better at social studies. Some struggle to be good at anything. My point is, our worth as human beings is never at question, regardless of how remarkable or unremarkable our strengths are relative to our weaknesses.

I also believe that we determine our own fate for the most part, and that we are responsible for living in accordance with our beliefs. I view our basic human nature in positive terms, and I think we strive to achieve positive goals and be persons of good character. Unfortunately, many have not had the privilege of knowing unconditional love, leaving them with insufficient self-esteem and self-love. Most well-meaning parents unwittingly keep their children in a box. Eventually, however, the box is not big enough to contain any of us. In a sense, then, we all need to "break out."

My philosophy of helping has been shaped by my philosophy of life, and by knowledge of various treatment approaches. The approach that can boast the greatest degree of demonstrated success is cognitive behaviour therapy. In fact, many insurance companies in the United States now require that psychological treatment be based on demonstrated success, known as empirically-validated treatments. This book is, in effect, my compilation of cognitive-behavioural techniques aimed at helping you develop a positive gay identity.

When I was in my twenties, I struggled with many life issues due to the large number of anxieties and insecurities I had developed from childhood. Through my own experiences with receiving counselling, I found cognitive-behavioural methods were most helpful in changing my view of myself and others.

The basic tenet of cognitive therapy is that the way we look at things affects the way we feel about them. In other words, our beliefs and interpretations of life events determine our reaction more than the event itself. For example, if you believe you can't live without your mate, and he or she breaks up with you, you feel desperate and depressed. But if your interpretation is that your mate is an over-controlling ass, the break up could be experienced as a positive event, and consequently you feel relieved and free.

Some of the basic assumptions underlying behaviour therapy are that: (1) our behaviour shapes and determines the way we look at things; (2) behaviour that is rewarded tends to be repeated, while behaviour that is ignored or punished tends to extinguish; and (3) some behaviour occurs after it is paired or associated with a signal. As an example of the first point, even if you don't initially share the beliefs of a group you are associating with, you will likely internalize some of their beliefs as you continue your association. If you attended a fundamentalist Christian church while growing up, you likely adopted some of their antigay sentiment.

As an example of the second point, if as a child you were punished every time you showed affection to another child of the same gender, but were praised for showing a child of the opposite sex affection, you learned that it was better to direct your affections one direction and not the other. Until you later challenged your beliefs, it is likely that you began showing more affection to the opposite gender.

Regarding the third point, if as a teenager whenever you talked about having a crush on someone of the same gender your guardian washed your mouth out with soap, you would probably find that later in life, you had to work at overcoming the "bad" taste in your mouth that occurred whenever you redeveloped crushes on same-sex individuals. Most of the exercises in this book follow the principles of cognitive-behaviour theory and therapy, the leading empirically-validated treatment for helping people to change.

My theory and practice has also been influenced by the psychodynamic approach, and I believe it has merit for working with gay people. However, it has not been traditionally gay positive in its approach. Its roots began with Sigmund Freud, who himself believed that gay people were developmentally inferior to heterosexual individuals. Many other theorists since him have seen homosexuality as a mental disorder, sickness or perversion. Philosophically, psychodynamic theory and practice is not based on human equality, and therefore I reject most of its tenets. Furthermore, its complexity does not lend itself well for use by individuals themselves. Consequently, it is not the best approach for use in a self-help book. The aspect of psychodynamic theory that I have retained, however, is in the area of defense mechanisms. For example, denial is one of the defense mechanisms used by gay people before they come out. Denial means not believing basic truths about oneself—truths that are too painful to acknowledge and accept.

A colleague of mine once noted that people change when they need to change. I am also aware that people often change without knowing they have a need or desire to change. People change both through conscious intent and unwittingly because of influences to which they are exposed. For example, many of us have been affected by societal messages that denigrate our gay souls. Nearly every message we hear is meant to force our deepest passions into hiding, while those around us who are heterosexual are often praised for having opposite-sex interests. In effect, we are emotionally abused and spiritually raped during our childhood years. And we change in response to the abuse we received—it pushes our love feelings into denial before our coming out journey can begin.

Within the limits of our genetic endowment, I believe we can become whatever we focus on becoming. The hope of change, and the practice of change, is what inspired me to write this book.

If you end up loving this book, please let me know: if you end up hating it, let my publisher know (just kidding). Either way, I would appreciate your feedback—especially any suggestions for how the next edition could be improved to be even more helpful to others who are building a positive gay identity. E-mail me at alderson@ucalgary.ca.

PREFACE

The world has seen much bigotry posing as morality, even myth posing as science. But the prejudice against homosexuality continues and must never be underestimated; it is one of the most destructive forces of our time.

(Herdt, 1997, 26)

Loneliness can feel like the worst enemy. It's not. The trouble is, you forget the enemy exists until the next time you encounter it.

It happened to me one Friday night—perhaps many Friday nights—as I stood watching the crowd of men two-stepping at a rodeo. I was okay, really, until Steve asked me to dance. Then came the familiar feeling of fear choking back gasps that nobody hears. I felt suddenly alone, yet I had to respond. The word "yes" spilled out, and the next thing I knew I was dancing. I could not take the lead out of fear, yet I did not know how to follow, either. My awkwardness was nothing compared to what my insides were telling me. If I had wanted to be a ballerina in this life, telling my dad would have been easier, far easier, than this. Although I survived that two-step experience, a part of me had to die. I call this part the enemy.

The enemy is commonly called internalized homophobia, and every gay person suffers from it. Our upbringing has helped us internalize the same heterosexual messages as everyone else. Chances are, even our parents are heterosexual, and they often have great difficulty accepting us after our coming out. Their challenge is nothing compared to our own. The oppression within ourselves is much scarier than anything they could possibly feel toward us. Coming out to ourselves is the first step, but what follows?

This is the book that I desperately needed to read after I came out. I know I'm not alone in this. I have met hundreds of gay men and lesbian women, both personally and professionally, each struggling with being positive in a society that relegates them to minority-group status. For many, in fact, the struggle is so deep that they have not been able to view their gay identities positively at all.

This book is for men and women, young and old. It will help you either build or enhance a positive gay identity. Based on thorough research about positive gay identity and on proven practices in self-help psychology, *Breaking Out* shows you how to improve yourself, whether you have been out for a day or for many years.

Don't let me give you a false impression, however, of what this book can do. Having a positive gay identity does not "cure" everything that's difficult about being gay. Some old issues remain, and new ones surface. Gay people, male and female, feel marginalized. Their minority-group status is a genuine obstacle, and results in inequality. This inequality means that many face job loss if "discovered," or that they experience the "invisible ceiling" in their employment, meaning that they are prevented from advancement or promotion. Family relationships can be strained, some-times indefinitely. They may be shamed by others who don't understand them, or by those who don't want to. Homophobia and heterosexism exist nearly everywhere, and their repercussions range from mild (noticing that others avoid you or smirk when you walk by) to life-threatening (gay bashings). Most people in our society do not understand us.

Why, then, would anyone want to develop a positive gay identity—isn't it too much to bear? Wouldn't you be better off if you just kept it to yourself and pretend-ed to be heterosexual for the rest of your life? The answer is absolutely NOT! The psychological consequences are simply too damaging.

The problems I've listed below can be caused by many different factors, but each of these can also be caused by not having developed a positive gay identity. In truth, none of us has been left unscathed. Consequences, and even symptoms, result from having a negative gay identity. Here are examples of problems, some of which you may be facing right now:

Struggling with internalized homophobia   (Chapter 1)
• Negative feelings: anxiety, guilt, shame, disgust, depression and self-loathing
• Poor self-acceptance
• Poor acceptance of others (being judgmental)
• Inability to love yourself completely
Experiencing a negative body image and self-esteem   (Chapter 2)
• Wanting and attempting to be heterosexual
• Feeling uncertain about your sexual orientation
• Motivation problems
Minimizing and denying your feelings   (Chapter 3)
Leading a "split life"   (Chapter 4)
Lying frequently or compulsively   (Chapter 4)
Stereotyping yourself and others   (Chapter 5)
Acting passively and trying too hard to conform   (Chapter 6)
Suffering from conflicts in your spiritual and religious beliefs (Chapter 7)
Having little sense of being part of a positive community (Chapter 8)
Feeling isolated and alone, and facing rejection from others (Chapters 9-10)
Feeling unhappy about dating and its outcome   (Chapter 10)
Having sexual problems, or feeling sexually dissatisfied (Chapter 11)
Encountering relationship difficulties   (Chapter 12)
Feeling afraid to tell others about your sexuality   (Chapters 13-14)
Feeling invisible   (Chapters 13-14)

The problems listed above are dealt with in the chapter(s) indicated to the right. Other problems, besides these, can occur for those who haven't developed positive gay identities. These problems I will call symptoms, meaning that they will likely disappear on their own once the underlying problem is corrected. By working through the exercises contained in this book, most of these symptoms will subside automatically. If that doesn't happen in your case, you probably need professional help. A few suggestions for finding a competent therapist are listed in Appendix B.

What symptoms am I referring to? Perhaps the scariest is if you are feeling suicidal. In this instance, please seek out professional help now, and leave this book for a later time. Every city has a suicide crisis line, and its number is listed on the first page or two of the telephone directory. They can provide some immediate assistance and refer you to those who can provide the necessary long-term help. Research also indicates that gay men are more likely than heterosexual men to attempt suicide. This really speaks to how hard it is to be gay.

Besides suicidal gestures, other symptoms include not having passion in life, lacking a sense of vitality and feeling drained of energy. Having a negative gay identity can lead to all kinds of emotional problems, especially anxiety and depression. These problems can range from mild to severe.

Acting out is an expression often used to describe adolescents who behave in unhealthy or destructive ways because of their underlying emotional distress. Gay adolescents and gay adults with unhealthy identities may also act out their disturbance. Examples include stealing, rampant or irresponsible sexual behaviour (including having unprotected anal intercourse and risking HIV infection), engaging in public sex (where this is their only same-sex outlet and where there is a significant risk of getting arrested), working excessively to avoid dealing with same-sex feelings, compulsive behaviour (addiction to various behaviours like sex, gambling and spending) and alcohol and drug problems.

After having researched the area extensively, I offer the following definition of "positive gay identity":

Individuals who have attained a positive gay identity have developed a high self-regard for themselves as gay persons. They view their gay status as equal to straight status. If given a choice, they would not prefer to be straight over gay, for they have come to value their uniqueness and the richness of life that comes from being themselves. They have integrated their gay identity with their other identities, and having accomplished this, they are "out" in most areas of their lives, except when it is dangerous to do so. They have largely overcome their own internalized homophobia, which frees them to fully love others of the same gender.

Positive gay identity is about liberation, inspiration, courage, strength, nonconformity, acceptance of self, acceptance of others, uniqueness and love. Having a positive gay identity allows you finally to be yourself in every sense of the word. Are you ready to see what that will feel like? Turn the page and begin to break out!

INTRODUCTION

How To Use This Book

This introduction looks at how you can use this book to either build or enhance a positive gay identity. If you haven't already done so, I suggest you read the Preface first. It includes a definition of positive gay identity and important information about this topic.

This book is intended primarily for those who already self-identify as gay or lesbian; those in the process of coming out; and therapists who work with gays and lesbians. If you are still uncertain about whether you are gay or lesbian, read Appendix A and answer the questions there. Regardless of your answers, you might find reading this book and working through its exercises helpful in broadening your mind and in making your decision.

If at the end of reading the book, you remain confused about your sexual identity and still find yourself vacillating, consider getting professional counselling from a therapist. A few suggestions for finding one are located in Appendix B.

As I mentioned in the Preface, this book is based on thorough research about positive gay identity and on proven practices in self-help psychology. The background to the therapeutic approach used throughout is explained in the Author Note section called My Beliefs About Change.

Each chapter begins with a case study that exemplifies its main theme. This is followed by a detailed examination of the problem or issue, providing you with important background information. Next is an overview of what needs to change for optimal functioning in this area. After that, you complete five questions that will help you quickly assess whether this is an area that you need to work on or not. The section following is the meat of the chapter, called Solutions, which suggests comprehensive practical exercises to help you overcome the particular problem or issue. Once you have made progress in working through the exercises, you are asked to answer the same five questions you answered earlier, thus allowing you to monitor your progress. Concluding each chapter is a pullout sheet of relevant positive affirmations. Before I explain how to use positive affirmations, I will tell you how to use the exercises in the Solutions section of each chapter.

How to Use the Exercises Contained in the "Solutions" Section of Each Chapter

The Solutions section of each chapter is broken into three parts: (A) Changing Your Thoughts; (B) Changing Your Behaviour; and (C) Changing The Way You Feel About It. Explained next is what you do in each part:

A. Changing Your Thoughts
1. Beliefs Chart

This section is broken into two subsections in each chapter: the beliefs chart and the visualization exercises. The beliefs chart looks like this:

SAMPLE THOUGHT	UNDERLYING BELIEF	QUESTIONING IT (you complete this column)	HEALTHIER BELIEF
"I don't deserve to have ~~person~~. a career." ~~as good~~	I am no good because I am gay.		I am a worthwhile ~person~ Being gay is just ~as good~ being straight.

The third column is called Questioning It, and you are asked to complete that column. This is how you do it:

1. Look at the Underlying Belief in the second column.
2. Using the 12 questions listed below under How to Question Your Beliefs, challenge the logic residing beneath each underlying belief. In the example above, challenging the logic might look like this:
   - What proof do I have that I am no good because I am gay? (Answer: I have no proof. Although some people might believe this, that doesn't make it true.)
   - Are there any competing 'truths?' (Answer: Yes, many people today believe that gay people are acceptable. It makes sense for me to believe this as well.)
   - What price do I pay for continuing to believe this? (Answer: I will continue to suffer from low self-esteem.)
   - What will be the advantages of believing something different? (Answer: My self-esteem will improve, and I will begin to like myself.)
   - If I knew I would be dead tomorrow, would I be happy believing this? (Answer: Definitely not! There is no reason for me to continue berating myself.)
3. Write the questions that have the most meaning to you in the Questioning It column.
4. At the end of each chart, there is room for you to write in your own entries, including Sample Thoughts. Follow the same procedure.
5. Periodically review the contents of the chart, focusing on the Questioning It column and the Healthier Beliefs column.

HOW TO QUESTION YOUR BELIEFS

The Questions

1. What proof do I have that this is true?
2. Do I have any evidence that indicates it is not true?
3. Are there any competing "truths"? Is another belief just as valid?
4. Does everyone think this way? Why not?
5. Does agreeing with the majority on this make it necessarily correct?
6. Where did I learn this message? Is it possible that the messenger was wrong?
7. What purpose is served in continuing to believe this?
8. What price do I pay for continuing to believe this?
9. What will be the advantages of believing something different?
10. Are my feelings about this providing an accurate gauge of what I should believe?
11. If I were helping someone else deal with this, what would I want him or her to believe?
12. If I knew I would be dead tomorrow, would I be happy believing this?

2. Visualization Exercises

The benefits of using visualization regularly are enormous. Visualization plays a central role in therapeutic hypnosis, for example. It is an effective means of producing change.

There are two types of visualization exercises suggested in each chapter. First are general visualizations, designed to have a general effect on helping you improve in the area designated by the respective chapter.

Second are specific visualizations, where you imagine situations you have actually encountered. These become a type of mental rehearsal for any future occurrence of a similar situation. Many people mentally rehearse how they will act and what they will say in an upcoming job interview, for example. This mental preparation can be helpful as actual practice.

The How to Visualize instructions on the next page explain how to get the most out of the visualization exercises. Refer back to this page as often as necessary.

How to Visualize

Visualization is like daydreaming, except you actively direct the dream. It is best accomplished while being relaxed. You relax deeply every night before you fall asleep. Consequently, relaxing is actually nothing new to you. There are many different ways to relax, and below I suggest the simplest way of doing this.

1. Lie down in a comfortable place. This could be your couch, bed or a recliner.
2. Close your eyes and let yourself become calm and relaxed. If you want to relax deeply, let it happen. In a deep relaxation, you will probably not want to move at all. You might also feel heavy, warm and tired.
3. Begin to visualize, as clearly as you can, what has been suggested to you in the chapter you are reading. This means to picture it in your mind's eye, similar to daydreaming.
4. The best visual images are detailed, so create as much detail as you can. For example, if you are visualizing a burning candle, see the shape and size of the candle, picture its burning wick, imagine the flame darting about, and see the wax dripping down its sides.
5. Allow as many of your senses into the visual image as possible. For example, imagine hearing people talk to you or other sounds (like ocean waves); bring in the sense of smell (What does ocean air smell like? What about the smell of melting chocolate?); add colour; allow the tactile to develop (In a beach scene, feel the sun's warmth upon your skin, and the sand under your feet); and even taste (Remember the taste of cotton candy?).

That's all you need to do to derive benefit from visualization exercises. Continue to do this daily, for 10 to 15 minutes, until you are satisfied with the improvement that you have made in the given area.

B. Changing Your Behaviour

The second part of the Solutions section looks at how you can change your behaviour, beginning with a number of general activities. Next come specific activities, where you focus on your own particular needs. The following explains what you will be asked to do:

1. Goal Setting

Begin by deciding upon a specific behaviour, or behaviours, that you will work on in the respective chapter. Write this down in the chart, similar to the example shown below (I have included the reasons in the chart so you understand the rationale behind the choices made):

GOAL: I am shy about asking guys on a date. I want to become more confident in doing this.

#	STEPS NEEDED TO HELP ME ACHIEVE THIS GOAL	DONE	REWARD
1	Decide on whom to ask out on a date (I will pick someone I'm not particularly attracted to—this will be easier than asking out a guy I think is really hot).		
2	Write out exactly what I want to say, and arrange the date over the telephone (This will help me stay calm).		
3	Ask him out for a drink after work (A drink will help relax me. I can keep the visit short, so I don't run out of things to say).		
4	Focus on asking him lots of questions about himself (This takes the focus off me—perhaps I will write out a number of questions as practice).		
5	As it gets close to an hour, tell him I need to get home soon.		
6	Tell him I have enjoyed the visit and leave.		
7	Next, ask someone that I am attracted to out for a brief date.		
8	Increase the length of the date.		
9	Have a date with someone I am really attracted to.		
10	Ask a hot guy out on a weekend getaway.		

2. Shaping

This is the idea of learning through successive approximations, in a step-by-step manner. When you were taught to ride a bike, the technique was likely used without either you or your teacher realizing it. If you began with training wheels, they soon became unnecessary. The wheels were then removed, but your teacher still helped you keep your balance. As you learned to correct your balance, your teacher held you less often, until you learned to ride on your own. Finally, you then learned to ride your bike safely, gaining awareness of traffic hazards and proper signalling. Shaping allows you to gradually increase your comfort level while learning a new skill.

In the example shown in the chart above, after you set your goal(s), you write out the steps that will help you overcome the problem. With shaping it is important that you make your steps sufficiently small so that moving from one step to the next doesn't feel like a "quantum leap." For example, jumping immediately to asking someone you find really hot on a weekend getaway (step 10) is going to stress you out and is unlikely to result in a successful outcome.

3. Rewards

Rewarding yourself is the technique of giving yourself something that you find pleasurable after accomplishing a certain task. If you decide that you will let yourself watch an hour of television after studying for two hours, watching television becomes your reward. Using the example of a smoker who quits, a long-term reward might be saving the money once spent on cigarettes for a year and then spending this on a vacation in Florida. Rewards can be something tangible, like the above examples, or they can be internal like telling yourself, Good job! Fantastic! Way to go! I did it!

The important thing about rewards is picking appropriate ones. A short-term reward should be simple, something you can easily give yourself. There is no point making your reward a shopping spree if you can't already pay this month's rent. Good examples of short-term rewards, some of which can be immediate, are:
- taking a short walk
- having a warm bath
- a few minutes of relaxation
- listening and dancing to music
- window shopping
- a hobby
- a tanning session
- jogging
- a telephone conversation
- a cup of tea or coffee

4. Environment Control

Environment refers to all of the external influences that affect you in some way, including people (friends, family, co-workers), locations (where you live, businesses you frequent, other destinations), and affiliations (church, clubs, organizations). Controlling the environment means making decisions about your participation within each environment, and changing its occurrence. Each chapter will have a chart that looks like the following:

#	PERSON OR GROUP THAT AFFECTS YOU	+ OR - EFFECT	PLANNED ACTION (Range: complete avoidance to frequent contact—be specific)
1	Peter	+	Increase contact from once-to-twice a week.
2	Natalie	-	Avoid having contact for the next month.
3			
4			

When you are beginning to work on a problem, it is helpful to avoid, or at least reduce contact with, the people and groups who are unsupportive of your efforts. Likewise, it will help to spend more time with those who are supportive.

The above chart in each chapter will help you decide what those changes will look like for you. List the person or group who affects you in the first column and indicate whether that influence is positive (+) or negative (-) in the second column. In the last column indicate what action you will take to help you accomplish your goal.

C. How to Change Your Feelings

The third part of the Solutions section looks at how you can change your feelings. You can work on changing your thoughts and behaviours directly, but not so with your feelings. For example, if you're feeling uptight before giving a speech, it will be difficult to stop the feeling from emerging: our feelings arise automatically from our unconscious.

The best way to try altering your feelings is to work on changing your thoughts and behaviours. Our feelings are an excellent indicator of our comfort level and therefore need to be understood. Changes in your feelings are also an excellent indicator of the progress you are making.

When you experience a negative feeling, complete the following chart, as in the example shown below:

NAME THE FEELING(S)	DESCRIBE THE TRIGGER	UNDERLYING BELIEF(S)	QUESTIONING IT	HEALTHIER BELIEF
shame embarrassment anxiety	My friend found out that I am gay.	He will think I am a sinner because I am gay, and that's awful!	Is another belief just as valid? Does everyone think this way? If I were helping someone else, what would I want him to believe?	My friend is entitled to his beliefs. Even if he thinks it's awful, tha's not my concern. It doesn't make it"awful" for me.

This is how you complete the chart and what to do with it afterward:

1. Write down the name of the feeling or feelings (e.g., shame, embarrassment, anxiety).
2. Write down what triggered the eruption of the feeling (e.g., "My friend found out that I am gay.")
3. Write down the belief(s) or the thought(s) that underlie the feeling (e.g., "He will think I am a sinner because I am gay, and that is awful!")
4. Refer to the How to Question Your Beliefs pullout sheet, and challenge the logic residing behind each underlying belief as suggested.
5. Write down a healthier belief or beliefs (e.g., "My friend is entitled to his beliefs.

Even if he thinks it's awful, that's not my concern. It doesn't make it 'awful' for me.")

6. Periodically review the contents of the chart, focusing on the Questioning It column and the Healthier Belief column.

7. Finally, you may want to incorporate the situation that triggered the feeling into a visualization exercise. To do this, refer to the How to Visualize pullout sheet.

Using Positive Affirmations

You will find a Positive Affirmations pullout sheet at the end of each chapter. This sheet includes five statements, called positive affirmations, that speak to the content of the chapter. An affirmation is like a suggestion, a message you give to yourself repeatedly. The intent is that, over time, the affirmation will become internalized, meaning that you begin to believe it. Earlier I wrote that visualization exercises are a type of hypnosis. So are positive affirmations.

I recommend that you keep the affirmations pullout sheet by your bed. Then read the list to yourself five times before you go to sleep, and five times when you wake up. Each time you read it, concentrate on it and think about what it means to you. The entire exercise need take only two or three minutes.

Pick the exercises that you think will be most helpful to you right now. Each exercise is meant to impact a number of life areas simultaneously, including the following:

- The mental domain
- The behavioural domain
- The emotional domain
- The social domain
- The spiritual domain

In each chapter, I begin with the mental domain. This includes your thoughts, values, attitudes and innermost beliefs. The way you think about yourself as a gay man, for example, is part of this area. Our thoughts have a significant effect on the way we choose to act. As you become more positive in your thoughts and beliefs, you will also want to behave differently. For example, when you believe you have equal rights compared to heterosexuals, you begin to act in a way that helps you assert your rights. Your feelings have also changed in this example, too. Instead of feeling passive and defeated, you now feel assertive and empowered.

Acting more positively is part of the behavioural domain. Just as our thoughts affect our actions, our actions also affect our thoughts. If you are shy, for example, the more you date, the more you develop confidence in dating. In this instance, you have changed your belief from I am too timid to date to I can do this. This example also shows how your emotions change as well. You have gone from feeling shy to feeling confident.

The emotional domain, as the previous two examples have shown, will change when either your behaviour or your thoughts change first. We cannot change our emotions directly. If you are feeling jealous because your ex-partner is now dating another guy, it is difficult, if not impossible, to change that feeling without changing the way you are viewing or thinking about your ex. Another way to change your feeling would be to change your behaviour by dating someone else yourself, or avoiding running into your ex until more time has healed the wound.

The social domain includes the people you hang out with, particularly the ones who are supportive of you. Especially in the early stages of developing a positive gay identity, it helps to surround yourself with people who accept you as you are, instead of being with people who want to change you. Later, you will have enough strength to be around anyone, regardless of how they view you, although I doubt if you will want to spend much time even then in their company.

The last domain this book addresses is the spiritual. By spiritual, I don't necessarily mean having a belief in a higher power, although it includes that. Here, spiritual simply means that which gives your life purpose and meaning. That might include belief in a higher power, or it might simply mean believing in and moving toward your own goals, regardless of whether or not they have cosmic significance to you.

Summary

This introductory chapter has shown you how to get the most out of the exercises contained in Breaking Out. Don't feel compelled to do every exercise, but pick the ones that you think will be most helpful to you right now. They are designed to help you in the mental, behavioural, emotional, social and spiritual areas of life. Each chapter follows a similar structure, beginning with an anecdote, an overview of the problem that the chapter addresses, a look at what needs to change to overcome the problem, a pre-test, a comprehensive section looking at solutions, a post-test, the chapter summary and a sheet of positive affirmations.

Part I
The Inside of Breaking Out

CHAPTER 1
Putting the Enemy to Sleep

"I was the embodiment of all those nasty things that have been said about gay people."

(Cody & Welch, 1997, 60)

Blaine has despised many of his behaviours since coming out three years ago. His Christian beliefs seem incompatible with his promiscuity, yet he finds himself unable to attain anything more enduring. The guilt and shame that result are painful, but he can't stop himself from seeking temporary companionship from other men, despite how empty it makes him feel.

He lives for the weekend—he feels it's his only chance to be himself. Nobody at work knows he's gay, and neither do his family nor his straight friends. Deep down, he harbours a great deal of animosity toward other gay people. He believes gay men are only looking for one thing, and he dislikes lesbian women for no apparent reason. His gay friends, Mike and Boyd, are similar to himself. When they get together, they love to gossip and criticize other gay people who look or act differently from themselves.

It's Saturday night, and Blaine gets ready to attend the hottest club in town. He takes as many precautions as he can think of to reduce the risk of being identified as gay by someone he knows. He arrives alone and cautiously scans every direction making sure no one sees him enter. The nervousness remains until he downs his first double. He looks over the growing crowd, thinking that he is the most attractive guy there. He soon hooks up with Mike and Boyd, and within minutes, the three of them start laughing at a couple of men they see making out in the corner. They tell each other they would never act so brazenly in public. In truth each of them have been in similar situations before, but in other cities where they are unknown. Blaine has also been to a few bathhouses during his travels, but he would never dream of telling anyone.

Many drinks later, Blaine becomes more aware of the aching in his groin, a reminder of how he hopes the evening will end. He notices a young guy checking him out, and he begins to reciprocate with frequent glances at the guy's crotch. The youth now looks more attractive than he did only a few hours ago. Blaine has another double, and he soon feels confident enough to go over and start talking to him. It doesn't take long for the other guy to make the advance. Blaine feels growing excitement mixed with anxiety, a familiar feeling. They go home together and soon begin frantically stripping off each other's clothes. The sex turns out to be hugely disappointing for both of them. Even after hours of stimulation, Blaine cannot come. Embarrassed and defeated, he dresses and leaves, never having found out the guy's name.

Blaine wakes in his own bed, feeling strangely empty and depressed. The familiar ache of loneliness resurfaces, hiding his desperate craving for intimacy. He doesn't understand why he is having so much trouble in the sexual arena. This wasn't the first time Blaine had become shy. Hesitantly, he admits to himself it has occurred often.

Deep down, Blaine desperately wants a boyfriend, perhaps even a life partner. But as usual, he ignores his feelings and pretends they aren't important to him. He opens the morning paper and notices the headline reporting a recent gay bashing. Without reading it, he assumes the guy deserved it, probably because he sported a gay look. Blaine looks at himself in the mirror and decides that would never happen to him.

The weekend ends, and Blaine is back to work. Jennifer asks him about his weekend and he tells her he went on a date with a woman he met a few days earlier. Jennifer wonders why Blaine always makes excuses in order to not meet the many attractive women she has tried to set him up with in the past. She knows him very well and she believes she knows his taste in women. To her knowledge, none of his dates have ever worked out, yet he still won't have anything to do with her friends. Does he have no faith in her intuition?

Before getting back to work, they tell each other a few jokes and have a good laugh. As soon as Jennifer leaves his office, though, the smile disappears from Blaine's face. Five more days till the weekend. He can't wait to be himself again.

The Problem

Although Blaine thinks he is being himself, something is preventing him from owning his feelings for other men. Blaine is consumed by internalized homophobia, the enemy that lives within him. Homophobia is fear, dislike, and/or hatred of gay people and homosexuality (Blumenfeld & Raymond, 1993). It includes discrimination and prejudice against gay persons and bisexuals. Internalized homophobia is the homophobia that resides within a gay person.

Blaine's story contains many examples of internalized homophobia. His dislike of himself is a theme throughout his story. His cautious scanning before entering the bar reflects his fear of being seen. The criticism of others that he and his friends make show his dislike of fellow gay bar patrons, which is a projection of his own self-abasement. Criticizing other gay people unconsciously serves to elevate his own feeling of inferiority. His inability to approach a guy in the bar before having a number of drinks exemplifies his personal discomfort with making an advance. Blaine's inability to ejaculate reveals his guilt or shame about what he is doing with another guy. When Blaine wakes the next day, his feelings of emptiness and depression indicate he feels bad about what happened. Blaine feels lonely because he is unable to connect emotionally with other men. After reading the paper, Blaine projects his own discomfort about being gay by blaming the victim of a gay bashing. Finally, Blaine waits for the next weekend— his only chance to become partly visible as a gay man.

His self-denigrating feelings have effectively kept him in the closet.

Imagining how internalized homophobia develops is not difficult. Until recently, nearly every message in society had a heterosexual bias, meaning that gay people were either absent, invisible, or made to appear inferior compared to heterosexual individuals. Media portrayals of gay men used to be negative, promoting unhappy, maladaptive images (Olson & King, 1995). Negative stereotypes were also abundant, suggesting that gay men were sissyish, bitchy individuals who walked with a girlish gait and spoke with a lisp.

Lesbian women were not immune to the bigotry either. Their media portrayals were often stereotyped and negative as well. More often than not, the media machine simply erased them along with gay men. Amazing how those in positions of power can make 10% percent of the population invisible.

We all grew up in a society that minimized who we are. Growing up in most societies was, and still is, unfavourable for gay individuals. Our same-sex feelings for other people are denigrated and condemned. Gay people are viewed by some as the most hated group in the United States today (Sapp, 2001; Unks, 1995).

Most of us knew that our feelings were not esteemed by society during our years growing up, so we learned to keep them to ourselves. We learned to dislike ourselves first and then others who had similar feelings to our own. This is internalized homophobia.

Parents were unable to prepare us for adulthood. Even if they knew our predispositions, they themselves were likely straight. How could they teach us about a subject they knew nothing about and probably preferred to know nothing about? Most of our parents did not respond with resounding joy when told their son or daughter is gay.

Internalized homophobia creates many problems for gay people. It is considered the number one obstacle preventing them from developing positive gay identities (Allen & Oleson, 1999; Gonsiorek, 1993). It produces feelings of shame, guilt, depression, demoralization and worthlessness. In response, gay individuals may try to hide, or worse, they may try to hurt themselves physically. Negative thinking, self-loathing and self-hatred prevent them from loving themselves and ultimately from loving others.

What Needs to Change?

Beneath the surface of internalized homophobia is the unconscious belief that gay is less than straight. This belief results in deep feelings of inferiority, shame and worthlessness. It's remarkable that internalized homophobia remains so prevalent, despite the finding that approximately 10% of men (Bagley & Tremblay, 1998) and 5% of women (Philipp, 1999) are gay. Remarkable, and tragic.

Overcoming internalized homophobia requires that you adopt within the deepest region of your psyche, the gay affirmative view—that being gay is equal to being straight. It is no better and no worse. For gay people, obviously it is better that they be gay. The converse is true for straight people. Why? Because most research has shown that sexual orientation is not something you can change (Drescher, 1998; Haldeman, 1994; Murphy, 1992b). You are who you are—period.

Consequently, it is normal for you to be gay. To try to be otherwise is to do yourself a grave injustice. If you are left-handed, you are left-handed. It will feel awkward for you to write with your right hand. As a gay person, you can have all the sex you want with people of the opposite gender and it won't change for one second your deepest affinity. Gay people can fall in love romantically only with members of the same gender (Money, 1988). Sure, you can love anyone. Think about your feelings for those who really matter to you—perhaps your mom, dad, siblings, and close friends. You may love these people, meaning that you care about them and are committed to them, but that's not the same as being in love romantically with them. Being in love romantically includes not only caring and commitment, but also the special ingredient that many call infatuation, lust, passion or chemistry (Sternberg, 1986). You cannot control who turns you on and who doesn't. Feeling sexually aroused and attracted to someone occurs automatically.

Breaking through internalized homophobia will allow you to love yourself deeply—with caring, commitment and passion. You can then externalize this passion, meaning that you have gained the ability to fall in love with a person of the same sex without guilt, shame or regret. Are you interested in learning how? That's what this chapter is about.

Where I'm At Now
Place a checkmark in the column that corresponds to your answer.

If your answer is "yes," use the following rating scale: 1=very slightly; 2=slightly; 3=moderately; 4=highly; 5=severely.

			YES				
		NO	1	2	3	4	5
1	I am ashamed of being gay.						
2	My fear is that others will find out I'm gay.						
3	Even if it were safe, I would not want to hold hands or neck with a date in public.						
4	I am uncomfortable when involved sexually with someone of the same sex.						
5	Some of my behaviour is self-destructive because I don't like being gay.						

If you respond "YES" to any of these questions, you would benefit from doing some work in this area. If all of your responses are "NO," you may want to skip this chapter.

The Solution

In Blaine's case, a solution to his internalized homophobia will require that he overcome his own self-loathing caused by his anguish over being gay. For this to occur, he needs to learn to love himself as a gay man, and come to see being gay as equal to being straight. It will take time for him to stop prejudging other gay people, and this will require his concerted effort. Learning to become tolerant of other gay people is really about learning to appreciate and value the various aspects of your own gay self. We usually don't like in others what we don't like in ourselves.

Blaine has a lot of work to do, and the sooner he does it the closer he will be to finding a suitable mate. In turn, this will help him deal with the conflict he currently feels about being promiscuous while trying to uphold Christian values. Beginning your own attack on the enemy begins now.

A. Changing Your Thoughts
1. Beliefs Chart

REMINDER: Complete the following exercise by using the How to Question Your Beliefs pullout sheet found in the Introduction.

SAMPLE THOUGHT	UNDERLYING BELIEF	QUESTIONING IT (you complete this column)	HEALTHIER BELIEF
I am ashamed of being gay.	I should be ashamed of being gay because it is inferior to being straight.		My worth is not dependent on my sexuality. Being gay is equal to being straight.
My fear is that others will find out I'm gay.	Being gay is horrible, and I should be concerned what others think of me.		Being gay is normal. I have every reason to be proud of who I am. If others don't like it, too bad.
Even if it were safe, I would not want to hold hands or neck with a date in public.	Touch between men or women is wrong.		I have every right to touch my partner, and it is good that I can express my affections for the one I care about.

I am uncomfortable when involved sexually with someone of the same sex.	Sex between men or women is wrong.	Having sex with a partner of the same gender is normal and natural when you're gay. Intimacy is intrinsically good.
Some of my behaviour is self-destructive because I don't like being gay.	I deserve to hurt myself because I am despicable.	My love for members of the same sex is a blessing, not a curse. I deserve to love myself for it.
(Write any addtional thoughts and beliefs you have.)		

2. Visualization Exercises

REMINDER: Complete the following exercises by using the How to Visualize pull-out sheet found in the Introduction.

(a) General Visualizations—Visualize yourself as a person who loves yourself and other people. Imagine white light emanating from your body, suggesting that you have much good inside of you. See yourself looking happy and contented, fully accepting the part of you that makes you gay. Picture yourself as though you are no longer fearful.

(b) Specific Visualizations—Think of a specific instance where you found yourself experiencing internalized homophobia. Imagine yourself acting in the situation without feeling any trace of fear, judgment, dislike or self-hatred. Do this for each example you can think of.

B. Changing Your Behaviour

Besides changing your thoughts, an effective method in self-change is to begin doing things that will help you change the way you act. Here is how to do it:

1. General Activities

These general activities will prove helpful in reducing your internalized homophobia:

• Read gay non-fiction books. Reading provides a great opportunity to learn more about being gay, which also helps to normalize the experience. The more gay positive literature you read, the healthier you become. A list of suggested readings is contained in Appendix D.

• Use other gay positive media. Watching movies containing healthy gay role models, such as Torch Song Trilogy, and listening to music with gay themes or by gay artists can be inspiring and therapeutic.

• Make a place for gay erotica. Whether it be watching explicit gay sex flicks or reading erotic novels, exposure to this material can help you increase your comfort with the sexual side of being gay.

• Make gay friendship a priority. If you haven't developed many gay friends, make the effort to do so: Chapter 9 will show you how. Good gay friends are fundamentally important (D'Augelli, 1991; Malyon, 1982).

• Increase exposure to the gay community. Attend gay events, like dances and marches, even if you feel ready only to watch. Support gay organizations where you live, and join one or more if you can.

2. Specific Activities

Using the four techniques of goal setting, shaping, rewards and environment control (explained in the Introduction), here are ways of overcoming specific aspects of your internalized homophobia:

Goal-Setting

Decide upon a specific behaviour you will target for change. Your best choice is a behaviour that you have already found is causing you trouble. Here are some examples:

• Feeling afraid to dance with another same-sex individual, especially intimately (e.g., two-step, waltz).

• Fear of being seen going into a bar.

• Drinking excessively just so you can "fathom" being sexual with a same-sex partner.

• Judging gay people more harshly than you judge heterosexual individuals.

Shaping

Write your goal in the chart below and then list the steps you will take to begin working on it.

GOAL:		
# STEPS NEEDED TO HELP ME ACHIEVE THIS GOAL	DONE	REWARD
1		
2		
3		

Rewards

In the chart above, decide which of your steps should have an accompanying reward for its successful completion. Write what the specific reward will be. After completing the step, place a checkmark in the Done column and be sure to give yourself the assigned reward.

Environment Control

Internalized homophobia is often "fed" by the people who know you, and within the groups to whom you belong. When you are beginning to work on reducing internalized homophobia, it is helpful to avoid, or at least reduce contact with, the people and groups who are unsupportive of your efforts. If a close friend is highly homophobic, his or her influence will not be beneficial to you. In the chart below, write the environmental changes you need to make until your goal is successfully achieved:

#	PERSON OR GROUP THAT AFFECTS YOU	+ OR - EFFECT	PLANNED ACTION (Range: complete avoidance to frequent contact—be specific)
1			
2			
3			
4			

C. Changing the Way You Feel About It

When you experience a negative feeling complete the following chart (REMINDER: instructions for using this chart are found in the Introduction):

NAME THE FEELING(S)	DESCRIBE THE TRIGGER	UNDERLYING BELIEF(S)	QUESTIONING IT	HEALTHIER BELIEF

Where I'm At After Working On It

Periodically re-test yourself to chart your progress in this area.

		NO	YES 1 2 3 4 5
1	I am ashamed of being gay.		
2	My fear is that others will find out I'm gay.		
3	Even if it were safe, I would not want to hold hands or neck with a date in public.		
4	I am uncomfortable when involved sexually with someone of the same sex.		
5	Some of my behaviour is self-destructive because I don't like being gay.		

If you are still responding "YES" to any of these questions, continue working on change in this area. If all of your responses are "NO," you have made significant progress! Continue to monitor any remaining problems in this area, and work on these as suggested in this chapter.

Summary

As we have seen with Blaine, and as you have probably noticed in your own experience, internalized homophobia creates nasty consequences. It diminishes your ability to love yourself and others, particularly other gay people. It leaves you feeling uncomfortable and anxious in your attempts to become intimate with a same-sex partner.

Internalized homophobia is the biggest obstacle faced in developing a positive gay identity. Its underlying belief is that being gay is inferior to being straight. Such a value judgment seems untenable, considering that a sizable percentage of the population is gay and that a homosexual orientation is not something we can change.

The bulk of this chapter has guided you through activities and exercises that will help you overcome this common, if not universal, problem. On the next page is the Positive Affirmations pullout sheet, which can be kept by your bed or in some other highly visible place. Spend a few minutes each day reflecting on what each affirmation means to you personally.

Positive Affirmations

[Also add your own from the *Healthier Belief* columns in this chapter]

My worth is not dependent on my sexuality. Being gay is equal to being straight.

Being gay is normal. I have every reason to be proud of who I am. If others don't like it, too bad.

I have every right to touch my partner, and it is good that I can express my affections for the one I care about.

Having sex with a partner of the same gender is normal and natural when you're gay. Intimacy is intrinsically good.

My love for members of the same sex is a blessing, not a curse. I deserve to love myself for it.

CHAPTER 2
Learning to Like Yourself

"it's all been for a good cause if only to learn the simple truth that accepting myself is more important than acceptance by others."

(Chuang, 1999, 40)

"One discovers that when you wish people love, especially on a regular basis, that it's hard to keep hating them."

(Herrman, 1990, 102)

Richard avoids mirrors because whenever he sees himself in one he feels uneasy and disappointed. Although others tell him he is attractive, he doesn't believe them. In Richard's mind, the mirror doesn't lie, and what he sees makes his stomach churn with disgust. His hips seem too large, his torso is too long, his muscles are small and undefined, his nose is slightly crooked and he is ten pounds overweight. Looking at the small amount of fat on his waist bothers him more than most people could imagine. It's like a curse, living in his body. The few aspects of his looks that he likes are overshadowed by every flaw that seems so pronounced. More disturbing is how his reflection symbolizes to him the deep feelings of dislike he has for himself. He feels ugly, inside and out.

Only his closest friends know that he is gay. In most settings, Richard is aware of his behaviour and the way he comes across to others. He censors anything that might appear "gay," doing his best to ensure that others think he is straight. Richard wants others to see him as macho. This means that although he loves creative pursuits, he avoids telling most people of his interests. Attending ballets, operas and plays is a definite taboo. Richard intentionally deepens his voice and holds back from showing any side of himself that others might think is "feminine." To add to his persona, he castigates others who display the slightest degree of effeminacy.

At work, Richard reminds himself that there is nothing wrong with being a dishwasher. After five years of this, though, he thinks he should soon quit. But then what? Richard doesn't believe he is capable of launching a successful career. His gay friends haven't accomplished much either, which reinforces his idea that gay men generally don't succeed. The exceptions, some of whom Richard has met before, never became friends with him. He concludes that they are arrogant, and that their success has happened either because of luck or inheritance.

Richard assumes people won't like him once they meet him. He also assumes that if they got to know him, they wouldn't like him either. Indeed, it's like a self-fulfilling prophecy: most people who meet Richard soon make their exit. He is unaware that the reason they don't spend much time talking to him is that he has nothing to talk about. Acquaintances soon find out he has little to discuss because he never challenges himself or tries new things. Richard has allowed himself to become boring, plain and simple.

When Richard is not at work, he often feels alone. He has trouble believing that being single is okay, and his mind obliges by reminding him of his lack of self-worth. Whenever he has dated someone, the other guy inevitably breaks up with him. Richard wants to know why, but is sick of hearing that it's because the other guy isn't sufficiently attracted to him. In truth, they get sick of hearing his complaints about life. Richard spends too much time complaining instead of doing.

To relieve his loneliness and negative thoughts, he occasionally calls his friend Elgin. Richard doesn't respect Elgin's lifestyle at all—Elgin smokes pot constantly and is rarely employed. Nonetheless, it's not like Richard's lifestyle is any better. Often when Elgin isn't available, Richard sits at home and smokes pot until he nearly loses his mind. Anything to numb himself when he is by himself.

He and Elgin once dated for a few weeks, but Elgin ended it. Richard begged to continue having some contact, and Elgin reluctantly agreed. They both know they are bad company for each other. Most of the time, they smoke up together, and then put each other down for being a loser. Neither understands why life is so lacklustre. Their fights at least remind them that they are still alive.

The Problem

Richard suffers from serious self-esteem problems. Self-esteem is whether one likes or dislikes oneself, and to what extent (Troiden, 1984-85). Consequently, it has both a valence (either negative or positive) and a rating (low to high). Luckily, most gay men and lesbians form a positive sense of self (Garnets & Kimmel, 1993), and consequently they do not experience problems with their self-esteem.

One aspect of self-esteem is body image—how one views one's own body. It can also be either positive or negative, and given a rating (low to high). Body image problems are common with gay men. The gay community idolizes the "perfect" male body—a chiselled physique with beautiful pecs, biceps and abs. Nearly every advertisement for a gay event proudly displays such godlike images of men, and today's fitness magazines for men remind us further of what we are supposed to look like. The obsession to become one of them can result in what I call the Adonis Syndrome.

The Adonis Syndrome results from internalizing the concept of the perfect male body, believing that you and others are lacking if you haven't achieved it. The first aspect of the Adonis Syndrome, which is where you believe you are lacking, affects self-esteem. The second aspect is where you believe others are lacking, which results in different consequences. These I will explain in Chapter Twelve.

The symptoms of the Adonis Syndrome, as applied to oneself, include the following:

- being too critical of your own body
- dissatisfaction with your body
- guilt and shame regarding your body
- doubting that others will find you physically desirable
- in those who exercise, a constant drive to develop the perfect male physique, resulting in compulsive workouts and guilt when a workout is missed

Although internalized homophobia influences self-esteem (Malyon, 1982b), they are different concepts. A homophobic gay male can have healthy self-esteem in areas unrelated to his gayness, just as a non-homophobic guy can have terribly negative self-esteem. An example where internalized homophobia and negative self-esteem occur together is in something I call heterofacsimile, which is a gay person's conscious and unconscious efforts to become and appear straight. It can take the following forms:

- Seeking the help of a therapist to try and alter one's sexual orientation (often called reparative or conversion therapy)
- Dating the opposite gender and having sex with them to try to alter one's sexual orientation (this may include getting married as an attempt to become heterosexual)
- In gay men, disengaging from anything that might appear feminine or "unmanly"; in lesbian women, disengaging from anything that might appear masculine. This includes avoiding:
  - certain mannerisms, clothing or adornments that the gay man views as feminine, or that the lesbian woman views as masculine
  - potential experiences, career choices and men who are deemed effeminate (by gay men); or potential experiences, career choices and women who are deemed   masculine (by lesbian women)
  - creating a macho persona if you're a gay man, and creating an exaggerated feminine persona if you're a lesbian woman

The gay person who displays heterofacsimile may or may not be aware of it. Either way, it is a problem in that it reduces people's freedom of choice to be themselves and feel good about themselves.

Self-efficacy, which refers to how one rates one's ability to perform specific tasks, is also related to self-esteem (Prochaska, Norcross, & Diclemente, 1994). Generally, people with positive self-esteem have confidence to take action to correct life circumstances they find undesirable. However, those with negative self-esteem are often less certain.

The consequences of self-esteem are enormous. When self-esteem is highly negative, depressive feelings and episodes are common (Otis & Skinner, 1996). When self-esteem is highly positive, it results in self-acceptance. Research has shown that self-acceptance is the single largest predictor of mental health in gay people (Hershberger & D'Augelli, 1995). It is fundamentally important.

Richard's story exemplifies many of the self-esteem issues commonly experienced by gay men. His avoidance of mirrors is a telltale sign of having a negative body image, caused by the Adonis Syndrome. He struggles with heterofacsimile and makes many choices based on trying to appear suitably masculine.

Richard's negative self-esteem is also expressed in his career choice. Although dissatisfied with remaining in his current job as a dishwasher, he lacks the self-confidence to change his circumstances. He doesn't believe, deep down, that he has the right to succeed, partly because he is gay.

Another corollary of this is that Richard doesn't believe that others will like him. This is a projection of Richard not liking himself. Consequently, he spends time with his "friend" Elgin, and together they verbally abuse one another. Richard knows he wants to develop healthier friendships and eventually have a sustainable relationship, but he doesn't believe he deserves to have either.

What Needs to Change?

First and foremost, you will never have optimal self-esteem as a gay person until you overcome internalized homophobia. If this still plagues you, return to Chapter 1 and continue working through the relevant exercises.

Have you ever met individuals who have achieved a great deal, yet continue to dislike themselves? Accomplishments have little to do with how you view yourself. To have positive self-esteem you need to believe that you have intrinsic worth, regardless of anything you accomplish. You will also need to overcome the Adonis Syndrome (primarily a gay male problem) and heterofacsimile. Both diminish your ability to accept yourself as you are.

Making comparisons to other people is a mistake. You will always come up short in some areas, and perhaps ahead in others—that is, until you meet your competition. If your feelings about yourself become based on comparison, you will always find yourself a victim of other people's circumstances. When surrounded by rich people, you will feel diminished if you are struggling financially. When surrounded by religious zealots, you will feel immoral and despicable.

You need to see yourself as unique. There is no one the same as you, and you are not the same as anyone else. And why would you want to be the same as anyone else? Even the person you most idolize has problems.

The happiest of people have come to accept themselves and their circumstances completely as they are right now. That doesn't mean they stop striving, but rather, it means maintaining an attitude of acceptance while working toward new goals.

Liking yourself as a gay individual means coming to see your gay self as a special part of you. It's a gift that you were born with. Believe it! Although comparisons are not personally helpful to you in improving your self-esteem, there are many gay people who have achieved greatness, both historically and today. Examples of famous individuals who have had significant same-sex relationships or who self-identify as gay include Gertrude Stein, Virginia Woolf, Leonardo da Vinci, Michelangelo, Queen Christina, King Richard II, Janis Joplin, k. d. lang, Melissa Etheridge, Aristotle, Socrates, Plato, Pope Julius III, Pope Sixtus IV, Margaret Fuller, Natalie Clifford Barney, Francis Bacon, Alexander the Great, Julius Caesar, Amelia Earhart, Eleanor Roosevelt, Hans Christian Andersen, Walt Whitman, Tennessee Williams, Oscar Wilde, Herman Melville, James Dean, Rock Hudson, Gore Vidal, Alice B. Toklas, Bessie Smith, Vita Sackville-West, Greg Louganis, Mark Tewksbury and Elton John (some names listed by Blumenfeld & Raymond, 1993; Rutledge, 1987) .

Some admirable traits have been ascribed to gay men and lesbian women, and being gay certainly has its own advantages. For example, gender role expectations are generally less pronounced compared to heterosexual relationships, and gays and lesbians are often more tolerant of differences within society. Given that gay people often like to do business with other gay individuals, there can be career advantages as well.

These are generalizations, but they are a good reminder that there is nothing intrinsically wrong with being gay—far from it. In their book, Uncharted Lives, authors Siegel and Lowe explain how gay males may become more independent, creative, compassionate and sensitive than heterosexual males. According to new research by Rothblum and Factor, lesbian women who are out not only view themselves as having mental health comparable to heterosexual women, they also report higher self-esteem. And Don Clark describes gay people as loving souls in his book, Loving Someone Gay.

Liking yourself is vitally important to your mental health. This chapter will show you how.

Where I'm At Now
Place a checkmark in the column that corresponds to your answer.

If your answer is "yes," use the following rating scale: 1=very slightly; 2=slightly; 3=moderately; 4=highly; 5=severely.

		NO	YES 1	2	3	4	5
1	I don't like myself.						
2	I don't like my body.						
3	I don't think I am capable of pursuing a better career choice.						
4	I don't feel worthy of having a relationship with a successful and attractive partner.						
5	I wish I could just blend in with everyone else and not be noticed for being "different" in any sense.						

If you respond "YES" to any of these questions, you would benefit from doing some work in this area. If all of your responses are "NO," you may want to skip this chapter.

The Solution

Richard has some intense work to do on himself. More than anything else, he needs to accept himself as the person he is and develop a realistic sense of his own self-efficacy. Richard needs to stop selling himself short, but to do so, he will need to stop believing he is inferior to other people. He is equal to others in terms of his human worth and potential.

Regarding body image, it will help Richard if he first gets some realistic feedback from others—those who will tell the truth. Is Richard attractive? Is there anything he can change about his appearance that will enhance his looks? Getting an honest appraisal is the first step. Next, he needs to begin programming the new belief about his looks into his self-concept, possibly through visualization exercises and questioning exercises. Whether Richard is considered attractive or unattractive by most people, the challenge will be for him to realize that attractiveness is more than just his looks. Many heterosexual and gay individuals are not especially attractive, but they still lead successful lives and have fantastic relationships with friends and their mate. It is time for Richard to begin challenging his beliefs, and develop the courage to take some chances and begin growing once more. The rest of this chapter will show you how to do the same.

A. Changing Your Thoughts

1. Beliefs Chart

REMINDER: Complete the following exercise by using the How to Question Your Beliefs pullout sheet found in the Introduction.

SAMPLE THOUGHT	UNDERLYING BELIEF	QUESTIONING IT (you complete this column)	HEALTHIER BELIEF
I don't like myself.	I have little intrinsic worth.		I have intrinsic worth and many likeable qualities.
I don't like my body.	Unless I look like a Greek god, my body is lacking.		I don't *need* the perfect body. I'm learning to love myself as I am.
I don't think I am capable of pursuing a better career choice.	I am inadequate.		I believe in myself and in my capabilities. I deserve to be the

		best I can be.
I don't feel worthy of having a relationship with a successful and attractive partner.	I am undeserving of love. Perhaps I am unloveable.	I am a loveable person who deserves to find love and nurture love.
I wish I could just blend in with everyone else and not be noticed for being "different" in *any* sense.	Being different is a bad thing. It's easier for people who "fit in."	I was never meant to be the same as everyone else. I embrace my uniqueness because it helps to define *me*.
(Write any additional thoughts and beliefs you have.)		

2. Visualization Exercises

REMINDER: Complete the following exercises by using the How to Visualize pull-out sheet found in the Introduction.

(a) General Visualizations—Imagine that you are looking into a mirror, examining every inch of your body. See your body as it really is, but with an attitude of complete acceptance. As you move from one body part to another, picture yourself saying to yourself, "This is okay; I accept this part of me." Focus especially on the parts of your body that you have been particularly displeased with. After a few minutes, switch to the inner self. See yourself looking into your eyes in the mirror, and imagine that you are looking at someone you really like. Notice the glow of acceptance in your eyes. Indeed, you have found a friend that you really deserve to know better and respect more.

(b) Specific Visualizations—Think of a specific instance where your negative or low self-esteem expresses itself. If pursuing a career has been an obstacle for you, imagine yourself working in a suitable career. You might also picture taking each step required in order to train and enter that particular career. To become a lawyer, for example, imagine enduring the many hours of study, and eventually practicing in a law firm. If heterofacsimile has been a problem for you, imagine accepting the more gentle sides of yourself. See yourself attending gay events, refusing to make judgments about others who appear different from you. Do this for each example you can think of.

B. Changing Your Behaviour
1. General Activities

These general activities will prove helpful in improving your self-esteem:

Focus on the Positive

• Use the mirror technique. Stand in front of a mirror, smile at yourself, and begin telling yourself—with authority in your voice—messages that you need to hear. For example, "I am a likeable person. My uniqueness is what makes me who I am. I accept myself completely." If you find yourself sometimes laughing when you do this exercise, good! Self-esteem will be enhanced if you stop taking yourself so seriously.

• Get in touch with the things you like about yourself. Write out a list of the qualities you like about yourself, and ask your friends what they like about you. Write these down later as well. Periodically review your list.

• Keep a journal of your positive experiences. Make a point of writing about your positive experiences, including things you do, things that happen to you and compliments you receive. Reread what you've written occasionally.

• Stop comparing yourself to others. When you catch yourself doing this, remind yourself that it is pointless to compare your life and your circumstances to others. What matters is that you set your own reasonable goals and that you work hard at attaining them.

• Attend gay events. Identifying with and integrating into the larger gay community is helpful to your self-esteem (Garnets, Herek, & Levy, 1990; Jacobs & Tedford, 1980). Individuals who view their gay identities as important and who participate in the community tend to have higher self-esteem than those who are alienated from it.

• Treat yourself in a special way. People who like themselves enjoy life to the fullest. Find ways to do this sensibly. For example, if you enjoy having a massage, go for it. The only caveat here is to avoid activities that on the surface look like "pampering" but actually hamper you from achieving your goals. If trying to lose weight, eating cheesecake every day doesn't cut it.

Work on Improving the Negative

No one likes everything about themself. Here is what you can do about it:

1. Using two columns, list the qualities that you don't like about yourself. On the left side, write down the qualities that are amenable to change (e.g., weight loss), and on the right, qualities that will not change (e.g., your height).

2. The qualities listed in the right column, which are unchanging, need to be accepted by you. If you have trouble doing this, return to the preceding section on Changing Your Thoughts and use the beliefs chart and specific visualization exercises that target this sensitive area for you.

3. The qualities listed in the left column can be targeted for change. Turn to the next section for instructions on how to accomplish a specific goal.

2. Specific Activities
Goal-Setting
From the left column of the list (referred to in the previous section), decide which problem you will work on now. You won't be able to change everything at once, so be patient. Get accurate information about the problem you want to work on. If losing weight is your goal, find out what is considered a healthy weight for someone of your height and frame. Then learn about the specifics of proper diet and exercise.

Here are some examples having to do with self-esteem:
- Pursuing an appropriate career choice
- Building a more desirable physique
- Losing weight
- Learning a new skill (be specific)

Shaping
Write your goal in the chart below, and then list the steps you will take to begin working on it.

GOAL:		
# STEPS NEEDED TO HELP ME ACHIEVE THIS GOAL	DONE	REWARD
1		
2		
3		

Rewards
In the chart above, decide which of your steps should have an accompanying reward for its successful completion. Write what the specific reward will be. After completing the step, place a checkmark in the Done column and be sure to give yourself the assigned reward.

Environment Control
Have you noticed that when you are in the presence of some people, you feel diminished, whereas you don't feel that way when you are with other people? There may be many reasons for this, some of which have nothing to do with you per se. Some braggarts, for example, may unwittingly leave you feeling less accomplished, less travelled or less anything. Until your self-esteem improves, you would do well to limit your contact with these people. Instead, spend time with those who have no effect on your self-esteem and who encourage you.

In the chart below, write the environmental changes you need to make until your goal is successfully achieved:

#	PERSON OR GROUP THAT AFFECTS YOU	+ OR - EFFECT	PLANNED ACTION (Range: complete avoidance to frequent contact—be specific)
1			
2			
3			
4			

C. Changing the Way You Feel About It

When you experience a negative feeling complete the following chart (REMINDER: instructions for using this chart are found in the Introduction):

NAME THE FEELING(S)	DESCRIBE THE TRIGGER	UNDERLYING BELIEF(S)	QUESTIONING IT	HEALTHIER BELIEF

Where I'm At After Working On It

Periodically re-test yourself to chart your progress in this area.

		NO	YES 1 2 3 4 5
1	I don't like myself.		
2	I don't like my body.		
3	I don't think I am capable of pursuing a better career choice.		
4	I don't feel worthy of having a relationship with a successful and attractive partner.		
5	I wish I could just blend in with everyone else and not be noticed for being "different" in any sense.		

If you are still responding "YES" to any of these questions, continue working on change in this area. If all of your responses are "NO," you have made significant progress! Continue to monitor any remaining problems in this area, and work on these as suggested in this chapter.

Summary

Richard needs to work on his self-esteem: he feels unworthy of self-love and respect from successful individuals. His body image has also been affected, and he needs to become aware that his attractiveness is more than just his looks. He has settled in his career choice and needs to become aware that he is capable of much more than he has thus far experienced. Perhaps you also relate to some of Richard's struggles.

This chapter has focused on self-esteem, which is whether you like or dislike yourself and to what extent. Self-esteem has huge consequences for an individual: when it is negative, depressive feelings often prevail; and when it is positive, self-acceptance usually results. Research has shown that self-acceptance is the single largest predictor of mental health in gay individuals.

The bulk of this chapter has guided you through activities and exercises that will help you improve your self-esteem. On the next page is the Positive Affirmations pull-out sheet. Spend a few minutes each day reflecting on what each affirmation means to you personally.

Positive Affirmations

[Also add your own from the Healthier Belief columns in this chapter]

I have intrinsic worth and many likeable qualities.

I don't need the perfect body. I'm learning to love myself as I am.

I believe in myself and in my capabilities. I deserve to be the best I can be.

I am a loveable person who deserves to find love and nurture love.

I was never meant to be the same as everyone else. I embrace my uniqueness because it helps to define me.

CHAPTER 3
Squashing Denial

"Every time a homosexual denies the validity of his feelings or restrains himself from expressing them, he does a small hurt to himself. He turns his energies inward and suppresses his own vitality. The effect may be scarcely noticeable: joy may be a little less keen, happiness slightly subdued; he may simply feel a little run-down, a little less tall. Over the years, these tiny denials have a cumulative effect."

(Fisher, 1972, cited in Blumenfeld & Raymond, 1993, 85, 86)

Without thinking about his motivation for doing so, Nelson would spend endless hours watching guys playing beach volleyball at the sand courts near his home. He often studied their bodies, but mostly—he told himself—he was interested in the sport. He also liked hanging out at the local outdoor swimming pool. The sun felt good on his mostly naked skin, and he would occasionally catch himself fantasizing about making out with some of the guys he observed.

Nelson also enjoyed wrestling and was thrilled when the school's wrestling team recruited him. Rubbing his body against other sweaty guys was a total turn-on, but he kept this to himself. He loved to watch and touch other guys, but he didn't want to indulge his feelings.

In fact, whenever Nelson felt attraction toward other boys, tremendous anxiety, guilt and shame ensued. The thought that he might be gay horrified him. He tried to diminish his feelings by telling himself that they weren't important. Whenever he felt a surge of homosexual attraction, he took a deep breath, told himself to forget it, and then carried on with his activities. However, this wasn't enough because sometimes the feelings were overpowering.

Nelson tried to block his feelings from emerging at all, but that didn't work. Unbeknownst to him, a coping style was developing—one which was less extreme than losing his feelings, but still managed to shelter him from the truth. Now when he felt aroused, he refused to believe that it was because of his homosexual feelings. He was always surprised when others thought he was gay, and after a while, became easily offended when asked.

Life seemed pretty boring through high school, and Nelson found little interest in dating. This made it difficult to talk to guys at school, and he became increasingly isolated from his peers. He felt so different from everyone else, but couldn't understand why. Thankfully, the heart only remains quiet for so long. In first-year university, Nelson developed a huge crush on a fellow classmate and through the romance that followed was able to come out to himself.

Nelson thought that was the end of it, but it wasn't. Often without realizing it, he found himself daydreaming about getting married, having kids and settling down with a woman. Nelson was now 28, and despite the fact that he had never fallen in love with or felt strongly attracted toward a woman, these thoughts periodically resurfaced. They became prevalent whenever he was unattached, and especially troubling during one specific episode.

Nelson has now been dating Davie for four months, and both think they are ready to make a deeper level of commitment to each other. For some reason, though, it is roughly at this point in a relationship when Nelson most entertains thoughts of heterosexual bliss. Furthermore, it often happens that during such milestones, Nelson will lose his attraction toward his partner, or he will feel a deadening of his feelings. How can his heart harden so quickly? A desire to run develops, but run from what?

None of his relationships have lasted more than six months. Nelson hopes that being with Davie will be different, but already his mind is telling him otherwise. Perhaps he will still develop feelings for the woman that lives in the next apartment. Perhaps he will find that he develops passion for her the way she seems to have for him. She always seems to be checking him out, smiling at him, and wanting to spend time together. Nelson has been afraid to let it happen. He knows what she wants from him. Can he deliver? Is it what he really wants?

Nelson knows he needs to end it with Davie, and sooner rather than later. He has become quite expert at it. In the last two years, he has dated at least 20 different guys. Soon Nelson will be alone once more. A part of him still needs to run.

The Problem

Nelson has actually been alone for a long time—alone with his thoughts, feeling, and urges. Even after coming out, Nelson continued to deny aspects of his sexuality, resulting in uncertainty about his sexual orientation. So long as Nelson doesn't commit himself to another guy, he can go on believing he is not gay. This is denial.

Gay men are experts at denial. They aren't born with this defense mechanism, but they soon master it. Denial is a method of coping whereby the individual refuses to believe information (such as thoughts, feelings and facts) that is true (Kalat, 1990). In other words, the individual learns to lie to himself and others, generally without realizing or acknowledging that he is doing so. Denial's purpose is to either help prevent or reduce anxiety about something the person doesn't want to face. When denial breaks, there is typically an outpouring of the anxiety that this defense mechanism was protecting one from.

For example, alcoholics in denial do not believe they have a problem with alcohol, even after it is abundantly clear to others. When confronted with the problems their substance abuse is causing, thereby breaking through the denial (at least temporarily), the alcoholic individual usually responds with defensiveness and other signs of anxiety and irritation.

Denial distorts reality, which is harmful to gay men and lesbian women in many areas of their lives. Before coming out, denial operates to keep "forbidden" homosexual thoughts, feelings and behaviours from having a label. In other words, while denial is operating, the homosexual person can avoid self-identifying as gay. After coming out, it remains easy for the individual to continue denying aspects of his or her sexuality that still create anxiety.

As an analogy, if people could "wish away" the parts of their bodies they didn't like, some would become quite harsh in their judgements, soon casting away most of what makes them human. If you wish away an arm, however, you'll have a hard time playing baseball. People in denial pay a huge price without knowing it. Each time a gay person refuses to accept feelings that are real, intense and loving, a piece of that person's emotional makeup breaks away. When loving, tender feelings are abandoned, gay men and lesbian women become increasingly less passionate about themselves, their interests and other people. For within this chemistry with others is the energy and passion that can be harnessed in many ways. Denial successfully robs the person of the best of what life has to offer. It also perpetuates feelings of low self-esteem and depression (Coleman, 1981-82).

Nelson's feeling of intense anxiety, whenever confronted with his developing homosexual awareness, was troublesome to him. This anxiety laid the foundation for denial. Although he felt different from other guys in high school, denial prevented him from understanding the source of his feelings. This only served to isolate him further. If Nelson could have accepted his feelings he may have met other teens with similar homosexual interests, which would have helped him establish a support network.

Nelson's thoughts about getting married and settling into a heterosexual lifestyle are similar to heterofacsmile, which was described in Chapter 2. The difference is that heterofacsimile is a behaviour or action, whereas denial is a mental process. In Nelson's case, thinking about being straight was a way to distance himself from the thought of being gay. In this way, some degree of denial was maintained. As long as he could think that being straight was still a possibility, he could unconsciously hope to someday reject his gay identity. Men with homosexual orientations who marry are, for example, in denial of their homosexuality (Isay, 1996). Most such marriages will result in divorce (Bohan, 1996).

Research indicates that sexuality is more fluid for women as compared to men, meaning that a greater percentage of women have the experience of being in love romantically with both genders, either simultaneously or sequentially, during the course of their lives (Dworkin, 2000; Golden, 1987). Furthermore, some lesbian women become involved in same-sex relationships for reasons other than sexual orientation (Friedman & Downey, 1999; Rothblum, 1994). These experiences should not be confused with denial.

What Needs to Change?

Overcoming denial and minimization, its counterpart, is a prerequisite to developing a positive gay identity. Minimization is where you downplay the importance of your feelings and attractions. If you are feeling aroused when you see a beautiful shirtless muscle god, minimization would involve telling yourself, These feelings don't matter, they aren't important. Denial, on the other hand, would involve refusing to acknowledge the effect the muscle god is having on you.

Like the proverbial onion, denial has many layers and you need to peel away each one. Removing each layer may make you feel more vulnerable at first, but it is vulnerability that allows you to grow emotionally. The fact is, heterosexual teenage girls also become vulnerable when they begin listening to their erotic attraction toward teenage boys (and vice-versa): some boys will rebuff them. You will also get hurt when you stop denying your homosexuality, but at least you won't be damaged for life, which denial virtually guarantees. Denial may be expressed in several ways, including:

- denial of same-sex interest and attraction
- denial of same-sex feelings
- denial of homosexual thoughts and fantasies
- denial of the meaning behind homosexual behaviour
- denial of the importance of becoming integrated

Almost any aspect of our sexuality can be denied, whether it is our attractions, thoughts, feelings or the meaning we attach to our behaviour. Yet another form of it is denying the importance of becoming an integrated gay man or lesbian woman. Gay individuals who practice this form of denial refuse to look at how their upbringing and indoctrination into heterosexism has deeply affected their gay souls and psyches. In turn, they are reluctant to do the work necessary to become happy and fulfilled gay men and lesbian women.

Before you can break denial, you need to be certain that you are, in fact, gay. What if you are bisexual, but made a mistake and prematurely labelled yourself as gay? Consider the "worst case scenario." If this occurred, you would date people of the same gender instead of the opposite gender. If you never ended up falling in love, what have you lost? Presumably you enjoyed meeting and having sex with some of the individuals you encountered along the way.

If you are bisexual, it is more likely that you would fall in love with one or more same-sex individuals that you date. If you fell in love with a same-sex partner, had a relationship that lasted for three years, and later fell in love with an opposite-sex partner, how much of a mistake did you make by calling yourself "gay" instead of "bisexual"? What have you lost during this three-year, same-sex relationship? If your relationship was characterized by mutual respect, integrity, honesty, and love, was that not worth the experience? If you had refused to follow your heart with this person, there is no assurance that you would have ever fallen in love romantically with someone else, male or female.

Furthermore, do you think if you fell in love with a same-sex partner, but denied your feelings, that this would help you to later fall in love with someone of the opposite sex, or might it actually diminish your ability to fall in love? There is no research to conclusively answer this question, but I suspect that to deny one love is to deny all love, because there can be no love in denial. Denial prevents you from owning whatever your thoughts and heart are telling you. This chapter will show you how to take back ownership of what is rightfully yours.

Where I'm At Now
Place a checkmark in the column that corresponds to your answer.

If your answer is "yes," use the following rating scale: 1=very slightly; 2=slightly; 3=moderately; 4=highly; 5=severely.

			YES				
		NO	1	2	3	4	5
1	I minimize my homosexuality by downplaying the importance of my feelings, behaviour or sexual attractions.						
2	I try to convince myself that I'm not gay.						
3	I find it easy to "turn off" my feelings when dating someone of the same sex.						
4	I don't feel much passion toward others.						
5	I don't feel much passion within myself.						

If you respond "YES" to any of these questions, you would benefit from doing some work in this area. If all of your responses are "NO," you may want to skip this chapter.

The Solution
For Nelson to overcome his denial, he needs to accept his feelings for guys and realize that for him, as a gay man, this is normal and natural, as it is for millions like him. He needs to stop denigrating his feelings and exalt them instead. Nelson is gay and that is beautiful. By accepting his feelings, he will become free to fully love others of the same gender.

Now that Nelson is 28-years-old, it is time for him to overcome his uncertainty about his sexual orientation. If his heart was going to go to women, it would have happened by now. At the least, Nelson would have felt some powerful crushes toward women. Most of us can remember many late childhood and adolescent crushes we had on others of the same sex. If Nelson continues believing that he just hasn't met the right woman yet, he will further delay the development of a positive gay identity.

Denial is unhealthy—whether it is hiding something harmful to a person, such as alcoholism, or hiding something that is good, such as same-sex feelings. Squashing denial requires having the courage to face the anxiety and the hidden feelings underlying it. This section will show you how.

A. Changing Your Thoughts

1. Beliefs Chart

REMINDER: Complete the following exercise by using the How to Question Your Beliefs pullout sheet found in the Introduction.

SAMPLE THOUGHT	UNDERLYING BELIEF	QUESTIONING IT (you complete this column)	HEALTHIER BELIEF
I minimize my homosexuality by downplaying the importance of my feelings, behaviour, or sexual attractions.	There is something wrong with feeling and acting the way I do.		My feelings tell me I am attracted to members of the same gender, and I accept this completely. Acting on my feelings is appropriate.
I try to convince myself that I'm not gay.	I can probably still become straight, which would be better than being gay.		I am gay, and that is okay. There is no substitute for being myself.
I find it easy to "turn off" my feelings when dating someone of the same sex.	Getting emotionally close to a person of the same gender is wrong.		Becoming a loving person is more important than pleasing others.
I don't feel much passion toward others.	This is just the way I am. I find it impossible to deeply connect with others.		Once I accept and love all parts of myself as a gay person, I will be able to accept and love others to an equal extent.
I don't feel much passion within myself.	There is nothing joyous happening in my life.		As I accept my feelings and attractions fully, I will reconnect to the passion in my life.
(Write any additional thoughts and beliefs you have .)			

2. Visualization Exercises

REMINDER: Complete the following exercises by using the How to Visualize pull-out sheet found in the Introduction.

(a) General Visualizations—Picture yourself at a gay beach, sitting comfortably in the sand. See yourself enjoying the sights of the scantily clad men or women around you. Look at each one, scanning each body from head to toe, paying particular attention to whatever grabs your eye. Create the feeling of accept-ance within you—that what you're feeling is good. Later imagine a conversa-tion with someone who particularly excites you. The two of you take an after-dark stroll together down the beach, still wearing only skimpy Speedos or a revealing bikini. Let yourself feel something for this person. Accept the feel-ing as legitimate.

(b) Specific Visualizations—Think of a specific instance where you found your-self denying some aspect of your homosexual experience, whether it involved denying your feelings, attractions or the meaning behind your actions. Replay the situation in your mind, but substitute the way you wish you had responded. Repeat visualizing this situation periodically during times you set aside for this exercise. Do this for each example you can think of.

B. Changing Your Behaviour

1. General Activities

These general activities will help you squash denial:

• Refuse to minimize or tuck away your feelings. When you're feeling same-sex attraction or other good feelings toward another person, express them to somebody, especially the particular person, if possible. At the least, write down your feelings in a journal so you can think about them later.

• Hang out in gay positive environments. Spend time in places where you can enjoy feeling same-sex attraction without repercussion (e.g., a gay bar, gay beach, or a gay resort).

• Watch gay erotica—For the same reason as the point above, watching gay erotica allows you to enjoy homosexual images without repercussion.

• Date other gay people. Dating gay individuals of the same gender will cre-ate all sorts of sexual and non-sexual feelings for you. Remember the first point in this section about expressing your feelings. If you have been dating someone for a while, and your feelings begin to dwindle, ask yourself why this is happening. If you cannot come up with a good reason, you might be slip-ping back into denial. Talk to a friend or professional before you decide on an appropriate action.

• Build passion in other areas of your life. Passion is a deep-rooted belief and commitment toward something or somebody. It is generally accompanied with emotion when thinking and talking about it, or when it is being thwarted in some way. How do you get in touch with your passion? There is no promise of when you will find it, but you might find the following helpful:

- *Self-Examination*—Come to know yourself better. How? Through personal experiences, listing your likes and dislikes, your admirable traits and less admirable traits and your values. Your career choice or career planning may shed some insights too. Which jobs do you most admire? Why? If you had no limitations on you, what career would you choose?
- *Visualization Exercises*—If you were to die tomorrow, what would you want to be remembered for? After visualizing, list these qualities, traits and accomplishments.
- *Purpose of Life*—What gives your life meaning? What is most important to you? How do you want to make a difference? Think of the most meaningful experiences you have had in your life. What made them so meaningful? List these.

• Become certain of your sexuality. There is no need to rush this decision. If you aren't ready to self-identify as gay, don't do it. Perhaps you need dating experience, sexual and otherwise, to help you decide whether you are gay or bisexual. This chapter is meant for those who have had enough time to decide, but then refuse to believe what their experience is telling them.

2. Specific Activities

Goal-Setting

Decide upon a specific behaviour that you will target for change. You might pick a specific instance of denial that has already caused you trouble. Here are some examples:

- Expressing caring, loving feelings toward other members of the same gender.
- Feeling certain that I am gay.
- Accepting my feelings of sexual excitement for other same-sex individuals.
- Developing passion in my life.

Shaping

Write your goal in the chart below, and then list the steps you will take to begin working on it.

GOAL:			
#	STEPS NEEDED TO HELP ME ACHIEVE THIS GOAL	DONE	REWARD
1			
2			
3			

Rewards

In the chart above, decide which of your steps should have an accompanying reward for its successful completion. Write what the specific reward will be. After completing the step, place a checkmark in the Done column and be sure to give yourself the assigned reward.

Environment Control

Others who know you may want to keep you in denial (e.g., family, friends, opposite-sex boyfriend or girlfriend). When you are beginning to work on reducing denial, it is helpful to avoid, or at least reduce contact with, the people and groups that would prefer you kept living a lie. In the chart below, write the environmental changes you need to make until your goal is successfully achieved:

#	PERSON OR GROUP THAT AFFECTS YOU	+ OR - EFFECT	PLANNED ACTION (Range: complete avoidance to frequent contact—be specific)
1			
2			
3			
4			

C. Changing the Way You Feel About It

When you experience a negative feeling complete the following chart (REMINDER: instructions for using this chart are found in the Introduction):

NAME THE FEELING(S)	DESCRIBE THE TRIGGER	UNDERLYING BELIEF(S)	QUESTIONING IT	HEALTHIER BELIEF

Where I'm At After Working On It

Periodically re-test yourself to chart your progress in this area.

		NO	YES 1 2 3 4 5
1	I minimize my homosexuality by downplaying the importance of my feelings, behaviour or sexual attractions.		
2	I try to convince myself that I'm not gay.		
3	I find it easy to "turn off" my feelings when dating someone of the same sex.		
4	I don't feel much passion toward others.		
5	I don't feel much passion within myself.		

If you are still responding "YES" to any of these questions, continue working on change in this area. If all of your responses are "NO," you have made significant progress! Continue to monitor any remaining problems in this area and work on these as suggested in this chapter.

Summary

Nelson did his best to avoid facing what his heart and soul had been telling him for years. He did this through the defense mechanism called denial, which is when a person consciously or subconsciously refuses to accept an aspect of his or her reality. There are consequences to living in denial. Perhaps the most obvious consequence is that a major part of what gives our life passion is missing—denial of the deepest of all emotions: consummate love for another person. If your life has felt devoid or lacking in passion, denial may be at work.

Denial can become so well learned by gay people that they become numb to their own feelings and needs, and to those around them (Colgan, 1987). Consequently, they become unable to love other people.

The bulk of this chapter has shown you how to eliminate denial so that you can fully own your thoughts, feelings and attractions. On the next page is the Positive Affirmations pullout sheet. Spend a few minutes each day reflecting on what each affirmation means to you personally.

Positive Affirmations

[Also add your own from the Healthier Belief columns in this chapter]

My feelings tell me I am attracted to members of the same gender, and I accept this completely. Acting on my feelings is appropriate.

I am gay, and that is okay. There is no substitute for being myself.

Becoming a loving person is more important than pleasing others.

Once I accept and love all parts of myself as a gay person, I will be able to accept and love others to an equal extent.

As I accept my feelings and attractions fully, I will reconnect to the passion in my life.

CHAPTER 4
Reclaiming Your Self

"Only by taking responsibility for one's self can one become free to choose and be authentic."

(Grodi, 1995, 12)

"Real happiness, self-actualization, is being yourself every waking moment."

(Herrman, 1990, 90)

"Less healthy personalities, people who function less than fully, who suffer recurrent breakdowns or chronic impasses, may usually be found to be liars. They say things they do not mean. Their disclosures have been chosen more for cosmetic value than for truth. The consequence of a lifetime of lying about oneself to others, of saying and doing things for their sound and appearance, is that ultimately the person loses contact with his real self."

(Jourard, 1968, 46, 47)

Mark came out at age 35 and soon started spending many nights at the local gay bar. He felt most attracted to the young cool kids with slender bodies. They became his role models, and before long, Mark shaved off most of his body hair and bleached what remained. Next came the body piercings—first both ears and later a nipple. Then the clothes changed. From a distance, Mark now looked like he was 19, and inside, he felt even younger. Before long, the young gay bar patrons were smitten with Mark's demeanour. He oozed raw sexuality. Mark was like the new kid in town, having as much sex and enjoying as much dating as he wanted. It seemed he had found exactly what he was looking for, yet deep down, he knew something was amiss.

Mark felt like an impostor. This wasn't anything new for he had felt that way long before coming out. The disappointment was in realizing that the feeling of fakeness had only diminished and not ended completely since coming out. Sometimes people would say to him, "Mark, just be yourself." That seemed so easy for others, but for Mark, it always sounded like an empty cliché.

Mark's life seemed like an endless web, but one with strands that didn't connect. With one friend, he might come across as prudish, yet he would accompany another friend to the bathhouse and enjoy the very activities he told his other friend that he despised. Similarly, Mark would tell his friends exactly what they wanted to hear. Behind their backs, however, Mark would occasionally say what he really thought or felt to a different friend. He didn't worry about the contradictions because his friends didn't know each other well. Mark wanted to keep it that way, partly because they were so different. Each friend brought out a different aspect of his personality, which to Mark seemed like very different parts.

Eventually he told his best friends that he was gay, which was uneventful. Some said they had already suspected, especially since he had adopted this new boyish appearance. However, coming out to his family then was not right. This meant that he had to repeatedly lie to them about why he had changed his appearance, why he never told them about his dates, why this and why that. A year later, Mark finally told them, but by then they had already pieced it together for themselves.

The lying, however, continued, and not just with family. Mark had lied so convincingly for so long that it was an ingrained habit. Whenever an untruth would suffice or it would lead to a more appealing consequence, Mark lied, and rarely questioned his reason for doing so. The trouble was, he couldn't always remember what he had said to whom. While his best friends began pulling away, new friends took their place, each sharing some of the same dishonest qualities that Mark had perfected.

Now at age 39, Mark remains primarily attracted to younger guys. He is beginning to feel some attraction to men closer to his own age, but having a relationship with anyone remains elusive. He still can't answer the question, "Who am I?" and therefore doesn't know what kind of person he would want in his life. Perhaps he hasn't just lied to others all these years— perhaps it's deeper than that. Although he came out four years ago, he still feels like an incomplete person and doesn't understand why.

The Problem

Mark has not formed an integrated identity: instead, parts of his identity have remained fragmented. The technical term for this is compartmentalization, which is when ideas, attitudes, values or feelings are kept blocked off and separated from each other. Like the word suggests, each part that the person perceives as threatening or contradictory is figuratively kept in a separate compartment. In this way, the person can avoid resolving internal conflicts. However, the negative spin off, is that compartmentalization prevents the person from forming a congruous sense of self. So long as a person's ideas, attitudes, values, beliefs and feelings are kept in limbo—usually because they haven't been sufficiently challenged or understood—there is no answer to the question, "Who Am I?"

In his book, Being-Being Happy-Being Gay, Bert Herrman wrote that it is not until a person becomes himself or herself in every moment that they become happy and fulfilled (Herrman, 1990). For many gay people, the quest to become authentic is an important catalyst for coming out to both themselves and others (Alderson, 2000).

Living a lie is painful. It can cause paranoid feelings because the person never knows when she or he might be found out. Just as gay people become expert at denial (see Chapter 3), they also become expert at lying. From a young age, gay individuals learn to lie about their deepest feelings. The later they come out to themselves, the longer they have practiced lying. When people lie to themselves so convincingly that they can avoid coming out, they have also mastered the fine art of lying to others.

Even after self-identifying as gay, the lying habit is so deeply ingrained that it takes concerted effort to stop. Unfortunately, the act of disclosing to others is often so emotionally charged, if not downright painful, that it often remains easier to hide, thereby necessitating an ongoing lie of the worst magnitude. To lie about something so basic as one's sexuality is to do the self the greatest hurt. Years of lying cause significant damage to our integrity (Martin, 1982). It also prevents us from being in touch with ourselves (Jourard, 1968).

Many men who do not come out until they are well into their thirties then experience something writers have called a delayed adolescence (Malyon, 1982a). It is a fitting term, because the person going through it often feels and acts like a teenager. He ignores his chronological age, which nevertheless periodically reminds him that there is something disconcerting about it all. Closeted homosexual teenagers often do not successfully navigate the identity crisis, which is natural and common for adolescents. While heterosexual boys date and learn about what turns on the other sex, closeted homosexual boys stymie their sexual interests. Once they come out, there is a lot of catching up to do.

Let's take a look now at what has happened to Mark. He came out at 35; experienced his own delayed adolescence, reflected by his interest in teens; he changed to a much more youthful appearance; and, his inner feelings were reminiscent of an earlier developmental stage. Mark felt like an impostor because he was still compartmentalizing his values, opinions and feelings. Instead of challenging his own contradictions, he avoided facing up to them. He still hasn't found a way to become honest with people, and his telling people what they want to hear likely reveals an old pattern of being a people pleaser. In doing so, Mark becomes less likely to be criticized. Criticism will bother anyone who has not already formed a strong sense of self, and the self-esteem to go with it.

Lying to self and others, combined with failing to challenge his contradictions or the fears underlying them, has had a tragic result. Mark has not achieved an integrated identity.

What Needs to Change?

The strands of your identity need to become intricately woven into their own unique creation. This means conquering the fear that has delayed your identity integration. If you remain afraid of your sexuality, you will also have trouble dealing with others, and loving others deeply (Helminiak, 1994). Consequently, overcoming internalized homophobia is the beginning step, which was covered in Chapter 1.

Once you have sufficiently reduced internalized homophobia, you will be less afraid to begin accepting the parts of your personality, behaviour and thoughts that you like, as well as the parts that you don't. Of course it makes sense to change aspects of yourself that you don't like, if they are amenable to change. This is not as easy as it sounds. If it were, there would be many people who are close to perfect. That is not the reality. In truth, most people remain pretty much the same throughout their adult years. Therefore, a more important task in life than self-change is gaining self-awareness and self-acceptance (Rogers, 1961). If you are an introvert, you are an introvert. Attempting to become extroverted is only going to frustrate you. If you enjoy a spontaneous lifestyle, but force yourself to become planned and deliberate, similar frustration will result. If you are gay, you are gay. You like and love others of the same gender—end of story.

Liking and loving anybody is an admirable trait. The love you give is the closest you will ever get to being divine. Love, therefore, is a good thing. Hold onto it, and accept it.

Face up to the ways you used to avoid looking at the aspects of yourself that you didn't like. A common practice is distraction, which simply involves keeping yourself focused on things other than challenging your contradictory thinking or confusing behaviour. More damaging is overcompensation, which is where you unconsciously try to make up for your "deficiencies" by excessively devoting your energy to other matters. Workaholics, those who overwork to avoid facing their inner conflicts, exemplify a common form of overcompensation.

To develop a clear identity, you need to enhance your self-awareness. You also need to become your own psychoanalyst. The person most qualified to examine and challenge your beliefs is you.

A trait you will need to develop, if it is not already there, is courage. Courage is acting in a positive and constructive manner, despite the fear it produces. As you discover parts of yourself you fear, you will still need to include these parts in your self-concept. Before you can become integrated you need to accept each petal attached to your flower, especially the ones that seem withered and otherwise disdainful. You were never expected to be perfect.

To become yourself you cannot be overly concerned with what other people think of you. The opinions of others count for little when you begin searching for answers regarding your likes, dislikes, beliefs, values and attitudes. The whole point of challenging your thoughts is for you to make your own decisions.

Developing a positive gay identity will also require that you become authentic, forfeiting lies for truth, choosing integrity over dishonesty. This, too, requires courage. Consequences will result when you begin telling the truth in all situations. The external consequence will generally be much less important than the internal consequence—the one we call integrity.

This chapter will show you how to improve or achieve a stronger sense of your own identity, and how to develop personal integrity. It will show you how to reclaim your self.

Where I'm At Now

Place a checkmark in the column that corresponds to your answer.

If your answer is "yes," use the following rating scale: 1=very slightly; 2=slightly; 3=moderately; 4=highly; 5=severely.

		NO	YES 1	2	3	4	5
1	I feel inauthentic, like an impostor.						
2	I cannot answer the question, "Who Am I?"						
3	I don't challenge my own ideas or beliefs about life.						
4	I am quite concerned about what other people think of me.						
5	I lie to others, even when telling the truth would not be that damaging to me.						

If you respond "YES" to any of these questions, you would benefit from doing some work in this area. If all of your responses are "NO," you may want to skip this chapter.

The Solution

Referring back to Mark, a solution will require that he continue working through his delayed adolescence. His emotional development is still that of a teenager, which is understandable given the later age of his coming out to himself. Growing emotionally occurs through our experience with others, which is what Mark is doing (i.e., dating younger men), but it also occurs through having our beliefs and contradictions challenged. Mark would do well to listen to what his insides are telling him and search for the sources of his feelings that don't feel quite right. The feedback he receives from people who accept him will be helpful too.

Mark needs to find himself. He needs to test the waters further, which is what he did when he changed his look. Trying on different roles is an important part of identity development. So is dating men with various traits and characteristics. Through this experience, Mark will eventually develop a clear sense of what he likes and dislikes in a partner.

While it will take Mark time to get a clear sense of who he is as a gay man, he can live his life with as much authenticity and integrity as he is currently capable. This means giving up the lies and noting the contradictions in his thoughts and behaviours so that he can later sort out the conflicting beliefs that underlie the discrepancies.

Mark missed out the opportunity to experience first love during his adolescence, and perhaps so did you. The most important thing is to develop your own unique identity, one that becomes integrated. In turn, this will leave you with a sense of wholeness and completeness. The exercises that follow will help you get there.

A. Changing Your Thoughts

1. Beliefs Chart
REMINDER: Complete the following exercise by using the How to Question Your Beliefs pullout sheet found in the Introduction.

SAMPLE THOUGHT	UNDERLYING BELIEF	QUESTIONING IT (you complete this column)	HEALTHIER BELIEF
I feel inauthentic, like an impostor.	I am not being true to myself.		I am determined to act in accordance with my beliefs, values and attitudes.
I cannot answer the question, "Who Am I?"	I don't know who I am.		I will commit myself to finding out who I am.
I don't challenge my own ideas or beliefs about life.	It is too difficult to challenge my ideas and beliefs.		I will do the necessary work to challenge my ideas and beliefs.
I am quite concerned about what other people think of me.	I need to please everyone who is important to me.		I need to feel comfortable with my own beliefs, values and attitudes. Other people's opinions are comparatively trivial.
I lie to others, even when telling the truth would not be that damaging to me.	Lying is easier than telling the truth.		Telling the truth leads to integrity. I am committed to truth.
(Write any additional thoughts and beliefs you have.)			

2. Visualization Exercises
REMINDER: Complete the following exercises by using the How to Visualize pull-out sheet found in the Introduction.

(a) General Visualizations—Reflect upon the various qualities that you have, both positive and negative. Include your personality traits, values, beliefs and attitudes. You might want to list these qualities, and continue adding to your list, after each visualization practice.

(b) Specific Visualizations—Think of a specific instance where you found yourself feeling incomplete or fragmented. Ask yourself what you would need to have worked out in that situation in order to feel whole and complete. Think through what the solution might look like, and then imagine yourself implementing that solution. Focus on feeling complete and whole. For example, if you tell people one thing and then do another, think about this contradiction and decide what you really want to believe. Then see yourself being consistent in what you say and do. Also imagine times where you have been dishonest, and see yourself telling the truth. Pay attention to the consequence of your honesty and ability to cope with its aftermath.

B. Changing Your Behaviour

1. General Activities

These general activities will help you reclaim your self:

• Don't let yourself off easy. Challenge your contradictory beliefs and behaviours. When you become aware of a discrepancy between them don't ignore it. Instead, stick with it until you find an answer, one that makes sense to you.

• Dig deep. Don't settle for a superficial understanding of yourself and others. Pay particular attention to your motives and feelings, listen to and learn from them. It helps to write them down so that you can see their recurring themes. Over time, this will help you come to understand yourself better.

• Foster the development of courage. This will automatically occur as you continue to face your fears. Push yourself into taking more difficult challenges in your personal and work life. Resist the temptation to flee difficult tasks in life.

• Enhance self-awareness. Take every opportunity to learn more about yourself. Writing down your beliefs, values and attitudes as you become aware of them can be helpful. Make a commitment to write daily entries in a journal.

• Develop friendships with many types of people. It is often through our interactions with others that we come to understand ourselves better. Through others we learn about what qualities we admire, and which ones we don't. Chances are, you will become more selective of who you pick as friends over time. That is a natural by-product of coming to know yourself better.

• Experiment. Try out many different roles and behaviours. Without experience you will have a hard time knowing what you like and don't like. Likewise, if you keep suppressing yourself by not doing what you want to be doing, you will continue to wonder how much of this desire is a defining trait of your identity.

• Don't delay your delayed adolescence. If you are going through this, go through it. Don't try and stop a necessary part of your development. If you are doing what I've suggested throughout this book, you will grow and mature in due course. Enjoy the journey.

• Speak only truth. Lying might be second nature to you, but being honest and speaking truth will put you on the path toward integrity. With integrity comes self-knowledge.

• Don't be that concerned with what others think of you. This is easier said than done. As this is a primary focus for Chapter 6, I will wait until then to offer suggestions on how to do this effectively.

2. Specific Activities

Goal-Setting

Decide upon a specific behaviour that you will target for change. Your best choice is a behaviour that you have already found is causing you trouble. Here are some examples:

• Disowning important interests (e.g., avoiding a career choice because you believe it will easily identify you as gay).
• Facing a specific contradiction (e.g., you want to be an accepting person, but find yourself harshly judging every drag queen).
• Saying things you don't mean so that others don't think less of you.
• Lying consistently to a close friend.

Shaping

Write your goal in the chart below, and then list the steps you will take to begin working on it.

GOAL:			
#	STEPS NEEDED TO HELP ME ACHIEVE THIS GOAL	DONE	REWARD
1			
2			
3			

Rewards

In the chart above, decide which of your steps should have an accompanying reward for its successful completion. Write what the specific reward will be. After completing the step, place a checkmark in the Done column and be sure to give yourself the assigned reward.

Environment Control

Becoming yourself is not easy if people insist you stay in the mould they have cast for you. As you test out different facets of your identity, you want to be with people who can accept the various dimensions of your personality. In the chart below, write the environmental changes you need to make until your goal is successfully achieved:

#	PERSON OR GROUP THAT AFFECTS YOU	+ OR - EFFECT	PLANNED ACTION (Range: complete avoidance to frequent contact—be specific)
1			
2			
3			
4			

C. Changing the Way You Feel About It

By paying attention to your feelings, you will increase your self-awareness, which is an important part of learning about yourself. Consequently, keep track of your positive and negative feelings in the following chart. You may not want to change a number of your underlying beliefs (column 3), however, as your main purpose here is self-awareness rather than self-change.

If you don't want to change the underlying belief, it will still be helpful to complete column 4 (Questioning It), as this will get you in touch with why you chose to maintain the belief. However, column 5 (Healthier Belief), will be irrelevant to you, as you have decided that the pros of this belief outweigh the cons.

NAME THE FEELING(S)	DESCRIBE THE TRIGGER	UNDERLYING BELIEF(S)	QUESTIONING IT	HEALTHIER BELIEF

Where I'm At After Working On It

Periodically re-test yourself to chart your progress in this area.

		NO	YES 1 2 3 4 5
1	I feel inauthentic, like an impostor.		
2	I cannot answer the question, "Who Am I?"		
3	I don't challenge my own ideas or beliefs about life.		
4	I am quite concerned about what other people think of me.		
5	I lie to others, even when telling the truth would not be that damaging to me.		

If you are still responding "YES" to any of these questions, continue working on change in this area. If all of your responses are "NO," you have made significant progress! Continue to monitor any remaining problems in this area, and work on these as suggested in this chapter.

Summary

Mark was slow in coming out and then found he had to make up for lost years. His attractions began at a developmentally appropriate level: he lusted after young men initially, a phenomenon known as delayed adolescence. Mark had to go in search of himself, rediscovering and discovering for the first time aspects of his self that were unknown to him. Mark still has work to do. Maybe we all do.

When ideas, attitudes, values or feelings are kept detached from each other, contradictions often result in the way one thinks, feels and behaves. The technical term for this is compartmentalization (Chaplin, 1975).

Reclaiming your self is about discovering your identity and staying true to it. Becoming authentic is an important aspect of becoming a positive gay man or positive lesbian woman. Shedding lies for truth is essential in that it allows you to form an integrated identity. Furthermore, honesty greatly enhances the quality of the relationships you develop with others.

On the next page is the Positive Affirmations pullout sheet, which can be kept by your bed or in some other highly visible place. Spend a few minutes each day reflecting on what each affirmation means to you personally.

POSITIVE AFFIRMATIONS

[Also add your own from the Healthier Belief *columns in this chapter]*

I am determined to act in accordance with my beliefs, values and attitudes.

I will commit myself to finding out who I am.

I will do the necessary work to challenge my ideas and beliefs.

I need to feel comfortable with my own beliefs, values and attitudes. Other people's opinions are comparatively trivial.

Telling the truth leads to integrity. I am committed to truth.

CHAPTER 5
Relinquishing the Lies That Haunt You

"In general, gay men are more similar to heterosexual men, and lesbian women more similar to heterosexual women, than to each other."

(Garnets & Kimmel, 1993, 25)

"Gay men and lesbians are as varied in their dress, mannerisms, and styles as their heterosexual counterparts."

(Blumenfeld & Raymond, 1993, 378)

Thomas had known of his sexual interest in guys since he was 10 years old. As he matured, however, he found that the stereotypes he held regarding gay men didn't apply to him—he was neither effeminate nor meek. He enjoyed competitive sports, especially hockey and football, and his looks and personality were rugged.

He also saw himself as a deep individual who wanted a long-term relationship, yet he believed that gay men were promiscuous and superficial. He viewed himself as emotionally well- balanced, yet he believed gay men were mentally unhealthy. He worked as an engineer, yet he believed gay men were destined to become hairdressers, dancers or interior decorators. The contrast between his self-image and the image he had of gay men was incompatible. Since he didn't share any of their characteristics, how could he be gay? Consequently, he dismissed his homosexual feelings for many years.

When Thomas was 25, he started working at a large industrial plant. Most employees were disgruntled with the company and bitch sessions became the norm during coffee breaks. Gordon, an accountant, was different—his optimism was refreshing, and Thomas wanted to know him better. Soon they became good friends. As they became closer, Thomas learned that Gordon was gay, and Gordon had assumed that Thomas was as well. Rather than confront him, he asked Thomas if he wanted to go with him to the local gay bar. Without giving it much thought, Thomas agreed. Later, amidst pangs of apprehension and fear, he considered cancelling his commitment, but a growing excitement was also surfacing. Thomas decided that he needed to become more open-minded about this.

At the gay bar, he was surprised by the variety of gay men he met, including some who did not define themselves as gay. He still noticed the flamboyant drag queens more than other bar patrons, but after frequenting the bar for a few months, Thomas understood that his stereotypes only applied to some individuals. After befriending a few more gay men, Thomas learned enough about being gay to come out.

Some months later when he told his parents, he was pissed off that they didn't believe him. They told him he's not the type, that it was merely a phase. It struck Thomas that this "phase" had already lasted for as long as he could remember. He decided to not make an issue of it, hoping that time would help his parents accept his disclosure.

Thomas now spends a lot of time on weekends with his new friends, meeting for coffee, taking walks through the park and cruising men that they pass on the street. As they walk by various men, Thomas is surprised by how confidently his friends label some of them as gay. After one such occurrence, Thomas asked Peter, "Do you know him?" Peter replied, "No, I've never seen him before." "Then how can you tell he's gay?" Thomas asked. "I can't explain it," responded Peter, "But you will eventually learn to do it yourself." Over the ensuing months, Thomas watched his friends closely, paying particular attention to their perceptions of other men. It didn't take long until Thomas had honed his own intuition. Like his friends, he enjoyed sharing his perceptions with others.

After spending an afternoon with Karen, his sister, Thomas sensed her growing annoyance. "What is bothering you, Karen? You're making me feel uncomfortable." Karen replied, "I guess you're picking up my discomfort, Thomas, with what you are doing. Do you realize that according to my calculations, you have labelled almost 30% of the men we have seen today as gay? Have you ever thought that your figures might be a tad bit high? I'm sick of hearing you cast judgment on people you don't know. Give it up."

Thomas felt hurt by Karen's terseness, yet he knew that she was hitting a deep chord inside. How does he know this about guys he hasn't even met? Why does labelling others make him feel better about himself? Before they parted company, Thomas apologized to her, and assured her that he would take a closer look at the meaning behind his behaviour.

The Problem

Karen has observed something that Thomas is only beginning to realize: although he has come a long way since his childhood, he is still stereotyping the people he encounters. This chapter is about stereotypes, both obvious and subtle. Stereotypes are the lies that haunt gay individuals before they come out, but because they are lies, they hurt all of us. Merriam-Webster's collegiate dictionary (1996) defines a stereotype as "a standardized mental picture that is held in common by members of a group and that represents an oversimplified opinion, prejudiced attitude, or uncritical judgment." Often stereotypes begin with some grain of truth, but that grain is sown into people's minds as though everyone in the targeted group shares the characteristic. The characteristic subsequently becomes over generalized, exaggerated and distorted.

In New York City, youth who are questioning their sexuality call a special hotline set up for them and the typical questions they ask are, "Does this mean I have to be a hairdresser or something like that?"; "Will I start messing around with little kids?"; "Am I going to get AIDS?" They're serious questions, and the stereotypes underlying them have driven some to both attempt and commit suicide.

Even today, some classified ads read, "Straight looking, straight acting, gay white male looking to meet same." Those who respond to such ads ought to ask what these words mean. There isn't a gay look. The trendy young man with two-tone hair and multiple earrings today is just as likely straight as he is gay. Statistically, in fact, he is more likely straight.

The vernacular expression, used by some gay men in North America, of having gaydar is little more than the flagrant use of stereotyping. Research has shown that the odds of distinguishing gay men from straight men by their looks are no better than chance (Dunkle & Francis, 1996). Only a small percentage of gay men engage in role-playing behaviour that would identity them (Slater, 1988), and because even this behaviour is based on stereotypes, one can easily make a mistake.

The gay stereotypes do not describe the majority of gay people, yet they persist. A smorgasbord of such stereotypes includes "mentally ill, emotionally crippled, neurotic, sexually confused, promiscuous, unfulfilled, parentally fixated, unhappy, obsessed, lonely, depressed, and incapable of relationships" (Dubay, 1987, 102). Other examples include undependable, narcissistic, shallow, effeminate, overly talkative and critical of others (Beard & Glickauf-Hughes, 1994; Hart, 1981; Lee, 1977). Individuals who believe in these negative stereotypes are more likely to develop pervasive negative attitudes toward gay people (Ben-Ari, 1998). Even in the Netherlands, which is generally viewed as gay positive, stereotypes concerning gay men and lesbians are common among the general population and among gay individuals (Hekma, 1998).

Each stereotype does describe some gay individuals, but the fact is, each stereotype also describes an equal proportion of heterosexual people. Gay individuals are as unique as heterosexuals. There is no evidence supporting any of the gay stereotypes (Bell & Weinberg, 1978; Blumenfeld & Raymond, 1993; Hart, 1981a; Herdt, 1997; Lee, 1977; April Martin, 1982; Morin, 1977; Slater, 1988). For example, the majority of gay men:

• are not effeminate (Lee, 1977)
• are capable of and interested in sustainable relationships (approximately 40% are in long-term relationships) (Cody & Welch, 1997; Peplau, 1993)
• work in traditionally masculine jobs, not in the arts or social services (Blumenfeld & Raymond, 1993)
• are psychologically healthy individuals (Gonsiorek, 1982; Morin & Rothblum, 1991; Richardson, 1993)

The majority of lesbian women:

• are more androgynous in their gender roles as compared to heterosexual women (Risman & Schwartz, 1988)

• are more independent in intimate relationships than heterosexual women (Elliott, 1993).
• have had heterosexual intercourse (Kitzinger & Wilkinson, 1995)
• appear to be more fluid and flexible in their sexual identity compared to gay men (Dworkin, 2000; Golden, 1987)
• are psychologically as healthy or healthier than heterosexual women (Falk, 1993)

Thomas' adherence to stereotypes delayed his coming out. His macho persona did not mesh with his view that gay men are effeminate. Furthermore, he viewed all gay men as promiscuous and superficial. Although he later realized that gay men come in every variety, he soon began typecasting passersby on the street, based on his simplistic notions of how a gay man looks and acts.

What Needs to Change?
Stereotyping helps people understand others in the simplest possible terms. Rather than see each person as an individual, stereotyping places people into categories, thereby pre-empting the process of needing to know more about the person. It's quick, efficient—and inaccurate.

Other motives for stereotyping include having feelings of superiority and believing in one's omnipotent ability to easily categorize others correctly. Another motive for some gay individuals is the desire to feel community by artificially inflating the number of perceived gay people out there. Thomas categorized 30% of the men he saw as gay because it helped him feel a sense of belonging—a sense that he is not alone.

In overcoming your own stereotyping behaviour, first remember that you are not alone. Gay men and women are everywhere, working in every occupation, sporting every kind of look, living on nearly every street. Your banker, lawyer, retailer, doctor, mechanic, uncle—gay individuals abound in every occupation. Even counsellors are often misinformed about gay people. Norton (1995, 157) lists a number of the myths commonly believed by counsellors:

(1) Gays want to be of the opposite gender
(2) Gay males are primarily artists, hairdressers, antique dealers and interior decorators;
(3) All gay males are promiscuous
(4) Gay males are weak, introspective and inactive physically
(5) Removing laws against homosexuality will increase its frequency
(6) Gays and lesbians hate those of the opposite sex
(7) Gays are a menace to children
(8) Just give a gay male some male hormones and he will want women
(9) Gays in role modeling positions, such as teacher or minister, will turn chil-

dren into homosexuals; and

(10) Homosexual partners take on male and female roles

As Norton points out, none of these myths have any validity whatsoever. They are simply promulgated by some misinformed heterosexual individuals. It seems that there is no greater difference between lies and truth in our society than those which are aimed at gay men and lesbian women. I also believe gay people have to take responsibility for this misinformation. The ongoing code of silence which has made gay people invisible to many heterosexuals is currently more our fault than it is theirs. If we want them to know us, we have to let them know we exist in the numbers that we do. Only then will they see how diverse and loving we are.

Unlike the members of other minority groups, who usually share a number of common beliefs, values or attitudes, members of the gay community are defined by their uniqueness and diversity. Gay individuals come from every conceivable ethnic, racial, cultural and socio-economic background—from rich to poor, from religious to atheist, from American to Southeast Asian. The key to overcoming stereotypes is in understanding the magnitude of this uniqueness and diversity. No two gay people are alike, unless they choose to create conformity between themselves. For this reason, being gay is about freedom to be yourself.

Along with this freedom comes the responsibility to accept the differences you will encounter. Learn to accept other gay people as they are, and remember that the differences are one of the defining features of being gay. Above all else, keep an open mind and challenge the stereotypes that haunt you.

Where I'm At Now
Place a checkmark in the column that corresponds to your answer.

If your answer is "yes," use the following rating scale: 1=very slightly; 2=slightly; 3=moderately; 4=highly; 5=severely.

		NO	YES 1	2	3	4	5
1	I believe most gay men are feminine, and most lesbian women are masculine.						
2	You can identify gay men and lesbian women by their looks.						
3	Nearly all gay men are promiscuous.						
4	Most gay people are emotionally disturbed.						
5	Gay people are incapable of sustaining long-term committed relationships.						

If you respond "YES" to any of these questions, you would benefit from doing some work in this area. If all of your responses are "NO," you may want to skip this chapter.

The Solution

Thomas has already eliminated a number of the stereotypes he had of gay men when he was a child. He now understands that some gay men, like heterosexual men, are promiscuous, some are superficial, and that they work within every career imaginable. He still needs to learn that their diversity is greater than he ever expected. Although he can accurately pick out some gay men who work at being visible through their mannerisms and behaviour, he still needs to learn that the majority of effeminate men are heterosexual. Instead of labelling people, Thomas needs to get to know people.

If you are gay and admit this to others, most other gay people will tell you if they are gay. There is no point second-guessing and no point categorizing. If you are still finding yourself stereotyping other people, you are doing everyone a disservice. The next section will show you how to stop stereotyping.

A. Changing Your Thoughts

1. Beliefs Chart

REMINDER: Complete the following exercise by using the How to Question Your Beliefs pullout sheet found in the Introduction.

SAMPLE THOUGHT	UNDERLYING BELIEF	QUESTIONING IT (you complete this column)	HEALTHIER BELIEF
I believe most gay men are feminine and most lesbian women are masculine.	The stereotypes propagated by society are accurate portrayals of gay people.		The gay community is extremely diverse. Stereotypes are over-generalizations and they do not apply to most gay people.
You can identify gay men and lesbian women by their looks.	There is one look for gay men, and another for lesbian women. It's easy to spot them.		Aside from a few who want to be identified through their dress and mannerisms, most gay people dress in a variety of ways.
Nearly all gay men are promiscuous.	Gay men are only looking for one thing—sex.		Many men, gay or straight, are promiscuous at

		certain stages in their lives. Research indicates that most gay men want to be in a committed relationship.
Most gay people are emotionally disturbed.	Heterosexual individuals are emotionally healthier than gay people.	There is little difference between the emotional health of the average gay person compared to his or her heterosexual counterparts.
Gay people are incapable of sustaining long-term committed relationships.	There is something inherently wrong with gay people that prevents them from sustaining relationships.	At least 40 % of gay men are in committed relationships, as are the majority of lesbian women.

(Write any additional thoughts and beliefs you have.)

2. Visualization Exercises

REMINDER: Complete the following exercises by using the How to Visualize pull-out sheet found in the Introduction.

(a) General Visualizations—Think about a world free of stereotypes and prejudice. What would be the benefits? What would be the costs? Imagine yourself being a person who no longer stereotypes people. What does it feel like? How have you gained as a person from this change?

(b) Specific Visualizations—Think of specific instances where you found yourself stereotyping other people, particularly examples where you later found out that you had misjudged the person. Think about the way you would dress if you wanted to be more readily identified as gay. What would you be wearing? Are there heterosexuals you know or have seen who sometimes wear similar clothes?

B. Changing Your Behaviour

1. General Activities
These general activities will help you stop stereotyping:

• Frequent a few gay bars. Once there, look around. What percentage of the men would you classify as feminine? What percentage of the women would you classify as masculine? Examine their clothing and hairstyles. How different are they compared to the heterosexual people you see around you?

• Attend a circuit party. A circuit party is a large rave-like event for gay people, held in various cities throughout Canada and the United States. These events are held annually and those who "play the circuit" attend a number of them. Once there, observe people. How many of them fit your stereotypes?

• Expand your friendship circle. Even now, you might be aware that most of your friends don't fit your stereotypes. If they do, connect with some gay people that don't. Challenge yourself.

• Be "straight looking, straight acting" for a day. How did you have to change to make this happen? How many gay people look and act this way most of the time? How many heterosexual people do not look and act this way most of the time?

2. Specific Activities

Goal-setting
Decide upon a specific behaviour that you will target for change. Your best choice is a behaviour that you have already found is causing you trouble. Here are some examples:

• Learn to appreciate effeminate gay men or masculine lesbian women. If you find that you automatically dislike these people before you even know them, you are struggling with varying degrees of internalized homophobia and/or heterofacsimile.

• Challenge a specific type of stereotyping that you engage in.

• Overcome your view that most if not all gay men are promiscuous.

• Talk to a gay man or a lesbian woman who works in a non-stereotypical career.

Shaping
Write your goal in the chart below, and then list the steps you will take to begin working on it.

GOAL:			
#	STEPS NEEDED TO HELP ME ACHIEVE THIS GOAL	DONE	REWARD
1			
2			
3			

Rewards

In the chart above, decide which of your steps should have an accompanying reward for its successful completion. Write what the specific reward will be. After completing the step, place a checkmark in the Done column and be sure to give yourself the assigned reward.

Environment Control

The stereotypes we internalize are taught to us and influenced by friends, family and media. In this section, you may want to list all of the people who have influenced the beliefs you have today, and then be specific in the next column regarding their influence on your development of gay stereotypes. Has the influence been positive (i.e., helping you overcome stereotyping tendencies), or negative (i.e., leading you to develop more stereotypes)? Are there people you can spend more time with who oppose stereotyping other gay people?

#	PERSON OR GROUP THAT AFFECTS YOU	+ OR - EFFECT	PLANNED ACTION (Range: complete avoidance to frequent contact—be specific)
1			
2			
3			
4			

C. Changing the Way You Feel About It

When you experience a negative feeling complete the following chart (REMINDER: instructions for using this chart are found in the Introduction):

NAME THE FEELING(S)	DESCRIBE THE TRIGGER	UNDERLYING BELIEF(S)	QUESTIONING IT	HEALTHIER BELIEF

Where I'm At After Working On It
Periodically re-test yourself to chart your progress in this area.

		NO	YES 1	2	3	4	5
1	I believe most gay men are feminine, and most lesbian women are masculine.						
2	You can identify gay men and lesbian women by their looks.						
3	Nearly all gay men are promiscuous.						
4	Most gay people are emotionally disturbed.						
5	Gay people are incapable of sustaining long-term committed relationships.						

If you are still responding "YES" to any of these questions, continue working on change in this area. If all of your responses are "NO," you have made significant progress! Continue to monitor any remaining problems in this area, and work on these as suggested in this chapter.

Summary
Thomas has made significant progress in overcoming the lies that haunted him about being gay. You can probably relate to many of his struggles as he began challenging deeply-entrenched stereotypes. Thomas still finds himself presuming that more people are gay than statistics would suggest. This probably helps him feel a sense of belonging—that he is not alone as a gay man.

A stereotype, according to Merriam-Webster's collegiate dictionary (1996), is "a standardized mental picture that is held in common by members of a group and that represents an oversimplified opinion, prejudiced attitude, or uncritical judgment." The gay stereotypes are no exception—they do not describe the majority of gay people, but they persist in the minds of both gay and non-gay individuals.

Most of this chapter has shown you how to eliminate stereotyping so that you can better appreciate each person's individuality and uniqueness. Gay people have been kept in a box long enough. On the next page is the Positive Affirmations pullout sheet. Spend a few minutes each day reflecting on what each affirmation means to you personally.

Positive Affirmations

[Also add your own from the Healthier Belief *columns in this chapter]*

The gay community is extremely diverse. Stereotypes are over-generalizations and they do not apply to most gay people.

Aside from a few who want to be identified through their dress and mannerisms, most gay people dress in a variety of ways.

Many men, gay or straight, are promiscuous at certain stages in their lives. Research indicates that most gay men want to be in a committed relationship.

There is little difference between the emotional health of the average gay person compared to his or her heterosexual counterparts.

At least 40 % of gay men are in committed relationships, as are the majority of lesbian women.

Chapter 6
Releasing Your Personal Power

"In [Nazi] Germany, they first came for the Communists, and I didn't speak up because I wasn't a Communist. Then they came for the Jews, and I didn't speak up because I wasn't a Jew. Then they came for the trade unionists, and I didn't speak up because I wasn't a trade unionist. Then they came for the Catholics, and I didn't speak up because I was a Protestant. Then they came for me—and by that time no one was left to speak up."

(Attributed to Pastor Martin Niemoeller, quoted in Bartlett, 1992, 684)

"I had lived my life letting others define me."

(Sapp, 2001, 18)

Janet and her partner Maureen became ecstatic when they opened the envelope. Janet was accepted into medicine at a prestigious school! A goal she had wanted since she was a child was finally becoming a reality. The summer seemed short as Janet worked hard to earn enough money to afford her educational pursuit. Sometimes working two or three jobs, she grew weary, but kept her heart focused on beginning classes.

Janet's first morning at university was remarkable. She felt such a glow inside as her soul told her she was accomplishing her dream. During lunch, she sat with several other medical students, some in their senior year, who began talking about what they did during their summer holidays. When it came time for Janet to talk, she hesitated for a moment. . .only enough for everyone to know she was uncomfortable. What should she tell them? She had only two weeks off work in the past four months, and this was spent going on vacation with Maureen. Janet was in love with Maureen and proud of her. Why should she hold this back? She decided not to. The reaction of her fellow medical students seemed positive. The next few years might be better than expected.

However, before leaving to catch her bus, Sue and Joan from the lunch group approached her. Sue said that she and Joan had been living together as roommates for the past four years and although their relationship was non-sexual, others in medical school suspected they were lovers. Both were tired of the smirks and stifled laughter they often noticed from other students. Most of the students wanted little to do with either of them after class. Janet felt panic as she realized that she could not take back what she had already disclosed.

Hoping that word would not spread, Janet pretended in class that nothing had been uttered. It soon became clear, however, that others now knew. Like Sue and Joan, she became the recipient of the smirks and laughter herself. As this slowly eroded her self-esteem over the ensuing weeks, Janet realized that she was having trouble coping. While still wondering if she should talk to a school counsellor about her feelings, an incident occurred which she would never forget.

Janet spent two days a week learning within the hospital itself. Each day there, she and Dr. Chives, her preceptor, were given a list of patients to visit. One of the patient names had been crossed off the list, and finding this curious, Janet asked Dr. Jones, the clinical supervisor, for clarification. Caught off guard, Dr. Jones replied, "This is common practice, Janet. Patients are routinely reassigned at the last moment." Janet was highly intuitive and knew his answer seemed suspicious.

Days later, Dr. Chives asked to speak to her in private. She had discovered that the clinical supervisor reassigned the patient after being told about Janet's sexual orientation. Dr. Jones felt it was inappropriate for a lesbian woman to see this particular patient. Janet wanted to know why, but even Dr. Chives was not provided with an answer. Holding tears back, Janet told Dr. Chives she needed to go home for the day.

Janet was having trouble controlling the crying. When Maureen arrived home from work, she was alarmed to find out how much trouble Janet was having with this. It took a few hours for Janet to recompose, but the damage to her ego had been done. A week later, she withdrew from medical school.

The Problem

There can be huge consequences to feeling marginalized. Recent research has shown that gay men are more prone than heterosexual men to stress-related conditions, including mood disorders and anxiety disorders (Cochran, 2001). These conditions may be caused by discrimination (Mays & Cochran, 2001).

Some encouraging research by Rothblum and Factor (2001) suggests that the mental health of lesbian women is no worse than their biological sisters. In fact, they found that compared to their sisters, lesbian women reported higher self-esteem.

Nevertheless, in Janet's case, we see that she has yet to develop enough ego-strength to deal with the externalized homophobia that she is experiencing in medical school. There are really two issues underlying Janet's problem: the first is how she chose to disclose to a group of strangers.

It is well-documented that medical schools are homophobic environments (Klamen, Grossman, & Kopacz, 1999; Risdon, Cook, & Willmns, 2000). Janet's decision to disclose during a casual lunch hour was costly—a decision that should have been carefully considered in advance. Before deciding to disclose, Janet should have first learned about the "climate" in her school. Was it a safe place for her to be openly lesbian? Would there likely be repercussions?

Before disclosing, one needs to ensure that the timing is right (Alderson, 2000). Some careers and professions are thought to be more difficult for out gay people (Chung & Harmon, 1994; Hewitt, 1995). If one is in a vulnerable stage of their training or their career, full disclosure is likely counterproductive. There is definitely a place for standing up for one's beliefs. It is a common characteristic of those who have developed positive gay identities (Alderson). But how much is worth risking? When the timing is right, one still needs to be prepared for the aftermath.

This raises the second issue underlying Janet's problem—her lack of ego-strength, or strength of character. Until Janet becomes strong enough to handle the criticism and rejection that will occasionally result after disclosing her sexual identity, she would do better to refrain from telling everyone. There is fragility in Janet's psychological makeup that she cannot be blamed for, but that needs to be addressed.

Most gay people have experienced some rejection for being gay, and often from a young age. For example, many gay boys have experienced rejection from their own fathers (Isay, 1996). Their fathers have often known that something is amiss with their son, something that makes them appear "different." Perhaps they detect that their sons have cross-gender interests, or perhaps they perceive at some level that their son is sexually attracted to other boys or men. In turn, it is easy to understand how some gay people become particularly vulnerable to rejection by others.

Janet has not learned adequate coping skills or assertiveness skills for dealing with the challenges of being gay in a mostly non-gay world. There are several areas she needs to change.

What Needs to Change?

Releasing your personal power is about developing autonomous thinking and strength of character, both in order to be yourself and to speak up when that is the best action to take. By definition, you are a nonconformist. Even if you blend in in every other regard, your sexual orientation makes you different from the majority. Autonomous thinking is about not accepting other people's interpretations about who you should be, what you should believe or what you should do. You are the only one who can provide these answers.

Think about it. How often have you heard one person suggest you do one thing, and another suggest you do exactly the opposite? Which is the "right" action to take? Every action you take occurs in a context, a situational perspective that is unique to you. For example, if you are trying to choose between two career possibilities—engineering or social work—how much will it really help you if some people suggest one choice and others recommend the other option? Who is the one that will eventually be doing the career every working day? You are! If the choice is not your best choice, you will be the one who feels the most regret. Particularly when it comes to defining yourself as a sexual being, others' opinions matter little. No one can tell you you're not attracted to the same gender and expect you to believe it. Once you're an adult, no one can tell you who you have the right to love.

Strength of character is having the intestinal fortitude to stand up for who you are and what you believe. It results from a combination of having healthy beliefs about yourself and having good coping skills and effective assertion skills. If you believe that you are inferior to others because you are gay, you are unlikely to feel adequate or act in an assertive manner toward others around you. By comparison, an example of a healthy belief would be "I have every right to express my opinions. Human worth cannot be measured, therefore I am equal to others." This belief will leave you less prepared to have your rights circumvented by others.

Good coping skills mean you have learned to deal with stressful events in a healthy way. For example, if you are thwarted from accomplishing a goal, you reassess your skills if necessary, decide if the goal is still important enough to you and redesign your action plan to increase your chances of succeeding next time. If you fail on the subsequent plan, you go through the same decision-making process as you did after the first failure. My point is, successful people never give up on themselves. It is tenacity that ultimately separates those who succeed from those who fail.

Assertion skills involve standing up for yourself when the situation warrants that you take action. It is a position between two extremes: passivity and aggressiveness. When you are assertive, you stand up for your rights (which passive people don't do) without taking advantage of the other person's rights (which aggressive people do). For example, if someone tells you a joke that you find offensive, a passive response would be to do nothing or to laugh at it. An aggressive response would be to launch into name-calling. An assertive response would be to tell the person politely yet firmly that you find the joke offensive and would prefer not hearing these kinds of jokes in the future.

When is the timing right to stand up for yourself as a gay person? This is not an easy question to answer. As a general rule, you may not want to stand up against others when it would be dangerous for you to do so. For example, I do not tell the 200-pound muscle-head steroid freak who butts in front of me at a movie theatre to move to the back of the line. However, if standing up to the same muscle freak is necessary to save someone who is getting gay bashed, I hope I would make a different choice. I also hope I never have to find out.

Where I'm At Now
Place a checkmark in the column that corresponds to your answer.

If your answer is "yes," use the following rating scale: 1=very slightly; 2=slightly; 3=moderately; 4=highly; 5=severely.

		NO	YES 1	2	3	4	5
1	I cannot be assertive, even when I should be.						
2	I deserve fewer rights than heterosexual people.						
3	I am highly influenced by other people's opinions of me.						
4	When the going gets tough, I begin shutting down.						
5	I don't know when to be assertive and when to keep quiet.						

If you respond "YES" to any of these questions, you would benefit from doing some work in this area. If all of your responses are "NO," you may want to skip this chapter.

The Solution

For Janet, a solution will require that she learn to assess environments carefully before choosing to disclose to others. She needs to think and learn before she acts. She might have assessed her medical school by first attending class for a few weeks and letting her intuition pick up clues regarding possible heterosexist beliefs and homophobic attitudes. She could have asked questions of the gay and lesbian group on campus regarding the overall school environment, or perhaps asked these questions of licensed physicians who have graduated from the same school of medicine. Another approach would be to wait until she had developed some trusted friends in the program, and then get their reading of how others would likely respond to her disclosure. If the timing of her disclosure is carefully considered it is also possible that Janet can help others to overcome their homophobia. Once the students know and respect her as a person, a disclosure then is more likely to result in a positive outcome. Gay professors, for example, who come out after students know them, have helped their students reduce homophobia (Waldo & Kemp, 1997).

Janet also needs to develop greater strength of character, a "thick skin" as it is sometimes called. This will occur once she deeply believes in herself and her right to succeed as much as anyone else. She will also need to become assertive. The remainder of this chapter will show you how to develop your own personal power so that you can release it whenever you decide it is appropriate.

A. Changing Your Thoughts

1. Beliefs Chart

REMINDER: Complete the following exercise by using the How to Question Your Beliefs pullout sheet found in the Introduction.

SAMPLE THOUGHT	UNDERLYING BELIEF	QUESTIONING IT (you complete this column)	HEALTHIER BELIEF
I cannot be assertive even when I should be.	My voice is not important.		Since my voice is important, I will learn to become assertive.
I deserve fewer rights than heterosexual people.	I am inferior to heterosexual people.		I am equal to other people and therefore have equal rights.

I am highly influenced by other people's opinions of me.	I should let other people make decisions for me.	I am becoming an autonomous person. I am capable of making my own decisions.
When the going gets tough I begin shutting down.	It is too hard to fight back. I must be the one that's in the wrong.	When the going gets tough I reassess my goals and priorities and then take action.
I don't know when to be assertive and when to keep quiet.	I can't or won't assess situations. Instead, I will be impulsive.	I assess situations carefully before deciding on appropriate action.
(Write any additional thoughts and beliefs you have.)		

2. Visualization Exercises

REMINDER: Complete the following exercises by using the How to Visualize pull-out sheet found in the Introduction.

(a) General Visualizations—Imagine how you would behave differently if you became a person of strong character. Also imagine how you would look at and feel things differently. As you visualize, allow a feeling of confidence to emerge. Imagine you have become an assertive person who stands up for yourself.

(b) Specific Visualizations—Think of specific instances where you did not act in an   assertive manner. See yourself handling these situations more effectively than you did. What do you wish you had said and done? Also do this with situations you have not encountered, but already know will be difficult for you. For example, if you know that walking in a gay parade would be hard for you right now, imagine yourself doing it. As you imagine the scene, allow a feeling of confidence to enter your psyche.

B. Changing Your Behaviour

1. General Activities

These general activities will help you increase your personal power:

• Practice assertive behaviours. When you first begin asserting your rights it will feel awkward and unnatural. Acknowledge that learning any new skill is like this. Learning to ride a bike was awkward at first too, but you gradually learned to master it. Then it felt natural to ride a bike. Begin with small acts of assertiveness (e.g., returning merchandise to the store that you don't like) and progress to more difficult scenarios (e.g., putting someone in his or her place who criticizes you for being gay).

• Keep a diary of times when you are and are not assertive. Record the times when you feel you did a good job of being assertive. How did you do it? Describe it in your diary. Also keep a record of the times when you slipped into either passive or aggressive behaviour. What did you do? How would you like to deal with similar situations in the future? Describe it in your diary.

• When you're feeling weak talk to yourself or a friend. We all experience times when we feel emotionally overwhelmed. At these times, talk to your-self—give yourself positive, healthy messages. For example, if you told some-one where to stick it and felt badly about it afterwards, tell yourself that you are not perfect, you are learning like everyone else on the planet, and that you can forgive yourself for acting the way you did. If this doesn't work, talk to a friend who can encourage you to see things differently.

• Practice autonomous decision-making. If you are used to relying on other people for making your decisions, begin to experiment by making some of your own. Pay attention to how you feel when you exert your own autonomy. Embrace the sense of independence it provides you.

• Learn to accept failure. No one is a master of everything, and most are mas-ters of nothing. Consequently, failure is more common in life than success. When you fail at something, remember you are not a failure. Then reassess your abilities, decide if the goal remains important to you and what your next action plan will look like. Then do it. If you fail again, go through the steps again. Within the limits of your potential (which is probably greater than you give yourself credit for) you can accomplish anything.

• Learn to succeed in life. Accepting your mistakes and failures is one thing, but refusing to stop until you succeed at something feels even better. Become the master of your destiny. Successful people have often failed at more attempts than those who have failed and quit trying. Don't give up on yourself

2. Specific Activities
Goal-setting

Decide upon a specific behaviour that you will target for change. Your best choice is a behaviour that you have already found is causing you trouble. Here are some examples:

- Backing off every time you hear someone stereotype gay people.
- Believing that you don't deserve to have equal rights because you are gay.
- Needing to deal more effectively with criticism.
- Learning to express your opinions openly and honestly.

Shaping

Write your goal in the chart below, and then list the steps you will take to begin working on it.

GOAL:		
# STEPS NEEDED TO HELP ME ACHIEVE THIS GOAL	DONE	REWARD
1		
2		
3		

Rewards

In the chart above, decide which of your steps should have an accompanying reward for its successful completion. Write what the specific reward will be. After completing the step, place a checkmark in the Done column and be sure to give yourself the assigned reward.

Environment Control

People who are already assertive usually respect this behaviour in others. You might want to tell your assertive friends that you are working on becoming more assertive yourself, and that you would appreciate their feedback when they see you acting assertively, passively or aggressively. Spending more time with strong people will help you become stronger yourself. In the chart below, write the environmental changes you need to make until your goal is successfully achieved:

#	PERSON OR GROUP THAT AFFECTS YOU	+ OR - EFFECT	PLANNED ACTION (Range: complete avoidance to frequent contact —be specific)
1			
2			
3			
4			

C. Changing the Way You Feel About It

When you experience a negative feeling complete the following chart (REMINDER: instructions for using this chart are found in the Introduction):

NAME THE FEELING(S)	DESCRIBE THE TRIGGER	UNDERLYING BELIEF(S)	QUESTIONING IT	HEALTHIER BELIEF

Where I'm At After Working On It

Periodically re-test yourself to chart your progress in this area.

1=very slightly; 2=slightly; 3=moderately; 4=highly; 5=severely	NO	YES 1 2 3 4 5
1 I cannot be assertive even when I should be.		
2 I deserve fewer rights than heterosexual people.		
3 I am highly influenced by other people's opinions of me.		
4 When the going gets tough I begin shutting down.		
5 I don't know when to be assertive and when to keep quiet.		

If you are still responding "YES" to any of these questions, continue working on change in this area. If all of your responses are "NO," you have made significant progress! Continue to monitor any remaining problems in this area, and work on these as suggested in this chapter.

Summary

As we saw with Janet, and as you have probably noticed in your own experience, there is an appropriate time to disclose to other people, as there are times when coming out is simply not a good idea. Like the rest of us, Janet wanted to be accepted for being gay. However, each environment and situation needs to be carefully assessed for signs that coming out to others will be relatively safe and will not cause you more problems than you can handle.

Releasing your personal power is about the times when it is appropriate to stand tall— proudly and confidently. It is about having good coping skills to deal with adversity, and it is about believing deeply in yourself as a person who has equal rights compared to non-gay individuals. It is also about learning to be assertive, not passive or aggressive, in most instances.

Positive Affirmations

[Also add your own from the Healthier Belief *columns in this chapter]*

Since my voice is important, I will learn to become assertive.

I am equal to other people, and therefore I have equal rights.

I am becoming an autonomous person. I am capable of making my own decisions.

When the going gets tough, I reassess my goals and priorities, and then I take action.

I assess situations carefully before deciding on appropriate action.

CHAPTER 7
Struggling with Spirituality and Religion

"I think the fundamental question is whether God made us this way. Everything has to come down to it. There is no way that anyone else can claim that they were made by God heterosexual and then say that I was not made by God homosexual."

(quoted from a respondent in Yip, 1997, 123)

"A human being has achieved much if his soul has felt the need for love and the growth of the soul of his beloved forms part of his happiness."

(Percy, 1996, 136)

"If Rome does have a lesson for the twentieth century, it is that a society can continue more or less efficiently despite the alarm of outraged moralists who equate nonmarital sexual expression with disaster."

(Karlen, 1980, 83)

For the past 22 years, Rose had sat through many Pentecostal Church services. Sitting there again recently, she anxiously awaited its end. Others noticed her discomfort, and some asked if there was anything wrong. Rose acknowledged that she wasn't feeling well, but that she didn't know why. But in fact Rose knew precisely why.

Rose had fallen in love with a friend. She always expected to someday marry, have children and please God. Her beloved friend's name, however, was Amy. Only a week earlier, they had shared their feelings for each other and kissed. What was she to do? Everything inside told her she was sinning, yet her heart was pounding at the thought of seeing Amy again.

Telling the minister was harder than anything Rose had ever done before. However, she knew it was necessary to cleanse her soul of this demon. The minister was sympathetic and caring. He suggested that Rose see a therapist he knew that could possibly rid her of these misdirected feelings. Dr. Knowles was his name, and he was touted as the best conversion therapist in the city.

There was nothing remarkable about Knowles' office except that Rose felt at home. Christian pictures and art were displayed sparingly throughout his office space. His questions seemed endless and deeply personal. Rose had to admit that she had never been attracted to a man, but that she had had many crushes on girls and women during her adolescent years. She assumed these feelings were transient, but they had now persisted for 15 years. Dr. Knowles knew this was an unfavorable sign, and he told her that the average length of conversion therapy was 3.4 years. Even then, her chances of successfully becoming heterosexual were less than 50 %.

Hearing this drove Rose into still greater panic—what now? How could God have given her such a cross to carry? She screamed at the top of her lungs, "Why did God make me this way? How could he have screwed me up like this. It's not fair!!!!" Dr. Knowles tried to calm her down, but Rose seemed to be impervious to his efforts. She was hysterical, and he was scared. An hour later, Rose's hysterical screams soothed into quiet yet desperate sobs. Dr. Knowles knew that Rose would be a challenge in therapy. More importantly, he knew she needed some reassurance right now. "Rose," Dr. Knowles said in a sedating voice, "You are not to blame for your feelings. Your feelings are not of God—they are of Satan. This is Satan's attempt to lead you into eternal damnation. Do not succumb to his manipulations." Rose understood. A calmness came over her as she realized what she had to do.

The next day, Rose got together with Amy and told her she could never see her again. Rose said this more strongly than in the many rehearsals she had practiced in her mind. In fact, Rose seemed strangely detached from herself, as though it were someone else speaking to Amy. Amy was devastated, not only by being dumped by a woman she loved deeply, but by Rose's distance. "What is going on, Rose? I don't understand." Rose said she now realized that she needed help, and she had begun getting it. The conversation soon ended as Amy became overwhelmed with emotion. Fleeing the restaurant, Amy held back tears that she knew would last for many weeks. Rose left soon after, numb to what her heart was once again rapidly concealing.

The Problem

Rose is in conflict between what her heart is telling her (she is in love with Amy) and what her head is telling her (same-sex romantic relationships are wrong). By telling Rose that her feelings are from Satan, the conversion therapist unwittingly creates in her a dissociative response. This means that Rose's personality splits so that her love feelings and what she believes this to infer (that she is gay) become detached from each other. The dissociation pushes Rose's feelings into a place she knows all too well—denial. Predictably, Rose will find that a part of what gives her passion in life diminishes—her spark becomes a little less noticeable, her enjoyment of life a little less rich, and her self-esteem begins to plummet. Grieving over her lost love relationship will not be easy as she pretends that Amy wasn't that important to her. With the help of a "therapist," she will only denigrate the essence of her gay soul.

Rose's conflict is common for those who subscribe to a belief system that does not honour homosexuality in any of its forms, including homosexual behaviour; desire or attraction; fantasies and dreams; feelings, including same-sex romantic love; orientation; and relationships. We are all raised with "scripts"—patterns of thinking and behaving that are considered appropriate by the culture and/or by one's caregivers. For example, the traditional female script was to marry, bear children and subjugate herself to her husband. The traditional male script was to marry, work and be the head of the household. When people attempt to override or overcome the influence of such scripts, a deep part inside reminds them they are supposed to follow the script. To do otherwise creates feelings of discomfort, apprehension, depression, anxiety or fear.

Religious scripts are no different. Usually these scripts were adopted early in life through the influence of one's family of origin and/or one's culture. Consequently, they are powerful and resistant to change. Furthermore, many people raised with religion do not want to reject these scripts—they help provide a foundation and a connection to others who share their particular faith. They also provide a sense of spiritual identity.

However, not all religions denigrate every form of homosexuality. Some churches, such as the Unitarian-Universalists, Society of Friends (Quakers), Ethical Humanists (Herrman, 1990), the United Church, the Metropolitan Community Church (Blumenfeld & Raymond, 1993), and some religions, like Buddhism, are supportive of gay people. Gay individuals who subscribe to such faiths will not likely experience much if any spiritual conflict.

The problem occurs for those who don't. Most religions are unsupportive of gay people (Blumenfeld & Raymond, 1993) and relegate them to an inferior, sinful, or pathological status compared to heterosexual individuals. For example, Rose belongs to a fundamental Christian faith that does not agree with her acting on her same-sex feelings. For her to be faithful to her church's interpretation of scripture, she must remain celibate for the rest of her life unless she marries. She is expected to uphold heterosexual privilege. What does Rose (and others who have similarly conflicting religious views) need to change in order to overcome the intense spiritual conflict? Does she need to give up the religion that has defined her for 22 years? Let's take a look.

What Needs to Change?

There are a number of ways to reduce or eliminate spiritual conflicts. You may feel that you need to reject your religion entirely to live freely as a gay person. That is one option within a myriad of possibilities. If you decide that you will not change your current faith, you will want to accept that some of your beliefs regarding homosexual relationships will not be in harmony with others who share the same faith. Appreciate that the written word is often different from people's interpretations of the written word. Consequently, the religion may have adopted some beliefs and practices that provide only one interpretation of scripture.

There are many sects within the Christian and Islamic religions. Sects create their own interpretations of scripture. "The Koran does not condemn homosexuality per se and does not recommend specific punishments for it" (Blumenfeld & Raymond, 1993, 185). Likewise, Jesus Christ never talked about homosexuality (Helminiak, 1994), and if anything, Jesus was a tolerant man who accepted people who were different from him. Scriptures from both the Old and New testaments that address homosexuality were written for specific reasons, and the translation of these scriptures and their original meanings are arguably not condemning of homosexuality (Helminiak, 1994). Furthermore, we now have a deeper psychological understanding of homosexuality and sexual orientation than did the writers of ancient scripture.

If you are suffering from spiritual conflict, you may want to read some of the books recommended by Dworkin (2000, 210): Twice Blessed: On Being Lesbian, Gay and Jewish (Balka & Rose, 1989), Coming Out Within: Stages of Spiritual Awakening for Lesbians and Gay Men (O'Neill & Ritter, 1992) and Just as I Am: A Practical Guide to Being Out, Proud, and Christian (Williams, 1992). Another book I would suggest is What the Bible Really Says About Homosexuality (Helminiak, 1994). These readings can help you better understand how your relationship with God is your relationship with God, and it doesn't need to end because you come out.

It might also be important for you to think about the difference between being spiritual, being religious, and religiosity. You can be spiritual (believing in God or in a higher power) without being religious (faithful devotion to an circumscribed set of beliefs about God or a higher power). Religiosity is a type of fanatical devotion whereby the individual lives compulsively by the doctrines laid down by the particular faith. You may choose to be spiritual or both spiritual and religious. It is only when you cross into religiosity that you will find that you cannot be who you are.

The bottom line is, don't let religion stop you from having a positive and healthy relationship with God or your higher power. You have probably been raised to believe that God loves you unconditionally. Since God made you the way that you are, and since God doesn't make mistakes, perhaps you ought to think about loving His creation unconditionally as well. Until you accomplish that, you will find it difficult to love others and your higher power with the passion they both deserve. A big part of any religion is learning to treat other people respectfully and lovingly. It must begin first from within.

Where I'm At Now
Place a checkmark in the column that corresponds to your answer.

If your answer is "yes," use the following rating scale: 1=very slightly; 2=slightly; 3=moderately; 4=highly; 5=severely.

			YES				
1=very slightly; 2=slightly; 3=moderately; 4=highly; 5=severely	NO	1	2	3	4	5
1 I feel conflict between being gay and being close to my higher power.						
2 I will have to give up my religion in order to be gay.						
3 God doesn't love me the way that I am.						
4 If I could be heterosexual, I would make the change.						
5 Gay people are inferior, sinful or pathological.						

If you respond "YES" to any of these questions, you would benefit from doing some work in this area. If all of your responses are "NO," you may want to skip this chapter.

The Solution

As mentioned in Rose's story, conversion therapy can take several years without any guarantee of success. One of the main proponents of conversion therapy recently reported that the average length of this treatment is 3.4 years (Nicolosi, Byrd, & Potts, 2000b). I believe that is possible to reduce the number of same-sex fantasies and the level of same-sex attraction through such approaches, but I severely doubt that conversion therapy can actually change a person's sexual orientation, which is about one's propensity to fall in love romantically with the same gender, the opposite gender or both. If one has a bisexual orientation, conversion therapy may push the envelope in the direction of opposite-sex interests. However, if one has a homosexual orientation, I believe such therapy is contraindicated. The last thing this world needs is more people living in shame and guilt over their tender passionate feelings for anyone, regardless of gender. You should be aware that there is no conclusive evidence to date either in support of or to refute conversion therapy.

I believe that Rose would benefit more from gay-affirmative therapy, which is therapy that respects the sexual orientation of the people it attempts to help. The view in gay- affirmative therapy is that being gay is no better and no worse than being heterosexual. The biggest obstacle for gay people is society's reaction to them. A gay-affirmative therapist will help Rose to love herself as she is, not as others want her to be. Furthermore, this type of therapist will help Rose overcome the conflict she feels with her spiritual beliefs, by helping her see that she can remain Pentecostal if she develops a thick-enough skin to appreciate that God's love is bigger than those who would try to change her. In addition, the therapist may help her to modify her beliefs to fit better with a church that will honour her feelings of same-sex love.

Because of how entrenched religious beliefs are for most people, you may not be able to change these on your own. If not, you would be well-advised to seek out a gay-affirmative minister who believes that gay people are equal before God or your higher power. You may need to seek out the services of a gay-affirmative therapist as well.

Nevertheless, you may be able to modify your own beliefs enough to conquer your conflict with spirituality and religion. That's the intention of the next section.

A. Changing Your Thoughts

1. Beliefs Chart

REMINDER: Complete the following exercise by using the How to Question Your Beliefs pullout sheet found in the Introduction.

SAMPLE THOUGHT	UNDERLYING BELIEF	QUESTIONING IT (you complete this column)	HEALTHIER BELIEF
I feel conflict between being gay and being close to my higher power.	Being gay is inconsistent with being spiritual and/or religious.		The conflict I feel is within myself. In reality, it has little to do with my relationship with my higher power.
I will have to give up my religion in order to be gay.	Because my religion has taught me its wrong, therefore it must be wrong.		The people who share my faith don't understand gay people. If they did, they would realize that love is what defines me as it does them.
God doesn't love me the way that I am.	God despises gay people.		My higher power knows unconditional love better than anyone I know.
If I could be heterosexual, I would make the change.	It is better to be heterosexual than gay.		If I were meant to be heterosexual, I would have been created that way.
Gay people are inferior, sinful or pathological.	Gay people are less than heterosexuals.		Gay people have equal worth compared to heterosexuals.
(Write any additional thoughts and beliefs you have.)			

2. Visualization Exercises

REMINDER: Complete the following exercises by using the How to Visualize pullout sheet found in the Introduction.

(a) General Visualizations—Picture yourself in the midst of your higher power. Imagine the love emanating from this being. What do you think is most important to your higher power: that you live your life without love, or that you give someone the deepest love of which you are capable? Do you think your higher power will be disturbed to discover that your deepest love is for someone of the same sex? As you visualize, feel the love between the two of you. No one can take that away from you.

(b) Specific Visualizations—Think of a specific instance where you found yourself feeling estranged from God or your higher power. What brought you to this place? Imagine how the situation could have been different if you were fully loving yourself at the time. If your perceived transgression is based on not treating someone in a loving way, think about how you could have behaved differently. If, however, you chastised yourself for feeling love for someone of the same gender, reflect on how beautiful it is to have been given the perfect gift of love from your creator.

B. Changing Your Behaviour

1. General Activities

These general activities will prove helpful in creating a closer bond between you and your higher power:

• Show your thankfulness in prayer. In prayer, thank your higher power for making you gay. Perhaps you have long prayed for the opposite. If that were your destiny, it would already be so. It's important to realize that not everyone was made in the same way, and really, what is so wrong with that?

• Practice rituals of thankfulness. If you feel you have ignored your higher power for a while because of guilt or shame, it's time to re-establish your relationship. Think of some ways you can become closer to your higher power again. For example, you might light some candles and allow your higher power to be felt in the room. Then you may want to have a conversation, expressing your fears and doubts. Remember: you are loved unconditionally. Only mortals have trouble with this concept.

• Practice humility. It is pride that makes you think you should be someone you are not. If you always think you should have been a movie star and work at the local theatre instead, it really won't help if you continue bemoaning the fact that you didn't make it to the top. Similarly, if you keep insisting that you should be heterosexual, and you're not, you're doing the same thing. Become humble in knowing that you are the way you are supposed to be. Gay is also beautiful.

• Read books that speak to being gay and spiritual. A number of these were mentioned earlier in the chapter. Not everyone has the need to question aspects of their faith—some are able to accept all parts of their faith blindly. As a gay person, you cannot take this route. You need to examine carefully what your scripture really says about gay people. I suspect you will be hard pressed to find anything that speaks to your ability to fall in love with others of the same gender. You may find passages that speak against homosexual behaviour amongst those who are heterosexual. After all, many religions have beliefs that are against acting on lust and ambition. Few religions, however, are against loving, committed relationships.

2. Specific Activities

Goal-setting

Decide upon a specific behaviour that you will target for change. Your best choice is a behaviour that you have already found is causing you trouble. Here are some examples:

- Not praying after coming out
- Continuing to feel guilt and shame after having sex
- Abusing myself because I am gay
- Not knowing how to live a gay life in a way that is pleasing to God

Shaping

Write your goal in the chart below, and then list the steps you will take to begin working on it.

GOAL:		
# STEPS NEEDED TO HELP ME ACHIEVE THIS GOAL	DONE	REWARD
1		
2		
3		

Rewards

In the chart above, decide which of your steps should have an accompanying reward for its successful completion. Write what the specific reward will be. After completing the step, place a checkmark in the Done column and be sure to give yourself the assigned reward.

Environment Control

If you subscribe to a faith that does not currently accept gay people, you already know the reaction you will get from others of your faith. They too have been indoctrinated into the same beliefs about sexuality. You are going to need people in your life who support you as a gay individual and who are spiritual or religious as well. In the chart below, write the environmental changes you need to make until your goal is successfully achieved:

#	PERSON OR GROUP THAT AFFECTS YOU	+ OR - EFFECT	PLANNED ACTION (Range: complete avoidance to frequent contact—be specific)
1			
2			
3			
4			

C. Changing the Way You Feel About It

When you experience a negative feeling complete the following chart (REMINDER: instructions for using this chart are found in the Introduction):

NAME THE FEELING(S)	DESCRIBE THE TRIGGER	UNDERLYING BELIEF(S)	QUESTIONING IT	HEALTHIER BELIEF

Where I'm At After Working On It

Periodically re-test yourself to chart your progress in this area.

1=very slightly; 2=slightly; 3=moderately; 4=highly; 5=severely	NO	YES 1 2 3 4 5
1 I feel conflict between being gay and being close to my higher power.		
2 I will have to give up my religion in order to be gay.		
3 God doesn't love me the way that I am.		
4 If I could be heterosexual, I would make the change.		
5 Gay people are inferior, sinful or pathological.		

If you are still responding "YES" to any of these questions, continue working on change in this area. If all of your responses are "NO," you have made significant progress! Continue to monitor any remaining problems in this area, and work on these as suggested in this chapter.

Summary

Rose encountered conflict in her spiritual beliefs after she fell in love with Amy. For 22 years, she had lived by the script that said it was wrong to fall in love romantically with someone of the same gender. Unfortunately, Rose had never fallen in love with a man before. She decided to try conversion therapy to overcome her homosexual orientation. After her first session, she was already fragmenting parts of herself and pushing into denial her love for Amy.

Perhaps you have already experienced something similar to Rose. By continuing to deny that which is part of your psychological and emotional makeup, you only hurt yourself deeper. If God or your higher power wanted you to be different, this would already be so. This chapter has been about helping you to challenge some of the core beliefs spawned by your faith. As every sect within Christianity and Islam share differences of opinion regarding scripture, it is evident that no one has the universal handle on spiritual truth. There is room for interpretation, and as a gay person, you will need to challenge some of the beliefs held by most members of your faith.

On the next page is the Positive Affirmations pullout sheet, which can be kept by your bed or in some other highly visible place. Spend a few minutes each day reflecting on what each affirmation means to you personally.

Positive Affirmations

[Also add your own from the Healthier Belief *columns in this chapter]*

The conflict I feel is within myself. In reality, it has little to do with my relationship with my higher power.

The people who share my faith don't understand gay people. If they did, they would realize that love is what defines me as it does them.

My higher power knows unconditional love better than anyone I know.

If I were meant to be heterosexual, I would have been created that way.

Gay people have equal worth compared to heterosexuals.

PART II
THE OUTSIDE OF BREAKING OUT

SECTION ONE
Stepping Into the Gay World

CHAPTER 8
The Joy of Being Gay

"Lesbians and gay men have made themselves an effective force in this country over the past several decades largely by giving themselves what civil rights movements had: a public collective identity."

(Gamson, 1995, 391)

"Because the gay man was not given the opportunities for participation in institutions like marriage and was forced out of the option to embrace such responsibilities as come with starting a family, he likely developed in his youth an advanced expertise in managing individual freedom and in exploring all the other aspects of life that are not traditionally associated with institutions— nightlife, personal entertainment, socializing, and, frankly, having fun and letting loose."

(Siegel & Lowe, 1994, 195)

"With freedom comes identity, self-acceptance, confrontation, responsibility, authentic communication, and choice."

(Grodi, 1995, 9)

Charlene grew up in a small town in northern Ontario. She knew by age 16 that her strongest attractions were toward women and that she could not come out where she lived. Finishing high school was one of the happiest moments in her life. Telling her parents she was moving was difficult because her dad wanted her to take over the family business. He was planning to retire soon and Charlene was his only child. Her parents also knew they couldn't hold her back from pursuing the education she wanted. Charlene had received acceptance to the University of Toronto. Becoming a schoolteacher was an important part of her life plan.

Moving to Toronto in late August was more difficult than she had anticipated. Toronto seemed overwhelming and she didn't know a soul. Charlene wanted this to be her time of exploring the gay world and what it had to offer, so after checking into one of the university's residences, she picked up a copy of the gay tabloid and began scanning it for places to meet other lesbian women.

Going out and meeting people was not easy for her. She soon realized that her small-town upbringing had given her values, verbal expressions and mannerisms that seemed vastly different from the people she was meeting. She simply didn't fit in. Charlene went to every bar in the tabloid, even those that catered to mostly gay men. Finding a sense of community seemed more elusive than ever. She couldn't understand how naïve she had been in thinking friendship would come easier for her than it did back home.

In her pursuit for a sense of belonging, she started hanging out with some heterosexual women from her part-time job. They were nice people, but they had their eyes on guys, and Charlene didn't feel comfortable checking out women at the straight bars they frequented. No dates and no girlfriend was leading to discouragement.

The real kicker was finding out that her boss was about the most homophobic man she had ever met. She was already out to her colleagues and knew it wouldn't be long until he found out she was a lesbian. She knew when the fateful day had arrived. Paul used to say hi to her in the morning. That stopped. Charlene knew then that getting promoted would now be highly unlikely. She couldn't remember the last time she felt this disillusioned with being gay. Here she was isolated and alone in one of the most gay-friendly cities in Canada.

Time to become more active. Charlene decided to attend the upcoming gay pride parade in late June. Pride day was absolutely beautiful, sunny, hot and humid. She and her friends found a great spot on Yonge Street to capture some of the excitement. Taking in the parade was great, but it made Charlene more deeply aware of her disconnection from these cool gay people who seemed so nonchalant and happy. Where would she meet them? How would she connect with them? Was she going to need to give up much of her upbringing to fit in? How would she do this?

After the parade ended, her friends suggested they have a drink together. Charlene declined, telling them that the heat had given her a headache. She went home and cried for hours. Not having gay friends was hard, and she felt isolated despite the closeness she felt toward her straight friends from work. As she reviewed her life through the ensuing days, she couldn't help but think how much happier she was living up north. It was nothing compared to this type of isolation—nothing at all.

The Problem

Growing up in a small town is a challenge for anyone who is gay or lesbian, and it's no coincidence that many decide to migrate to a larger city (Bagley & Tremblay, 1998). Charlene is having trouble coping with the change as she finds herself with different attitudes, values, beliefs, verbal expressions and mannerisms compared to those who grew up in the city. Combined with her isolation from other gay people and having to cope with homophobia in her job, Charlene is having a hard time seeing anything positive about being a gay person.

Even if Charlene were heterosexual, she would still experience a huge adjustment in moving to the largest city in Canada. Instead of changing her strategy for meeting gay people, Charlene appears to have given up, at least temporarily. Consequently, she has created a scenario whereby she has only heterosexual friends. If Charlene were to take a deeper look, maybe she would conclude that the gay "bar scene" may not be fit for her right now. However, something seems to be preventing her from taking appropriate action.

Charlene's problem is that she has allowed herself to become isolated from other gay people. She has rejected other gay people who are different from her, believing that if she stays away from them, the problem will go away. Indeed, Charlene will need to make some adjustments, but probably not as many as she thinks. Gay individuals are so diverse in their personalities, interests, values and attitudes that her problem may simply come down to finding the right venue to meet like-minded people.

Besides this rejection of other gay people, which Charlene projects by believing that they are all rejecting her, she is unable to see the advantages of being gay. Being gay for Charlene is disillusioning because of this unawareness. No one finds it easy to experience life alone when they are part of a stigmatized group. And what a shame to deny being part of what the gay community offers.

Despite their incredible diversity, gay people have a collective sense of identity (Valocchi, 1999) that provides them a sense of belonging and culture. Allegiance to the gay community helps offset the effects of stigmatization that is still prevalent throughout most parts of the world. The Internet has brought gay people together, sometimes from thousands of miles. Today, gay people need not be alone, whether they live in large cities or small towns. Becoming connected and enjoying the richness of the gay community is just one of the many "perks" of being who you are.

Being gay is also about learning to celebrate. The joy of being gay develops as one learns about the breadth and depth of the gay community, its history, and its interrelatedness and connectedness; becomes involved in organized and spontaneous celebrations; gives something back to other gay people, through volunteering and participating in gay events and activities; enjoys the freedoms and special privileges that result from being gay. Each of these will be considered in turn.

What Needs to Change?

If you are not feeling the joy of being gay, it's time to do some work. Gay people who suffer from internalized homophobia, poor self-esteem, denial, fragmented identity and self-lies, negative stereotypes of gay people, unassertiveness and/or religious or spiritual conflicts will not experience much joy in being gay. Instead, they are apt to suffer from varying degrees of anxiety and depression, and perhaps drug and alcohol abuse in their attempts to numb the psychic pain. If any of these apply to you, go back over the first seven chapters of this book, respectively, to deal with these issues first. If you have done your work to this point, you are ready for this chapter.

Referring back to the previous section, the joy of being gay develops as one:

- learns about the breadth and depth of the gay community, its history, and its interrelatedness and connectedness
- becomes involved in organized and spontaneous celebrations
- gives something back to other gay people, through volunteering and participating in gay events and activities

- enjoys the freedoms and special privileges that result from being gay

The breadth of the gay community is reflected in sheer numbers, given that approximately 10% of men and 5% of women are lesbian. A city with a million adults will have approximately 50 thousand gay men and 25 thousand lesbian women.

The depth of the community results from gay people meeting one another who work in every occupation. Unlike most heterosexual parties and events, which tend to have people attend who are relatively homogeneous (having similar characteristics, such as age, religion, occupational background or socio-economic status), gay functions tend to be far more heterogeneous, with people attending who are themselves diverse. This provides opportunity to connect with many people from divergent backgrounds. Attending gay social events and having a positive group identity is also associated with having better self-esteem and feeling less psychological distress (Frable, Wortman, & Joseph, 1997). The gay community can provide social support, professional contacts, and access to social networks and activities whether at home or when travelling or relocating (Garnets & Kimmel, 1993).

Celebrating one's gayness by developing a celebratory spirit and by attending organized celebrations is also important. Gay pride marches and parades, gay dances, gay fundraisers, gay art shows and festivals, and travelling to destinations known for their gay culture or gay festivities are all a part of enjoying being gay. If you've already attended any of these, you know that gay people know how to have fun.

As I wrote in Beyond Coming Out, gay people with positive identities also act as ambassadors of change within the gay community. They give something back to gay people whether it be through philanthropy, volunteering, or acting as mentors to younger gay individuals who are still learning about being gay. In giving we often feel the greatest joy in being alive.

Lastly, enjoying the freedoms and special privileges of being gay is another way to feel good about who you are. Heterosexual scripts have had a long history and serve to define much of our behaviour as a society. For example, the traditional marriage script was about clearly defined spousal roles, commitment for life, monogamy and raising children. Although this is changing to some extent, the scripts governing heterosexual behaviour are relatively constrictive.

Gay scripts have not had as long a history, and they are still not clearly defined, and hopefully never will be. One of the advantages of being gay is not having to fit into a box. Gay people have tremendous freedom in constructing their own lifestyles and in negotiating their own relationships. If anything, stereotypes are far more applicable to the heterosexual community than the gay community because of this freedom we have to define ourselves.

Gay people are sexually freer than most heterosexual individuals. Because of what it has taken us to overcome the heterosexual conditioning to which we were all exposed, gay individuals have had to relinquish sexual taboos. Any sexual behaviour is appropriate so long as it is consensual between adults. Gay people can still enjoy having sex with the opposite gender if they want, in contrast to many heterosexual individuals who would find homosexual behaviour too anxiety provoking.

Now is the first day of the rest of your life, and you want to feel good about each day that you spend here. If you have had trouble celebrating the joy of being gay, it's time to turn a new leaf and find yourself blossoming once more. The Solutions section will show you how.

Where I'm At Now

Place a checkmark in the column that corresponds to your answer.

If your answer is "yes," use the following rating scale: 1=very slightly; 2=slightly; 3=moderately; 4=highly; 5=severely.

			YES			
1=very slightly; 2=slightly; 3=moderately; 4=highly; 5=severely	NO	1	2	3	4	5
1 I do not experience being gay as a positive thing.						
2 I do not find ways to celebrate being gay.						
3 I do not attend or participate in gay events or activities.						
4 I do not give of myself in some way to gay people.						
5 I have established few, if any, gay friendships.						

If you respond "YES" to any of these questions, you would benefit from doing some work in this area. If all of your responses are "NO," you may want to skip this chapter.

The Solution

Charlene has only tried meeting other gay people in bars, and bars are not likely her best starting place. Every sizable city has a gay and lesbian information service that is listed in their telephone book. The number might also be available over the Internet or from a gay tabloid or gay establishment. Charlene should give them a call and find out what services, clubs and organizations are available. Introverted people, like Charlene, often have trouble in unstructured environments. Joining a gay club or gay organization is often an easier way to meet people.

Besides this, Charlene needs to questions her beliefs about gay people. Why is she judging everyone at the bar as being inappropriate for friendship? The "bar scene," as it is typically called, is not one scene, but instead includes people patronizing the bar for a multitude of reasons. Some are there to get drunk, others to get laid, some to dance, others to socialize with their friends (or meet new friends), some go to hang out, and others want to meet a mate. It's unfair and inaccurate to paint everyone with the same brush.

Charlene is denying herself the opportunity to experience the joy of being gay. If you find yourself doing the same, work through the exercises in this chapter.

A. Changing Your Thoughts

1. Beliefs Chart

REMINDER: Complete the following exercise by using the How to Question Your Beliefs pullout sheet found in the Introduction.

SAMPLE THOUGHT	UNDERLYING BELIEF	QUESTIONING IT (you complete this column)	HEALTHIER BELIEF
I do not experience being gay as a positive thing.	Being gay is a vice more than it is a virtue.		Being gay is about being myself—therefore it is a virtue.
I do not find ways to celebrate being gay.	There is nothing to celebrate about being gay.		Celebrating my gayness is about celebrating the deepest part of who I am. I deserve to love myself and enjoy life.
I do not attend or participate in gay events or activities.	Attending or participating in gay events is a waste of time.		Being involved in the gay community is about strengthening my positive gay identity.
I do not give of myself in some way to gay people.	There is no point in giving back to the gay community.		Giving back to the community reflects the love I have for myself and others like me.
I have established few, if any, gay friendships.	I don't like the gay people that I have met.		Gay people are so diverse that I will like many of them, if I give them a chance.
(Write any additional thoughts and beliefs you have.)			

2. Visualization Exercises

REMINDER: Complete the following exercises by using the How to Visualize pullout sheet found in the Introduction.

(a) General Visualizations—Picture being filled with joy and happiness because you are gay, and view yourself becoming an active member of the gay community. Visualize the excitement of meeting many new people and making new friends, or focus on the freedom you have to live your life in whatever way you choose. Also imagine the various ways you could give of yourself to help other gay people who are perhaps struggling more than you.

(b) Specific Visualizations—Think about the times you have wished you weren't gay and ask yourself what was going on that created those feelings. Then substitute more gay-affirming messages. For example, if you regret not having children, think through this carefully. After all, you can have your own children as a gay person. If you are convinced that your life will never feel complete without having a child, begin to visualize the ways that you can make this a reality (e.g., artificial insemination, or working out an arrangement with someone of the opposite gender).

B. Changing Your Behaviour

1. General Activities

These general activities will help you begin to experience the joy of being gay:

• Read books about gay people and their history. For a list of recommended readings, see Appendix D. Reading will help you learn about gay culture and the vibrancy of the gay community.
• Get involved in the gay community. Join at least one gay club or gay organization. Besides enjoying the activities of the specific club, you will meet lots of like-minded people.
• Find a way to help other gay people. Besides helping others, you will be helping yourself. Giving back adds greater meaning and purpose to the gay experience.
• Be ready to celebrate and then do it. It begins with a mental mindset that says you deserve to celebrate who you are. It continues with taking part in gay celebrations, either by creating your own (e.g., theme parties, celebrating the day you came out to yourself or the anniversary of being with your mate) or by attending and participating in those created by others.
• Be proud of who you are. You've worked hard to come out and live authentically. That is honourable and deserving of respect. Begin by respecting yourself and appreciating the beauty that resides within your gay soul.

• Refuse to think negative thoughts about being gay. Whenever you have a negative thought, challenge it and then replace it by focusing on the positive aspects of being gay. As you get into this exercise, you may become aware that there are more advantages to being gay than there are to being heterosexual. If this seems like a big stretch for you right now, it only shows how much work you have to do in this area.

2. Specific Activities

Goal-setting

Decide upon a specific behaviour that you will target for change. Your best choice is a behaviour that you have already found is causing you trouble. Here are some examples:

• Never attending gay events, activities, or celebrations
• Avoiding contact with other gay people
• Feeling that there is nothing to celebrate in being gay
• Not knowing how to approach potential friends

Shaping

Write your goal in the chart below, and then list the steps you will take to begin working on it.

GOAL:		
# STEPS NEEDED TO HELP ME ACHIEVE THIS GOAL	DONE	REWARD
1		
2		
3		

Rewards

In the chart above, decide which of your steps should have an accompanying reward for its successful completion. Write what the specific reward will be. After completing the step, place a checkmark in the Done column and be sure to give yourself the assigned reward.

Environment Control

Some people seem to keep a positive attitude about most things in life, whereas others approach life with trepidation. It is helpful for you to associate with positive people most of the time, especially those who love being gay and see it as something to celebrate. In the chart below, write the environmental changes you need to make until your goal is successfully achieved:

#	PERSON OR GROUP THAT AFFECTS YOU	+ OR - EFFECT	PLANNED ACTION (Range: complete avoidance to frequent contact—be specific)
1			
2			
3			
4			

C. Changing the Way You Feel About It

When you experience a negative feeling complete the following chart (REMINDER: instructions for using this chart are found in the Introduction):

NAME THE FEELING(S)	DESCRIBE THE TRIGGER	UNDERLYING BELIEF(S)	QUESTIONING IT	HEALTHIER BELIEF

Where I'm At After Working On It

Periodically re-test yourself to chart your progress in this area.

1=very slightly; 2=slightly; 3=moderately; 4=highly; 5=severely	NO	YES 1 2 3 4 5
1 I do not experience being gay as a positive thing.		
2 I do not find ways to celebrate being gay.		
3 I do not attend or participate in gay events or activities.		
4 I do not give of myself in some way to gay people.		
5 I have established few, if any, gay friendships.		

If you are still responding "YES" to any of these questions, continue working on change in this area. If all of your responses are "NO," you have made significant progress! Continue to monitor any remaining problems in this area, and work on these as suggested in this chapter.

Summary

Charlene grew up in a small town and found it difficult to connect to gay people once she moved to Toronto. Instead of taking this on as a challenge, she withdrew from gay people and established friendships with heterosexual people only. This contributed to her feeling negative about being a lesbian.

For Charlene to feel happy, she needs to change her attitudes about being gay. Beyond developing a positive gay self-concept, Charlene needs to begin celebrating the fact that she is a lesbian. Becoming involved in the gay community is also a prerequisite for her continued happiness.

The bulk of this chapter has guided you through activities and exercises that will help you experience the joy of being gay and help you appreciate that what you have been given is one of life's greatest virtues. On the next page is the Positive Affirmations pull-out sheet, which can be kept by your bed or in some other highly visible place. Spend a few minutes each day reflecting on what each affirmation means to you personally.

POSITIVE AFFIRMATIONS

[Also add your own from the Healthier Belief *columns in this chapter]*

Being gay is about being myself—therefore it is a virtue.

Celebrating my gayness is about celebrating the deepest part of who I am. I deserve to love myself and enjoy life.

Being involved in the gay community is about strengthening my positive gay identity.

Giving back to the community reflects the love I have for myself and others like me.

Gay people are so diverse that I will like many of them, if I give them a chance.

CHAPTER 9
Friendships That Count

"Indeed, research indicates that gay men are more able to create and sustain close friendships with other men than are heterosexual men."

(Bohan, 1996, 206)

"Every gay man needs a gay family or gay support group."

(Beane, 1981, 226)

"Besides our own blood, gay people learn to make family out of ex-spouses, ex-lovers, lovers' ex-lovers, and even past and present roommates. Once we have given our love to a person, that love and a little bit of us is always with that person."

(Herrman, 1990, 108)

Some people had told him that after the initial high of coming out to himself, he would eventually see the gay scene more realistically, and this would end the mental bliss he had been feeling. Claude hoped they were wrong—after all, their descriptions of gay life sounded like many marriages after the "honeymoon" phase passed. Sure enough, 18 months later, Claude was feeling disgruntled and discouraged. He still loved going to the bar and getting it on with other guys, but it was dawning on him that his life had never seemed more superficial.

As he reflected on the past 18 months, Claude realized that although he had had more sex than he had ever had with women, he still didn't have a gay friend of any substance. Were all gay men like this? Claude had tried to become friends with most guys he slept with, and the majority never wanted to see him again. Claude concluded from this that he was also bad in bed. Some said let's be friends, but friends get together now and then. These guys never called, or returned calls. Even when he met guys through other guys that he knew, the results were generally the same: after sleeping with them, they bolted.

Claude also got the feeling that the entire bar crowd were gossipers. He became aware that he had developed a reputation of being a "slut," a term he never used to describe other people's behaviour, including his own. Why were people judging him for being single? It was nearly enough to dissuade Claude from ever going to the bar again, but if he chose that, where would he meet guys?

Claude knew that the gay friends he had now were "fair-weather" friends. He couldn't count on these people for anything, other than drinking and having a few laughs. They were more like bar buddies than friends. He didn't think his heterosexual friends would understand him either. If he thought the bar crowd was judgmental, most of his straight friends would be as bad if not worse.

In his pensive state, Claude also realized that he didn't know one gay person, male or female, whom he admired. Was being gay about being unsuccessful in life? Was it about abusing drugs and alcohol to make yourself feel better? He knew he needed to try a different approach to meeting gay men. It was time to try the telepersonals and the chat lines. It didn't take long before Claude was meeting more guys than he had ever imagined. Nor did it take long for him to discover that most were dishonest. The attractive guy with "nine inches" must have taken ugly pills before getting together with him. In bed, reality was much more shrivelled than the ad had stated. They weren't all like that, of course. He met some decent people too, but he wasn't attracted to any of them. Furthermore, they were as equally disconnected from the kind of guys he wanted to meet as he was. The gay world started to look more desperate than Claude had ever dreamed. And frankly, he was feeling desperate. If this was to be his reality, perhaps he would go back in the closet and at least be surrounded by people who cared about him.

Now more morose than ever, Claude decided to withdraw for a while from his gay life. He stopped returning the calls of those he felt were wasting his time, which meant all the bar buddies he had befriended. Soon they stopped calling entirely. Claude knew he needed to make some changes, but he didn't have a clue what these changes would look like.

The Problem

Claude is seeing one side of the gay community, and he is going about making friends in all the wrong ways. On the one hand, he wants to develop close friendships with gay men, but on the other, he treats them like sex objects rather than as friends. Although he judges the people he meets as superficial, it is really he that has become superficial. Our best clue that this is occurring is when we read that Claude has met some decent guys through ads and the Internet, but wasn't attracted to them. If Claude is looking for friendship, why does he need to be attracted to them? In fact, being sexually attracted to one's friends usually complicates matters.

Gay men and lesbian women often do end up making friends with some of the people with whom they have had sex (Herrman, 1990), and supportive friendships are important to gay people, especially if they feel tension with their biological families (Bohan, 1996). However, many people see having sex with someone as primarily a casual experience or as part of initiating or sustaining an intimate relationship. If one beds a potential friend during an initial encounter, the intention of each person is unclear. Although Claude says he wants friendship, having sex suggests to the other person that he wants more than that. The one he beds may have completely different intentions from friendship. Having sex during the first encounter is usually part of the casual sex script or the initiation of a relationship script. Consequently, once the other person becomes aware that Claude is looking for friendship, the sexual behaviour that has just occurred only fits into the casual sex script: fuck and move on.

Besides treating others as sex objects, Claude is not using the best strategy for meeting other men. As Hermann (1990) mentions, meeting guys at the YMCA, bars or on the streets is not the ideal location for making sustainable friendships. Instead, Herrman suggests meeting people who likely have their "heads together": those attending gay churches, organizations and professional groups. He also recommends letting "it be known that you are seeking to give of yourself, not to be taken care of. Don't let sex be your first priority; self-respect must come first" (112).

Claude has also had trouble finding positive role models, gay people that he admires. Where is he most likely to meet these people? Perhaps not at the bar. Again, he may be more likely to meet potential mentors at gay churches, organizations and professional groups. Once Claude becomes friends with at least one person he admires, he will likely meet others through this person who share common attributes. This is how friendship circles generally develop—one friend introducing you to other friends.

The judgment that Claude describes (people calling him a "slut") seems relatively common in gay bars, and it is unfortunate. It is a carry-over label from the heterosexual script, and it is generally applied to women who enjoy promiscuity. Obviously created by men with double standards, the label is sickening in both the straight and gay worlds. Sex is a wonderful gift of caring and should never be denigrated (unless it is between non-consenting adults or between adults and minors). Those who make such judgments ought to question their behaviour. Even if they themselves believe in monogamy or celibacy, it lacks tact to impose their beliefs on those who follow a different path.

Early on, Claude was told that the "mental bliss" he was feeling would soon end. It doesn't have to. What has to end is his superficiality. The next section looks at how to develop friendships that count.

What Needs to Change?

In their book about gay etiquette, Petrow and Steele (1995) offer some good advice for making friends: "You need to be out there and visible, with a positive attitude. Simplistic as it may seem, people are drawn to others who appear open, content, and happy. . .Trust, the basis of all healthy relationships, builds over time and is earned through respect, loyalty, sensitivity, and caring." You are also most likely to develop sustainable friendships if you meet people who are mature and who have depth of character. Consequently, you need to develop good intuition—the ability to discern the type of person you are considering having as a friend. If you spend time with fair-weather people, they will likely become fair-weather friends. If you are associating with deep individuals who are looking to meet similar sorts of people, then you are more likely to develop lasting and deep friendships.

Remember: you don't need to be sexually attracted to your friends. They come in all shapes, sizes, genders and sexual orientations for that matter. If you are sexually attracted to someone who becomes a friend, or if he or she is attracted to you, you will likely need to deal with this openly at some point. Sexual attraction mixed with admiration can lead to falling in love. I have worked with several heterosexual women in my counselling practice who have fallen in love with a gay male friend. Working through the grieving is as painful as having been in love with someone with whom they have had a romantic relationship. Some people are better at creating boundaries than others. You need to know which group you fit into.

As a general rule, it is best that you don't have sex with your friends. It takes truly liberated people to navigate through such a scenario without leaving hurt feelings on one or the other side. Some gay men, more so than lesbian women, establish friendships with a sexual element, colloquially called "fuck buddy" relationships. These can work so long as both understand the ground rules. These relationships usually end when one or the other man becomes intimately involved with someone with whom they hope to have a long-term, committed relationship.

Accept that building a viable friendship circle will take time. When you start meeting the kind of people with whom you wish to associate, let them introduce you to some of their friends at get-togethers, house parties and other social events. If you are also looking for a mate, such activities are often ideal meeting places for this purpose as well. Given that you like the people you call your friends, you will likely enjoy meeting their friends too.

It is important that you establish friendships with at least some gay people. If you don't, you will likely feel a sense of isolation, and this increases the likelihood that you will develop a negative gay identity (Beane, 1981; Frable, Wortman, & Joseph, 1997). Gay friends often provide a greater source of emotional support for us as compared to our family of origin (Bohan, 1996), and gay friends add significantly to our gratification in life (Prochaska, Norcross, & Diclemente, 1994).

Where I'm At Now
Place a checkmark in the column that corresponds to your answer.

If your answer is "yes," use the following rating scale: 1=very slightly; 2=slightly; 3=moderately; 4=highly; 5=severely.

			YES				
1=very slightly; 2=slightly; 3=moderately; 4=highly; 5=severely	NO	1	2	3	4	5
1	I have trouble making and keeping heterosexual friends.						
2	I have trouble making and keeping gay friends of the same gender.						
3	I need to feel sexually attracted to my friends.						
4	I only make friends at the bar, over the internet, or through telepersonals.						
5	I only make friends after I first have sex with the person.						

If you respond "YES" to any of these questions, you would benefit from doing some work in this area. If all of your responses are "NO," you may want to skip this chapter.

The Solution

If Claude is looking for casual sex, the approach he is using is just fine. If he wants a mate, he will likely want to begin meeting men in venues where they are more apt to have their heads together. The same is true if he wants to establish enduring friendships. Claude needs to learn the specific art of making friends.

Sexual attraction between friends can complicate matters, and the friendship will remain strained while the chemistry and admiration peak. Friends are people you like with whom you share a common interest. Claude is giving mixed messages to the men he hopes to have as friends—having sex with them enacts the casual sex script or the initiation of a relationship script, neither of which is Claude's intent.

Perhaps you have struggled as well in establishing friendships with gay people of the same gender. This chapter will help you make friendships that count.

A. Changing Your Thoughts

1. Beliefs Chart

REMINDER: Complete the following exercise by using the How to Question Your Beliefs pullout sheet found in the Introduction.

SAMPLE THOUGHT	UNDERLYING BELIEF	QUESTIONING IT (you complete this column)	HEALTHIER BELIEF
I have trouble making and keeping heterosexual friends.	I don't know how to treat heterosexual friends properly.		I need to learn how to treat heterosexual friends properly.
I have trouble making and keeping gay friends of the same gender.	I am giving gay friends mixed messages and not treating them respectfully.		If I want gay friends of the same gender, I need to avoid giving mixed messages. All friends need to be treated respectfully.
I need to feel sexually attracted to my friends.	I don't want to hang out with unattractive people for fear of being judged by others.		Friends are people with whom I share a common interest. It doesn't

			matter what they look like.
I only make friends at the bar, over the Internet or through telepersonals.	I believe that these are the best ways to make new gay friends.		The best places to make friends are where I will meet people who have their heads together.
I only make friends after I first have sex with the person.	A person won't want to be my friend if he or she is not sexually attracted to me.		People will choose me as a friend because they like me. I am worthy of having good friends.
(Write any additional thoughts and beliefs you have.)			

2. Visualization Exercises

REMINDER: Complete the following exercises by using the How to Visualize pullout sheet found in the Introduction.

(a) General Visualizations—See yourself surrounded by people who want to spend time with you. Then think about the traits you have that other people will admire. What are your positive qualities? What draws, or could draw, other people to you? Alternatively, what are your negative qualities? Can any of these be altered in some way?

(b) Specific Visualizations—Think of a specific instance where someone rejected your offer of friendship. What was going on at the time? What factors were within your control? Could you have improved your chances of developing a friendship with this person? Do this for each example you can think of.

B. Changing Your Behaviour

1. General Activities

These general activities will help you begin developing sustainable friendships:

• Show interest in others. This is one of the tried-and-true methods for increasing the chances that people will like you. You may know from your own experience that when someone really listens to you when you're talking, and asks thoughtful questions based on what you have said, it is difficult not to like them. Contrast that with the many times you know that others are paying lip service to you, and that they can't wait to move on to someone else.

- Be humble. Few people like a braggart. Even if you are well-accomplished, let others do the bragging for you.
- Avoid giving mixed messages. If you want sex, go for it. If you want a lasting friendship, leave it alone.
- If you are shy or introverted, get involved in structured activities. You will find it easier to meet people if you join a club or organization. The structure it provides will allow you to get to know the same group of people gradually.
- Practice approaching people. The best way to overcome shyness is to get extensive practice in approaching people and talking to them. This can be an ideal exercise to use in the Shaping section that follows. You don't want to expect much of yourself at first. If all you do is approach people initially by introducing yourself and asking how they are doing, you have made a successful first attempt. Gradually increase your expectations of yourself.
- Be visible. You won't meet people if you stay at home. Get out there and start making the friends you always wanted.

2. Specific Activities

Goal-setting

Decide upon a specific behaviour that you will target for change. Your best choice is a behaviour that you have already found is causing you trouble. Here are some examples:

- Talking to one person you don't know when you go out to a bar
- Joining one gay club or gay organization
- Asking one person if he or she would like to plan on enjoying a mutual interest (be specific about date, time and activity)
- Become acquainted with at least one gay person whom you admire

Shaping

Write your goal in the chart below, and then list the steps you will take to begin working on it.

GOAL:		
# STEPS NEEDED TO HELP ME ACHIEVE THIS GOAL	DONE	REWARD
1		
2		
3		

Rewards

In the chart above, decide which of your steps should have an accompanying reward for its successful completion. Write what the specific reward will be. After completing the step, place a checkmark in the Done column and be sure to give yourself the assigned reward.

Environment Control

You are most likely to develop a supportive friendship circle if you begin hanging around people who have their heads together and who are the kinds of people you like and respect. Through them, you will meet others of like mind. Similarly, if you hang around people who aren't living in accordance with your values, you are unlikely to be successful. In the chart below, write the environmental changes you need to make until your goal is successfully achieved:

#	PERSON OR GROUP THAT AFFECTS YOU	+ OR - EFFECT	PLANNED ACTION (Range: complete avoidance to frequent contact—be specific)
1			
2			
3			
4			

C. Changing the Way You Feel About It

When you experience a negative feeling complete the following chart (REMINDER: instructions for using this chart are found in the Introduction):

NAME THE FEELING(S)	DESCRIBE THE TRIGGER	UNDERLYING BELIEF(S)	QUESTIONING IT	HEALTHIER BELIEF

Where I'm At After Working On It

Periodically re-test yourself to chart your progress in this area.

1=very slightly; 2=slightly; 3=moderately; 4=highly; 5=severely	NO	YES 1	2	3	4	5
1 I have trouble making and keeping heterosexual friends.						
2 I have trouble making and keeping gay friends of the same gender.						
3 I need to feel sexually attracted to my friends.						
4 I only make friends at the bar, over the Internet or through telepersonals.						
5 I only make friends after I first have sex with the person.						

If you are still responding "YES" to any of these questions, continue working on change in this area. If all of your responses are "NO," you have made significant progress! Continue to monitor any remaining problems in this area, and work on these as suggested in this chapter.

Summary

Claude wants to develop close friendships with gay men on the one hand, but on the other hand he treats them like sex objects rather than as friends. This generally enacts a casual sex script or the initiation of a relationship script in the other man, which means that friendship will not likely result. Besides providing mixed messages, Claude is not meeting the kind of people he wants to befriend. After 18 months of being unsuccessful, Claude has become disillusioned with the "gay community," which is really his disillusionment with a small sample of people he has attracted sexually.

You may be facing your own challenges in developing sustainable friendships with heterosexual and/or gay individuals. If so, this chapter has provided many suggestions to improve your attitude and skill in this important area. On the next page is the Positive Affirmations pullout sheet, which can be kept by your bed or in some other highly visible place. Spend a few minutes each day reflecting on what each affirmation means to you personally.

Positive Affirmations

[Also add your own from the Healthier Belief *columns in this chapter]*

I need to learn how to treat heterosexual friends properly.

If I want gay friends of the same gender, I need to avoid giving mixed messages. All friends need to be treated respectfully.

Friends are people with whom I share a common interest. It doesn't matter what they look like.

The best places to make friends are where I will meet people who have their heads together.

People will choose me as a friend because they like me. I am worthy of having good friends.

Chapter 10
The Art of Successful Dating

"Taking chances means that some conversations and some guys will turn out to be duds. If that happens, it's perfectly fine to say "no thanks" to an invitation and continue on with the conversation. Whatever you do, don't lie. Lies beget more lies and more complex lies."

(Petrow & Steele, 1995, 52)

"Showing affection publicly is the same for gays as it is for straights. No matter where, handholding, eye gazing, and light kissing are acceptable behaviours. However, when in public, be wary of open-mouth kissing, excessive fondling, and having sex."

(Petrow & Steele, 1995, 20)

"Charm is the ability to make someone else think that both of you are wonderful."
(Quote by Edgar Magnin, cited in Petrow & Steele, 1995, 57)

Janine has always been very shy. At age 21, she has never asked a woman out on a date, and she rarely gets asked out herself. Her social awkwardness is obvious to everyone who meets her. This means that generally, only the extroverts have enough confidence to date her. At the bar, her friend Cheryl introduces her to Petula. Petula is gregarious and can talk anyone's head off. Janine has learned to be a good listener, and Petula loves an audience. She invites Janine out for dinner, and during the three-hour four-course meal, Janine speaks for no more than 10 minutes total, uttering more u-huhs and u-hums than ever. Petula talks non-stop, and by the end of the meal, Janine is so exhausted she asks to be taken home immediately. As Petula reaches over to give her a goodnight kiss, Janine responds (while thinking inside she can't wait to get away from Petula). The goodnight kiss itself becomes nearly as drawn out as the conversation, but Janine doesn't know how to pull herself away. When finally she is given a moment to catch her breath, she excuses herself and leaves.

The next day, Petula calls her and asks her out on another date. Janine is stunned and doesn't know what to say. While Janine tries to compose herself on the phone to spit out a "no thank you", Petula says she will be over at 7 p.m. to pick her up. Once off the phone, Janine freaks. She can't stand the thought of hearing another diatribe like the last one. Before Petula arrives, Janine takes a cab to the downtown library to have some peace and quiet. Over the next few days, she lets her answering machine pick up all the calls. Sure enough, there is one message after another from Petula wondering what is wrong. The calls eventually end.

Janine feels badly about how she treated Petula, but she can't imagine telling her how uninterested she is in seeing her again. Besides, it doesn't take long before Donna approaches her at the bar. Janine has met Donna before, and although there isn't any attraction, she likes the way Donna is a take-charge sort of person. In fact some would call her downright aggressive. Donna barges into Janine's personal space and steals a French kiss from her. Janine is so startled, she succumbs to the advance. Donna moves in further, and tells Janine she is coming home with her. Before she can think twice about it, Donna has grabbed her hand and escorts her to her half-ton. Janine is turned on by the rough treatment. After all, it's been eight months since her last sexual experience.

When they arrive, Janine follows Donna into her apartment. Donna immediately grabs Janine's top and rips it open. Then she pops Janine's bra open so her ample breasts fall prey to Donna's hard-handed clutches. Janine's head is now spinning, and she lets Donna do whatever she wants to her for the next two hours. At the end of it, Donna leaps out of bed and offers to call her a cab. Janine is out of there within minutes, wondering if she did the right thing. Donna never calls her again, and when she sees Janine at the bar, she ignores her like she didn't exist. Janine feels hurt but doesn't know how to respond to it. She keeps it to herself and decides to forget the whole incident.

There is one woman Janine has fantasized about at the bar. She is there whenever Janine is, and she is usually alone. After observing her for months, Janine musters enough courage to go over and introduce herself. Her name is Karen, and she seems really nice. Eventually Janine pops the question, "Karen, do you want to go out with me sometime?" "I would really enjoy that," Karen replies. They set up a date for Friday evening, and Janine leaves, already beginning to feel anxiety creep over her in anticipation.

As the days pass, Janine's anxiety increases as she tears herself apart wondering what to suggest they do. She decides to propose that they go out to a movie. Karen agrees. When Janine arrives to pick her up, Karen can see how anxious Janine is feeling. As the evening progresses, her tension lessens. By the end of the night, Janine is having a much easier time talking to an understanding Karen about her many problems. The next day, Janine calls Karen to tell her how much fun she had. She leaves a message on her answering machine, and suggests another date. A few days later, Janine wonders if she received the message—still no reply. She leaves another message and waits patiently at home for the phone to ring. It doesn't. The next time at the bar, she storms over to where Karen is standing and demands an explanation. Karen said she thinks it would be best if they were just friends. Janine is not stupid... she knows exactly what this means.

Discouraged and disappointed, Janine heads home, wondering if she will ever find someone. It doesn't seem to be getting any easier. In fact, she is starting to feel jaded and bitter.

The Problem

Janine doesn't know how to be assertive. Consequently, she becomes victim to whomever approaches her, and because of her own deep-rooted insecurities and loneliness, she is apt to go out with women who are not well-suited to her personality. Her lack of assertiveness is evident in failing to be direct with Petula. As Janine is inexperienced in dating, feeling stunned is not surprising. After she hung up the phone and began thinking about it, however, the assertive response would have been to call Petula back and tell her she is not sufficiently attracted to her to want another date. Nearly everyone understands this because nearly everyone has had the same experience at one time or another. And if they don't understand, their naiveté is not your problem.

If Janine was attracted to Petula and simply found her non-stop talking annoying, she should have let her know how she felt. For example, she could say, "Petula, I think you're really hot, but I must admit, I found it hard to be around you last night because you talked so much. If we are going to date, I need to have the opportunity for equal air time." This provides Petula the chance to apologize and decide if she wants to correct her behaviour on a subsequent date. If she chooses not to, then the dating is not going to prove beneficial to either of them.

Janine is also unassertive with Donna. Although we are unclear if Janine really wants a dominatrix for the night, there are clues that she is befuddled and unable to assert herself against Donna's aggressive approach. At the least, Janine could have spoken up when Donna rushed out of bed to call her a cab. Most of us would feel used after having had a wild sexual experience and immediately being sent home.

Beyond her lack of assertiveness, Janine doesn't know how to date someone. When she finally becomes more comfortable with Karen, she begins talking about her problems. This is not what people want to hear on a first date. Karen tries to be supportive, but probably thinks that Janine is too messed up to date again. Nothing kills attraction faster than hearing about how rough life is from someone who was initially perceived as cool and sexy. Petrow and Steele (1995) recommend that first dates should be on a weeknight, not on a Friday or Saturday. They suggest that expectations are lower then and ending the date early is easier if either party wants out.

Janine is not the only one making mistakes in dating. Petula's insensitivity in not allowing Janine more opportunity to talk is a quick date breaker. Donna's aggressiveness will leave a lot of women feeling mistreated and used. Dating occurs in stages, and what is appropriate in the intermediate and later stages is not appropriate during the beginning stages. The emphasis throughout needs to be on open, honest and direct communication.

Two people that don't know each other need to do a lot of talking to each other in a sensitive and respectful manner. Why did Petula assume that Janine wanted her to keep talking? She probably wasn't reading clues. Most people who are bored will begin yawning or they will develop a glazed look, or their eyes will wander. Why did Donna assume that Janine wanted to be French kissed? Before dragging her away to have sex with her, why didn't she ask if that is what Janine wanted? After sex, why did Donna rush her out of her apartment? If Donna needed to get ready for work, or whatever, some communication would have helped ease the transition. Because of poor or absent communication, each person was left guessing as to what the other person was thinking, feeling and wanting.

What Needs to Change?

There is no substitute for learning to be assertive. Successful dating is about being honest, open, direct and respectful in your communication. Your feelings, thoughts and wants are important, and it is unfair to expect your date to read your mind. Although it may feel as though the worst thing would be to never date the person again, it is actually worse if you end up suppressing yourself and lying in the process. One of the biggest contributors to lost passion in relationships is resentment. Resentment develops when people hold back their feelings, thoughts and wants from one another, or are not respected when they do express their opinions.

Petrow and Steele (1995) recommend that you provide at least three days notice in asking someone out on a date. Furthermore, they suggest you not rush things—allow the relationship to develop naturally. Before asking for a second date, wait until the first date has ended. Rushing the "do you love me?" question is also a fatal mistake unless sufficient time has passed for real love to have matured.

If you are now dating, you are probably looking for something more enduring than a one-night stand. The best advice I ever heard regarding dating is to use the "H-H-H" approach. The three Hs are an acronym for big head, heart, and little head. When looking for a mate, first determine if the person has the qualities you are looking for (big head), then see if you develop feelings for the person (heart) and then move into the sexual arena (little head). Although the approach was told to me in relation to dating men, the third H applies equally to lesbian women.

Most gay men start with the third H, and then work in reverse. Many women, heterosexual or lesbian, begin with the second H and then incorporate the other two. Many relationships have failed because people have not adequately discerned who they are with before becoming sexual or before allowing their emotions to run wild. Relationships are hard work, even when you are with someone who is well put together. But they are a disaster when either or neither of you have first carefully ascertained the other person's qualities, including his or her traits, characteristics, attributes and shortcomings.

It's important to have fun on a date while beginning to carefully assess the other person. Humour and lightheartedness are well advised in the early stages of dating. Increased intensity and depth generally occurs as you begin to bond with one another. The later stages of dating usually involve planning for having a life together.

Dating has a rhythm, similar to dancing. If one of you keeps making the other move before he or she can respond to the previous step, both of you will soon be falling over each other. The rhythm of dating requires that mutual effort be made. For example, if you find yourself always the one to request a date from the same person, the natural balance is disturbed. If this pattern continues, you will find that you are investing more in the relationship than the other person. If he or she wants to date you, he or she needs to make some effort too. Another example: if you are always giving and the other person is always taking, you have created a one-sided relationship. Don't be surprised when this person doesn't develop as strong feelings for you as you develop for him or her.

In effect, both people have to work at a relationship if it is to develop the cement that binds people together. If you make it too easy on the other person, he or she will not reciprocate as an equal partner, and without equality, the relationship will not develop in a healthy manner. Furthermore, it increases the likelihood that the other person won't develop enduring feelings for you.

Now for a few dating ideas. Below are 20 ideas, some of which may really appeal to you, arranged in three groupings: Recreate, Communicate and Vegetate. Enjoy:

Recreate

1. Share a mutual athletic interest (cycling, rollerblading, tennis, swimming).
2. Attend an event or do something unique to both of you (horse races, car races, bungee jumping, whitewater rafting).
3. Go for a walk barefoot in the park.
4. Have a water fight with giant soakers.
5. Get in sync together on the dance floor—one of you attempts to do the same dance moves as the other.
6. Feed ducks, skip stones across a river or lake or enjoy nature in some other way.
7. Have a wear-what-you-dare date, and go out dressed like that.
8. Go window shopping together.
9. Organize a picnic.
10. Take your date to a gay event or gay celebration.

Communicate

11. Talk about yourself (your favourite foods, activities, your past or upbringing.
12. Get philosophical—share your views on spirituality, the meaning of life, and your life goals.
13. Take turns asking each other one question at a time.
14. Share a coffee or meal at the funkiest place you know.

Vegetate

15. Share a bottle of wine under moonlight or candlelight.
16. Spend an evening listening to music.
17. Take a drive to the country or somewhere romantic in the city.
18. Attend a live stand-up comedy show.
19. Rent a movie and give each other brief back massages while watching it.

20. Have a sleepover. Decide with your date what you will wear to bed, if anything.

Where I'm At Now
Place a checkmark in the column that corresponds to your answer.

If your answer is "yes," use the following rating scale: 1=very slightly; 2=slightly; 3=moderately; 4=highly; 5=severely.

1=very slightly; 2=slightly; 3=moderately; 4=highly; 5=severely	NO	YES 1	2	3	4	5
1 I have trouble asking someone out on a date.						
2 I have a hard time being honest with people who I have dated or want to date me.						
3 I don't know how to act appropriately when I'm on a date.						
4 Instead of clarifying, I make assumptions about what my date is feeling, thinking and wanting.						
5 I cannot show any public display of affection toward my date.						

If you respond "YES" to any of these questions, you would benefit from doing some work in this area. If all of your responses are "NO," you may want to skip this chapter.

The Solution

A. Changing Your Thoughts

1. Beliefs Chart
REMINDER: Complete the following exercise by using the How to Question Your Beliefs pull-out sheet found in the Introduction.

SAMPLE THOUGHT	UNDERLYING BELIEF	QUESTIONING IT (you complete this column)	HEALTHIER BELIEF
I have trouble asking someone out on a date.	I am afraid of people.		I am entitled to ask anyone out on a date. The worst they can say is "no."
I have a hard time being honest with people who I have dated or want to date me.	The truth will hurt them, and I am the cause of their pain.		Lies generally hurt more than the truth. Furthermore, I am not responsible for other people's reactions to my honesty.

I don't know how to act appropriately when I'm on a date.	I haven't learned the basic etiquette of dating.	I will learn how to act when I am on a date. I will treat my date the way I would want to be treated—with respect.
Instead of clarifying, I make assumptions about what my date is feeling, thinking and wanting.	It is impolite or improper to ask about a person's feelings, thoughts or desires.	The most important thing is to ask rather than assume and not to rush anything.
I cannot show any public display of affection toward my date.	Any public display of affection for gay people is wrong.	The same public displays of affection deemed appropriate for heterosexual people are appropriate for gay people as well.
(Write any additional thoughts and beliefs you have.)		

2. Visualization Exercises

REMINDER: Complete the following exercises by using the How to Visualize pullout sheet found in the Introduction.

(a) General Visualizations—Imagine asking the hottest guy or woman you have seen at the bar out on a date. Picture yourself as confident, self-assured and nonchalant. Think about the approach that works best for you. What would your non-verbal communication look like? What expression would you have on your face? How would you carry your body? Then imagine what you could say to strike up a conversation. Also imagine what the ideal dating situation would look like. Where would you go, what would you do and how would you feel?

(b) Specific Visualizations—Mentally rehearse aspects of dating that you have struggled with. For example, if you find yourself awkward at the end of a date when a sexual advance may be made, think about how you could deal with these advances better in the future. Rehearse assertive responses, whether you want sex or have decided to decline the offer. Do this for each example you can think of.

B. Changing Your Behaviour

1. General Activities

These general activities will help you master the art of successful dating:

• Read Petrow and Steele's 1995 book, *The Essential Book of Gay Manners and Etiquette*. The authors provide sound advice regarding etiquette in a number of settings and situations in which lesbian women and gay men find themselves. A thoroughly enjoyable read.

• Become assertive. There is no place for acting like a doormat when it comes to dating. Your rights are just as important as the rights of the person you date. That means your feelings, thoughts and desires are to be taken seriously, especially by you. No one can stand up for your rights like you can, and no one else should have to try. If you want to ask someone out on a date, ask, and do not hesitate. If you don't want to date someone, tell her or him. Don't keep the person guessing. If you want sex, ask for it. If you don't, decline it. Be as straightforward as these words sound. But also be tactful and respectful of the other person's feelings.

• Create your own list of date ideas that you think are cool. You may want to include some ideas from the list provided in the What Needs to Change section of this chapter. Then check with your date as to which ideas are a match.

• Do not stray from a commitment to honesty. Sometimes it may seem easier to lie to someone you barely know, but even if the person doesn't like to hear what you're saying, he or she will respect you for it (and if they don't, then you know even more clearly that this person is not mature enough for you right now).

• Keep conversations lighthearted and well-humoured in the early stages of dating: become more serious once you have developed positive momentum. Remember that no one, including yourself, wants to hear all about a date's problems when you are first getting to know him or her. We know that everyone has struggles and challenges in this life. But early on in dating, why kill the growing attraction and excitement? Keep them guessing for a while.

• If you hope that dating will lead to something more enduring, use the H-H-H approach. Size up the person (big head), see if your heart engages (heart) and then become sexual (little head). Reversing the order of any of these will increase the likelihood that one or both of you will become hurt or jaded over time.

2. Specific Activities

Goal-setting

Decide upon a specific behaviour that you will target for change. Your best choice is a behaviour that you have already found is causing you trouble. Here are some examples:

- Feeling afraid to ask someone out on a date
- Not dealing well with rejection
- Not telling the truth about how I feel
- Never showing any public display of affection toward a date of the same sex

Shaping

Write your goal in the chart below, and then list the steps you will take to begin working on it.

GOAL:			
#	STEPS NEEDED TO HELP ME ACHIEVE THIS GOAL	DONE	REWARD
1			
2			
3			

Rewards

In the chart above, decide which of your steps should have an accompanying reward for its successful completion. Write what the specific reward will be. After completing the step, place a checkmark in the Done column and be sure to give yourself the assigned reward.

Environment Control

Through modelling, you can learn how to date by watching others and spending time with others who have a style that you admire. If you have friends who are socially awkward and uncomfortable in dating situations, they will not be of much help to you in this area. In the chart below, write the environmental changes you need to make until your goal is successfully achieved:

#	PERSON OR GROUP THAT AFFECTS YOU	+ OR - EFFECT	PLANNED ACTION (Range: complete avoidance to frequent contact—be specific)
1			
2			
3			
4			

C. Changing the Way You Feel About It

When you experience a negative feeling complete the following chart (REMINDER: instructions for using this chart are found in the Introduction):

NAME THE FEELING(S)	DESCRIBE THE TRIGGER	UNDERLYING BELIEF(S)	QUESTIONING IT	HEALTHIER BELIEF

Where I'm At After Working On It

Periodically re-test yourself to chart your progress in this area.

		YES					
1=very slightly; 2=slightly; 3=moderately; 4=highly; 5=severely		NO	1	2	3	4	5
1	I have trouble asking someone out on a date.						
2	I have a hard time being honest with people who I have dated or want to date me.						
3	I don't know how to act appropriately when I'm on a date.						
4	Instead of clarifying, I make assumptions about what my date is feeling, thinking and wanting.						
5	I cannot show any public display of affection toward my date.						

If you are still responding "YES" to any of these questions, continue working on change in this area. If all of your responses are "NO," you have made significant progress! Continue to monitor any remaining problems in this area, and work on these as suggested in this chapter.

Summary

Janine neither knows how to act assertively nor how to date effectively. Because she relies on others to approach her, she is missing the opportunity to approach those to whom she feels attraction or affinity. On a date, she doesn't express her opinions or take charge of her own behaviour. After a bad date, she doesn't deal with the person honestly and directly.

When Janine is on a date, she doesn't know what and what not to say. She becomes an open book on the first date, which is usually more than the other person wants to hear. Dating should not be rushed—it is a gradual process of getting to know each other, with both parties deciding along the way whether to increase the commitment or end the liaison.

If you have struggled with dating, you can relate to some of what Janine has experienced. Remember to use the H-H-H approach if you are looking for a mate or life partner, and also remember that successful dating has a rhythm created by both people making an effort toward developing a positive relationship.

The bulk of this chapter has guided you through activities and exercises to help you master the art of successful dating. On the next page is the Positive Affirmations pullout sheet, which can be kept by your bed or in some other highly visible place. Spend a few minutes each day reflecting on what each affirmation means to you personally.

Positive Affirmations

[Also add your own from the Healthier Belief *columns in this chapter]*

I am entitled to ask anyone out on a date. The worst they can say is "no."

Lies generally hurt more than the truth. Furthermore, I am not responsible for other people's reactions to my honesty.

I will learn how to act when I am on a date. I will treat my date the way I would want to be treated—with respect.

The most important thing is to ask rather than assume and not to rush anything.

The same public displays of affection deemed appropriate for heterosexual people are appropriate for gay people as well.

CHAPTER 11
Having Great Sex

"Would human freedom be enhanced if the sex-biology of our partners in lust was of no particular concern, and had no name? In what kind of society could we all more freely explore our desire and our flesh?"

(Katz, 1990, 30)

"It is important to recognize that not all gays fall in love (or bed) the instant they meet another gay of the same sex. Selectivity occurs in the homosexual as well as the heterosexual world."

(Norton, 1995, 162)

"Intercourse is just one tiny aspect of 'sex,' like one tiny planet in a vast galaxy of possibilities."

(Judy M. Hancock, Health Education Coordinator, University of Alberta)

Most men thought of Sean as a hot stud. He had a body to die for: hard pecs, ripped abs, and bulging biceps. It took him ten years to achieve his chiselled physique, and he proudly displayed as much of it as he legally could at various bars.

Sean was also incredibly cute with his cropped blonde hair and seductive blue eyes. He got off on watching guys give him a second and third take. He was hard not to stare at and lust over. He could have almost anyone, and according to most reports, had had almost everyone.

Beneath his confident and muscular exterior, however, you would never know how unsettled Sean felt. He knew he was attractive and hotly pursued by guys, but his sex life seemed so lacklustre. After a sexual encounter, he couldn't wait to get rid of the guy he had fucked. It often seemed to Sean that his sex partner felt the same way. Sean never felt sexually fulfilled or compatible. He used his entire arsenal of sex techniques with each guy he brought home, but they never pleased him sufficiently. Most people at bars thought he was promiscuous, and he was, but what he was really pursuing was a guy who could satisfy him sexually. If he ever met such a guy, Sean was convinced he would settle down. At age 28, he now feels ready for something more committed.

Sean has a ferocious appetite for sex, but most of the time, he ends up frantically masturbating at home. He can't hold back his ecstatic screams. Thank God he lives alone, he thinks to himself, or he would be razed nearly every day. What really gets him off is when he inserts the nine-inch dildo up his ass. And that is no longer enough it seems. He loves doing it by attaching nipple clamps and jerking himself using both hands. However, masturbation has become boring and Sean feels desperate to figure out why he can't get his needs met.

Sean knows he is mostly a bottom. Because of his muscularity and size, most guys assume he is a top, and Sean delivers. But even the men he sleeps with sense that Sean is not enjoying himself that much. Afterwards, most never want to have sex with him again, which suits Sean just fine because he can't wait to get rid of them either.

On Monday, he gets on his bike and rides to Dr. Scott's, his physician, to get the results of his yearly physical. Dr. Scott has asked another health professional to join her, which Sean finds more than a little unusual. He blurts out, "Are you going to hold me down for the news, Dr. Scott?," intending the comment to be taken lightly. Dr. Scott is not smiling, however, and the guy with her looks sober. He introduces himself as Mr. Johnson from the STD clinic. He gives Sean the worst news he has ever heard: Sean's test result came back HIV positive. Sean never thought it could happen to him. Despite the fact that he hasn't used condoms in months, he has been the top, for God's sake. There must be a mistake. But no, a mistake has not been made.

Over the next few months, Sean becomes increasingly depressed, eventually culminating in admittance to the psychiatric ward of the General Hospital. His recovery from depression seems slow as he needs to try three antidepressants until finding one that works. Although his depression lifts, he knows his HIV status can never change. Being HIV positive feels like the beginning of the end, and deep down, he knows that is exactly the score.

The Problem

This chapter is about having great sex—great, responsible, safer sex that is. Sean was under an illusion that he couldn't become infected with the HIV virus because he was the penetrator in anal intercourse. Unfortunately, that is not true. All sexual behaviour between two people that involves physical contact with contaminated semen, blood, vaginal secretions and breast milk carries some risk of HIV transmission (U.S. Centers for Disease Control and Prevention, 2001). That is why receptive anal sex is considered the highest risk sexual activity. The rigorousness of anal sex leaves the bowels open to minor hemorrhaging (bleeding), and the efficient absorption ability of the intestinal lining provides still more opportunity for contraction of the virus into the bloodstream. The penetrator is also at risk because of having contact with the receiver's blood.

To date, there is no cure for HIV/AIDS. Do not deceive yourself into thinking that today's drug cocktails will save you. They prolong life, but they do not kill the virus that eventually causes AIDS.

If you are not thoroughly familiar with HIV/AIDS, more information is found in Appendix E. Detailed information is available from the U.S. National Center for HIV, STD and TB Prevention at http://www.cdc.gov/hiv/dhap.htm. Another excellent Web site is http://www.sfaf.org/aids101/transmission.html.

Besides Sean's unsafe and irresponsible sexual behaviour (remember: Sean has likely infected other guys as well), he doesn't know how to be himself in the sexual arena. Partly he has become the victim of stereotyping because the men he beds have pegged him as a top simply because he is muscular. But Sean has not communicated his preference either. Why doesn't Sean tell these men he prefers receptive anal sex? Furthermore, he likes his nipples clamped, and perhaps he would enjoy having them sucked on, bitten or chewed lightly as well. Sean neither communicates what he likes sexually nor does he ask his sexual partner what he likes either. Consequently, sex becomes a mechanical routine that both people believe the other will enjoy.

Open communication about preferred sexual practices is difficult for many people. Paying attention to what a sex partner does to you often provides clues as to what he or she prefers as well. For example, if your partner massages your shoulders, this may suggest that he or she would enjoy the same. Regardless, the preferred approach is still to ask directly.

Sean has also become bored with his own masturbation because he is not sexually satisfied with men, and sees masturbation as a poor second choice to what he could enjoy if he found the "right" man. Nonsense! Masturbation does not need to be seen as a second choice at all. Perhaps Sean needs to become more diverse in his masturbatory practices. Sean may be craving the closeness that comes from having a relationship, but he assumes that the "right" man is someone with whom he will have outstanding sex. In truth, the right man is someone with whom he can establish a sustainable relationship. As this is the focus of Chapter 12, I will leave that discussion until then. The point is, nearly any two people can improve their sex lives by communicating openly and directly with each other.

What Needs to Change?

First and foremost, remember to wear condoms when participating in vaginal sex and anal sex. As condoms do occasionally break, some recommend wearing two rubbers. There is also minimal risk of HIV infection through oral sex (see Appendix E). Women are advised to use dental dams or cut-up, stretched-out condoms during oral sex with their female partners.

Now that you've taken adequate precautions, you are ready to begin having the best sex ever. Let's review how that might look in a "cookbook" fashion:

1. Before agreeing to sex, talk about what you want with your partner. This is particularly a good idea with one-night stands and remains common practice in the leather community. When you get to that place of thinking about sex with a potential partner, and it becomes clear that sex will transpire, talk to him or her about what he or she is into and what it is you are looking for as well. If a lesbian woman, for example, wants you to wear a strap-on dildo and fuck her anally, and you are strictly into vaginal penetration or oral sex, then you have some negotiating to do. If, on the other hand, you are a guy into receiving

head but not giving it, and your potential partner loves giving head and is less into getting it for the night, you have a near-perfect match.

2. Talk to your partner about desired ambience. Does your partner prefer the lights on or off? No music, relaxing music or thumping dance music? Candles, incense or a glass of wine before sex? Create the desired atmosphere.

3. Begin sex with foreplay. Before you start, ask your partner what he or she likes and doesn't like. Encourage him or her to be explicit with you, and to let you know when to move to something else. Especially if this is someone you have not had much sex with before, you really don't know what this person enjoys. Don't be afraid to ask directly. Talking during sex is not only okay, it is a necessity, particularly with a new partner.

4. Take turns at foreplay. One-sided sex is rarely what either of you wants, unless this was negotiated and agreed upon in step 1. Give equal time to enjoying foreplay with each other. If anal sex is on the menu, don't forget the condiments. Spend plenty of time slowly lubing and stretching the anus, gradually inserting one finger, two fingers, and finally three fingers. When there is enough lube for insertion of three fingers, you're ready.

5. Proceed with what you had agreed on experiencing together. Again, don't forget to communicate. Although you may have agreed on one thing, you or your partner may have had a change of mind. You also need to talk about the point when you have had enough of whatever is happening.

You can also enjoy great sex by yourself. In this case, let your imagination run wild. You may want to visit a sex shop to buy some great masturbation toys. The only caution is to avoid doing anything that may cause you permanent damage. Most guys have probably thought of using a vacuum cleaner at one time or another, but they are really made for floors. Vacuum cleaners may damage a guy's penis, and that is not a good thing.

The biggest sex organ is your brain. If you are inhibited when it comes to sex, or suffer huge performance anxiety, sex won't be the best until you work on the disturbed underlying beliefs. This chapter will help you make those changes.

Where I'm At Now

Place a checkmark in the column that corresponds to your answer.

If your answer is "yes," use the following rating scale: 1=very slightly; 2=slightly; 3=moderately; 4=highly; 5=severely.

1=very slightly; 2=slightly; 3=moderately; 4=highly; 5=severely	NO	YES				
		1	2	3	4	5
1 I am inhibited either when getting naked with someone else or when it comes to having sex.						
2 I am hung up about some or several sexual practices—they seem wrong and dirty to me.						
3 I usually do not ask my partner about what he or she wants either before or during sex.						
4 I usually do not communicate what I want before or during sex.						
5 I do not fully enjoy masturbation, or I feel guilty about it.						

If you respond "YES" to any of these questions, you would benefit from doing some work in this area. If all of your responses are "NO," you may want to skip this chapter.

The Solution

Sean's failure to practice safer sex led to his becoming HIV positive. Now that he is infected he needs to ensure that he protects future sexual partners from contracting the virus from him. If Sean is going to enjoy great sex, he needs to begin communicating with his partners, telling them what he wants and finding out what they want. It seems that most of the men Sean takes home stereotype him as a top. If Sean doesn't want to consistently act in this capacity, he would do well to tell them this before they agree to have sex together.

Sean hasn't learned that sex is not just about technique. In fact, the communication that occurs between two people is more important than technique will ever be. Each person will teach the "technique" that he or she finds most satisfying if their partner really listens. The remainder of this chapter will help you enjoy better sex.

A. Changing Your Thoughts

1. Beliefs Chart

REMINDER: Complete the following exercise by using the How to Question Your Beliefs pullout sheet found in the Introduction.

SAMPLE THOUGHT	UNDERLYING BELIEF	QUESTIONING IT (you complete this column)	HEALTHIER BELIEF
I am inhibited either when getting naked with someone else or when it comes to having sex.	I should be ashamed of my body. Having sex with someone of the same gender is wrong.		My body deserves my fullest appreciation and acceptance. Having sex is a beautiful way of expressing affection for another person.
I am hung up about some or several sexual practices—they seem wrong and dirty to me.	Sex is dirty and it is wrong to fully enjoy it.		Sex is a good thing and I deserve to enjoy it fully, and so does my sex partner.
I usually do not ask my partner about what he or she wants either before or during sex.	People are supposed to know what their partner wants sexually without having to ask.		I cannot read other people's minds. Especially when it comes to sex, I need to ask what my partner wants from me.
I usually do not communicate what I want before or during sex.	My sexual wants are not important.		It's important that I communicate what I want out of a sexual experience.
I do not fully enjoy masturbation, or I feel guilty about it.	Masturbation is wrong, or it is a poor second choice for sex.		Masturbation is a good thing because I have a right to enjoy the pleasures of my own body. There is nothing second-rate about it—it's okay to fulfill my needs.
(Write any additional thoughts and beliefs you have.)			

2. Visualization Exercises

REMINDER: Complete the following exercises by using the How to Visualize pullout sheet found in the Introduction.

(a) General Visualizations—Imagine yourself as though you are completely comfortable getting naked with a sex partner. Then see yourself completely immersed in having sex, enjoying every minute of it. Particularly see yourself enjoying activities that you have felt hung up about.

(b) Specific Visualizations—Think of a specific instance where you found yourself not responding as you wanted in a sexual experience. What was behind it? If you can arrive at the cause, correct it in your visual image. Replay the sexual experience repeatedly the way you wanted it to turn out. If you struggle with having a good body image, do some exercises addressing this in Chapter 2. If you are simply shy when it comes to sex, visualize yourself as you want to be—cool, calm and confident. Practice these images repeatedly.

B. Changing Your Behaviour

1. General Activities
These general activities will help you improve your sex life:

• Expand your sexual repertoire. If you are unaware of the vast number of sexual possibilities when you get together with a partner, learn more. A good place to start is by reading a book about sexual techniques for gay people (refer to Silverstein & Picano, 1992, in Appendix D). You might also begin by using your imagination to come up with ideas you would like to try.
• Introduce varied methods into masturbation. If you always masturbate the same way, try something different. Use various sex toys or household objects (remember my warning about using only those that are safe!). A firm English cucumber works as well as a dildo, for example.
• Spend more time being nude. The more time you spend being naked, the more comfortable you will feel in someone else's presence.
• Practice communicating with your partner before and during sex. Start small, and gradually become more verbal. The best sex occurs when two people know what they each want, and the best way to learn is by asking and telling.
• Experiment with enacting sexual scripts. If you have a regular sex partner and always wanted to enact a bondage script with one of you being tied up, talk to your partner about it and do it. It will add spice to your sex life.
• Pull the rabbit out of a hat. If you and your regular sex partner have become irregular when it comes to sex, you need to work at restoring your sex life. First, forget about spontaneity for a while. Decide which days of the week you will have sex, and at what time of day. Second, each of you can write out as many ideas you can think of for how you would like to have sex, each idea

written on a separate paper or card. You might include sexual scripts as in the preceding exercise. Third, you place an equal number of ideas from each of your collection into a hat. Fourth, when the day and time arrives for having sex, one of you draws one of the ideas from the hat and you are both committed to doing whatever is on the paper or card. Enjoy!

2. Specific Activities
Goal-setting

Decide upon a specific behaviour that you will target for change. Your best choice is a behaviour that you have already found is causing you trouble. Here are some examples:

- Feeling afraid to get naked with someone
- Not comfortable with performing oral sex
- Inconsistent use of condoms when having anal or vaginal sex
- Never telling my sex partner what I want from the sexual experience

Shaping

Write your goal in the chart below, and then list the steps you will take to begin working on it.

GOAL:		
# STEPS NEEDED TO HELP ME ACHIEVE THIS GOAL	DONE	REWARD
1		
2		
3		

Rewards

In the chart above, decide which of your steps should have an accompanying reward for its successful completion. Write what the specific reward will be. After completing the step, place a checkmark in the Done column and be sure to give yourself the assigned reward.

Environment Control

Spending time with people who are hung up about sex or think of it as wrong in most contexts, won't help you develop the freedom of spirit and liberation necessary if you want to enjoy great sex. Likewise, having sex with people who are inhibited sexually won't help you overcome your own fears in this area. In the chart below, write the environmental changes you need to make until your goal is successfully achieved:

#	PERSON OR GROUP THAT AFFECTS YOU	+ OR - EFFECT	PLANNED ACTION (Range: complete avoidance to frequent contact—be specific)
1			
2			
3			
4			

C. Changing the Way You Feel About It

When you experience a negative feeling complete the following chart (REMINDER: instructions for using this chart are found in the Introduction):

NAME THE FEELING(S)	DESCRIBE THE TRIGGER	UNDERLYING BELIEF(S)	QUESTIONING IT	HEALTHIER BELIEF

Where I'm At After Working On It

Periodically re-test yourself to chart your progress in this area.

1=very slightly; 2=slightly; 3=moderately; 4=highly; 5=severely	NO	YES 1 2 3 4 5
1 I am inhibited either when getting naked with someone else or when it comes to having sex.		
2 I am hung up about some or several sexual practices—they seem wrong and dirty to me.		
3 I usually do not ask my partner about what he or she wants either before or during sex.		
4 I usually do not communicate what I want before or during sex.		
5 I do not fully enjoy masturbation, or I feel guilty about it.		

If you are still responding "YES" to any of these questions, continue working on change in this area. If all of your responses are "NO," you have made significant progress! Continue to monitor any remaining problems in this area, and work on these as suggested in this chapter.

Summary

Sean was highly sought after as a sex object, but he didn't enjoy the sex he had that much. Masturbation also seemed lacking. Sean was a victim of his own sexual scripts, which were full of prescribed methods for having sex. More importantly, he neither communicated with his sex partners about what he wanted nor did he ascertain what they wanted. Consequently, both were left with incomplete and unsatisfying sexual experiences. Later Sean received the worst news he could imagine: because of his unsafe sexual practices, he had become HIV positive.

You might be experiencing your own problems in the sexual area. If so, this chapter offered a number of ways to improve your outlook regarding sex and your sex life itself. On the next page is the Positive Affirmations pullout sheet, which can be kept by your bed or in some other highly visible place. Spend a few minutes each day reflecting on what each affirmation means to you personally.

POSITIVE AFFIRMATIONS

[Also add your own from the Healthier Belief *columns in this chapter]*

My body deserves my fullest appreciation and acceptance. Having sex is a beautiful way of expressing affection for another person.

Sex is a good thing and I deserve to enjoy it fully, and so does my sex partner.

I cannot read other people's minds. Especially when it comes to sex, I need to ask what my partner wants from me.

It's important that I communicate what I want out of a sexual experience as well.

Masturbation is a good thing because I have a right to enjoy the pleasures of my own body. There is nothing second-rate about it—it's okay to fulfill my needs.

CHAPTER 12

Creating Sustainable Relationships

"Love and romance, intimacy, and lifelong vows of commitment and partnership could never be part of homosexuality, it was mistakenly believed. Now a generation of people in many countries, making their lives together as partners in life, have proved this bias to be wrong. This false conception of homosexuality in the past reduced the whole person and his or her goals and aspirations to nothing more than sex, denying all of the full and loving person as well as his or her creativity, civility, and spirituality."

(Herdt, 1997, 178)

"In sum, gay and lesbian relationships are in many ways strikingly similar to hetero-sexual ones. Old myths about unhappy, transient, and loveless unions are clearly false; gay men and lesbians form loving, lasting, richly satisfying partnerships. They also face relationship problems, as do heterosexual couples."

(Bohan, 1996, 196)

Some people think Robin is a sex addict, but they don't know him very well. There is no denying that Robin goes through men like many people go through underwear, but in his heart, he knows that he wants a long-term relationship. He is just having trouble meeting the right guy.

Robin admits that his standards are quite high. The guy has to be buff, attractive and well hung. Sadly for Robin, he doesn't have all of these traits himself. He has developed a good physique from frequent workouts at the gym, but most guys would judge him to be of average attractiveness. And as for being well hung. . .well, maybe in his fantasies.

So Robin has sex with a lot of men. It's the only way he can find out if the guy meets all of his criteria. Even the perfect penis is hard to find. Many times they are too small, too thin, too big (not often, Robin thinks), too bent and even too small when flaccid. Given his expectations, it's amazing that he has actually dated five men over the past two years. However, none of the relationships have lasted more than two months. The other guy ended two of these short relationships. Robin dumped the other three.

After the steamy-passionate-sex phase has ended, which for Robin takes between two and three weeks, he loses interest in the guy. This disturbs him because he wants a long-term relationship. So he keeps trying to re-kindle the flaming passion that seemed so pronounced at first. It's easier paddling a boat upstream, Robin concludes, after having gone through this experience time after time.

Robin really wanted his relationship with Tony to sustain itself. But the old pattern soon returned. Two weeks after having lost interest, Robin ended the relationship. Tony wasn't that upset either—he knew Robin wasn't connecting with him. Tony felt he was with someone who could not get beneath the surface.

So back to the bars and baths to look for Mr. Right. As usual, though, Robin only found Mr. Right Now. Robin's friends could see the agony that he was experiencing, but they had stopped introducing their attractive friends and acquaintances to him. Inevitably, Robin would have sex with them and then move on, sometimes leaving them confused and hurt. This left Robin's friends to deal with the emotional pain and anger of having introduced him to them.

Some of Robin's friends had actually withdrawn their friendship from him for this reason. But they had also lost respect for him. It was hard not to think of Robin as self-centred and superficial. Robin never saw it this way, though, because he knew it was worth waiting for the right guy. It had only been 10 years of waiting by this point, and he knew lots of gay men who remained single longer than him. He had no doubt that Mr. Right was out there, but he still never expected it would take this long. He had to admit he was lonely most of the time, but he could not settle for less than he deserved. Who could blame him, he thought. He could get laid whenever he wanted, and that helped to ease his loneliness.

After another five years of this, however, Robin was nearly beside himself with self-doubt and anxiety. God, he was now 33-years-old, and he realized that the only friends he had left were friends he had known less than a year. His other friends were all coupled off and always seemed to have excuses for why they couldn't get together. Maybe it was time to lower his standards. Robin couldn't understand why this was so difficult for him to actually do.

The Problem

Robin is suffering from the projected or externalized form of the Adonis Syndrome, which was first described in Chapter 2. Remember that the internalized form is about trying compulsively to attain the perfect physique. The result of this obsession and compulsion is diminished self-esteem and a disturbed body image. The externalized version means that the desire for a perfect physique becomes projected or externalized to potential partners. The result is that he or she is only satisfied with establishing a relationship with someone else who has the perfect male or female body.

The externalized Adonis Syndrome, which is one of Robin's problems, produces inordinate difficulty or inability to find a suitable mate. It more commonly occurs with men, regardless of their sexual orientation. The other result is that if one is so lucky as to find a mate who qualifies, constant pressure will be placed on the mate to maintain at least the same level of attractiveness. This pressure can lead to conflict if the mate is unable to sustain this due to stress or aging.

Besides the Adonis Syndrome, Robin experiences another problem I call Chasing the Dragon Syndrome. Chasing the Dragon is a term used to describe drug users who begin "chasing" greater and faster highs by heating heroin and then inhaling it (Strang, Griffiths, & Gossip, 1997). Applied to the sexual context, Chasing the Dragon Syndrome includes the following symptoms:

- A compulsive need to pursue the next sexual high
- As this sensation wears off with one individual, loss of interest in the person as a sexual partner
- Obsessive desire to chase the feeling again with a new sex partner, followed by active pursuit of that individual
- Inability to stop the cycle

Those who suffer from the Adonis Syndrome and/or Chasing the Dragon Syndrome will come across as superficial to most people. As others come to know them, it will become increasingly difficult to believe that they really want a committed relationship. Yet consciously, that's exactly what they want. Subconsciously, however, a different picture emerges.

Beneath the externalized form of the Adonis Syndrome is a problem of self-esteem in gay and heterosexual individuals, which can be further compounded by internalized homophobia in gay people. If afflicted individuals have a relationship with the stereotype of male or female beauty, it enhances their feeling of self-worth. The underlying belief is "If I can attract such a beautiful person, I must be okay too." They may feel an increase in status as others notice and comment on their mate's beauty. If afflicted gay people have a relationship with someone gorgeous, they may believe that it is not so bad to be gay because of their partner's attractiveness. In other words, such individuals don't feel good about being gay deep down, but having a beautiful partner helps to compensate for these feelings. It is also easier, in their minds, to introduce such a same-sex partner to their friends and family.

Chasing the Dragon Syndrome, on the other hand, has a different set of dynamics. Afflicted individuals equate sex with love. When sexual passion diminishes, even temporarily, they assume that they do not love the person anymore. In actuality, not enough time has elapsed for them to know. As mentioned in Chapter 1, romantic love is not just about chemistry and passion; it is also about caring and commitment. These elements take time to develop. If a relationship becomes based on caring, commitment, respect, trust and honesty, passion will likely persist for many years. But it's not always going to peak, as anyone knows who has been involved in a long-term relationship. Another problem with people suffering from Chasing the Dragon Syndrome is that they don't know what comprises real relationships. Sex is only a small part of a relationship. More time is spent communicating and spending time together. For those suffering from this syndrome, the sexual component of a relationship becomes grossly exaggerated in importance.

Many people, including many gay individuals, are misinformed about gay relationships. "Most lesbians and gay men want intimate relationships and are successful in creating them" (Peplau, 1993, 414). Gay couples are just as psychologically healthy and happy as compared to heterosexual couples (Smith & Brown, 1997), and relationships between gay men enhance their psychological health and well being (Simonsen, Blazina, & Watkins, 2000). Although I am unaware of similar studies with lesbian women, the same is likely the case for lesbians as their relationships are usually based on equality (Risman & Schwartz, 1988). Compared to heterosexual women, lesbians tend to be more androgynous in their gender roles (Fassinger, 1995). Such characteristics are related to establishing healthy relationships.

Long-term relationships are common with gay individuals, including durations of twenty years or more (Bohan, 1996). One survey, which included responses from 560 gay male couples and 706 lesbian couples, found that lesbian relationships were less enduring compared to relationships between gay men (Bryant & Demian, 1994).

Gay couples generally refer to their mates as lover, partner or life partner (Bryant & Demian, 1994). Most lesbian women and gay men would not prefer to be legally married, even if this were an option (Bohan, 1996).

It is important to understand that there are different types of sustainable relationships in the gay world. Here are a few of the possibilities:

• Monogamous relationship, with or without children
• Open relationship (varying degrees of openness exist with many gay couples, particularly men)
• Living together or apart
• "Daddy-son" or "mommy-daughter" relationship (between two men or women of   significantly different ages where each assumes somewhat different roles)
• "Sugar daddy" or "sugar mommy" relationship (where one is financially capable and willing to look after the other, who is often younger, but not necessarily)
• Threesome or foursome relationships (Herrman, 1990)
• Casual-sex relationship, often known crudely as a "fuck buddy" relationship. These relationships usually include some level of friendship, and sometimes intense friendship, along with a sexual component. Either person is still free to date others and remains open to falling in love with someone (usually not the fuck buddy)
• Companionship relationship. These relationships often began with a combination of caring, commitment and passion (or chemistry), but over time the passion dwindles, whereas the love does not. Often gay companions stay together, but lead separate lives in the sexual area

As you can see from the above list, there is a smorgasbord of possibilities in gay relationships. Each of the above forms is sustainable so long as the relationship is based on mutual respect, honesty, trust, and clear communication. Many relationships, gay or straight, dissolve when two people are unable to work through their conflicts. Conflict is inevitable, and if you and your partner are unsuccessful in resolving it, please see a gay or gay-positive counsellor. Such conflicts are beyond the scope of this book.

What Needs to Change?

If you are suffering from either the externalized Adonis Syndrome or Chasing the Dragon Syndrome, or both, the first step is to work on these problems and overcome them. The next section of this chapter will provide some solutions.

Assuming that you don't suffer from either of these syndromes, but you have had trouble sustaining relationships, here are 10 helpful suggestions:

1. Carefully assess what you are doing wrong—Until you know what mistakes you are making, it will be difficult to correct the problem. The two most common mistakes are not picking an appropriate person to be your mate and not treating the person properly once the relationship is underway. If you don't pick appropriate mates, you are probably following your heart and/or your "little head" more than your big head. Go back and read the H-H-H approach described in Chapter 11. It will show you how to start making better choices. You need to become discerning to find a suitable mate. If you find yourself making good choices but your relationships don't survive, the ideas that follow will help.
2. Appreciate that appropriate behaviour depends on the stage of the relationship and the type of relationship—There are helpful suggestions in Chapter 11 regarding the various stages of dating. As a relationship grows, deeper levels of commitment occur, and this requires making greater efforts to maintain the highest level of integrity and truthfulness.
3. Be sincere and honest—Relationships do not survive if they are based on varying degrees of dishonesty. You need to be yourself with the other person, and that means not holding back the truth, even if it might be hurtful to your partner. Better to be hurt and real than to be placated by lies and deceit.
4. Build trust—Trust is the building block of any relationship. Besides being honest, trust builds as you deliver what you say you're going to deliver. If you agree to pick your partner up at 10 p.m., and show up at 11 instead without having called to say you'll be late, you are doing the relationship a small hurt. If enough hurts accumulate, the foundation of the relationship erodes.
5. Be respectful of your partner at all times—Even if you are fighting, learn to disagree in a cordial, respectful manner. Remember that your anger is directed at some aspect of your partner's behaviour, not at the person himself or herself. While talking about the behaviour that you find inappropriate, don't lose sight

that it is a person you are talking to. Forget name-calling, back-stabbing and drudging up the distant past.

6. Learn to negotiate—Conflict is inevitable between any two people. Conflict resolution will usually fit into one of the following categories: (a) the person doing the behaviour in question decides that it is wrong or inappropriate, and consciously chooses not to repeat it; (b) you reach a compromise, and each of you gives a little so that you can agree on a middle ground position; or (c) neither of you can budge on the issue in question, which means you are dealing with a "bottom-line" crisis. In this case, the only solution is deciding to respect (or at least tolerate) this difference between you. An example of (a) is you begin cheating on your partner, your partner finds out, and you decide to stop cheating because you realize it is harmful to your relationship. An example of (b) is you find yourself doing all the housework and soon begin to resent it. You raise the issue with your partner, and together you work out a fairer arrangement. Finally, an example of (c) is one of you is a dedicated pot smoker, and the partner is completely against all drug use. The only viable solution to this, unless the pot smoker wants to stop using, is to respect or tolerate this difference. Two management strategies would be to either turn a blind eye to the pot smoking or to negotiate an arrangement where the smoking only occurs when the partner is not at home.

7. Don't expect your partner to change for you—Big, big mistake. Accept or at least tolerate your partner as he or she is, not as you want him or her to be. Remember: you started this relationship with a person already entrenched with habits and attitudes, just like you. If you made a bad choice of picking your partner, accept that and move on. But if you love this person, accept that not everything will be to your liking. People change when they want it, not because someone wants it for them.

8. Establish ground rules in your relationship—Recall the eight different types of relationships mentioned in the previous section. Each relationship style will have different ground rules, some by definition (e.g., a "sugar" relationship means the one with the money will do the spending). Even within a relationship style, additional ground rules will need to be discussed and negotiated. There are many types of open relationships, for example, and the rules surrounding outside sexual activity need to be agreed upon.

9. Encourage your partner—Ideally, relationships are about two people growing together and individually as well. Support your partner's growth by showing plenty of praise and encouragement. We all thrive when surrounded by positive energy and love.

10. Talk about issues as soon as possible—Don't let issues percolate until they become blown out of proportion. When something happens that upsets or angers you, talk about it. This is the time to be assertive, not days or weeks later when your partner can barely remember the incident.

If you practice these 10 suggestions, you will work through most of what your relationship throws at you. You'll still get hit by the occasional sidewinder, and after the initial shock or upset subsides, go back over the list of 10 suggestions and work through the problem.

Don't be afraid to ask for help either. Relationships are tough work. Sometimes the first year or two of being together are the hardest. If both of you communicate with each other honestly and directly, you are going to encounter conflict around every corner. Accept this as normal and healthy—it's the only way you're going to get into better sync with each other. But sometimes the conflict is more than you can handle on your own. Talk to friends, family or a professional counsellor when the two of you become stuck. Don't let staying stuck become the theme of your relationship. What you have may become more beautiful than anything you've ever experienced, and that can sustain each of you for a long time, perhaps even forever.

Where I'm At Now
Place a checkmark in the column that corresponds to your answer.

If your answer is "yes," use the following rating scale: 1=very slightly; 2=slightly; 3=moderately; 4=highly; 5=severely.

			YES				
1=very slightly; 2=slightly; 3=moderately; 4=highly; 5=severely	NO	1	2	3	4	5
1	I must have a partner who is extremely attractive and almost perfect physically.						
2	I soon get bored with a partner sexually and want to move on to someone else.						
3	I tend to keep issues to myself instead of sharing them with a partner, or once disclosed, I have trouble negotiating a solution.						
4	I have a hard time being totally honest, sincere, and respectful toward a partner.						
5	I have trouble creating sustainable relationships.						

If you respond "YES" to any of these questions, you would benefit from doing some work in this area. If all of your responses are "NO," you may want to skip this chapter.

The Solution
Most importantly, Robin needs to overcome both the externalized Adonis Syndrome and Chasing the Dragon Syndrome if he is ever going to be happy and settled in a relationship. Let's begin with how you overcome the externalized Adonis Syndrome:

1. Develop positive self-esteem—Chapter 2 shows you how to do this.
2. Overcome internalized homophobia, if this is partly to blame—Chapter 1 shows you how to do this.
3. Focus on the person, not the body—Although we all need to feel some degree of physical attraction for our partner, the question is one of degree. Have you ever noticed how you often develop greater attraction for someone who is a kind, loving person, and lose attraction for someone who has undesirable traits? The same principle applies here. Get to know the person you feel some attraction for and see if it builds over time.

To overcome Chasing the Dragon Syndrome, do the following:

1. Learn as much as you can about real relationships—Do some reading in this area and watch couples that you admire. Learn from them.
2. Accept that sexual passion naturally goes through changes in a relationship—If you want to keep the fire burning, get to know the person and establish a genuine relationship based on all the positive qualities mentioned throughout this chapter. Give it a chance. You'll likely find that as you come to establish a meaningful commitment, the sex gets better, even if it doesn't always "blow you away" in the figurative sense.
3. Put sex in its proper perspective—It is only one aspect of a relationship. Learn to lighten up a little, and begin enjoying other activities with your partner.

If Robin works through these two syndromes, he will have a chance at developing sustainable relationships. The following exercises will help you do the same.

A. Changing Your Thoughts

1. Beliefs Chart

REMINDER: Complete the following exercise by using the How to Question Your Beliefs pullout sheet found in the Introduction.

SAMPLE THOUGHT	UNDERLYING BELIEF	QUESTIONING IT (you complete this column)	HEALTHIER BELIEF
I must have a partner who is extremely attractive and almost perfect physically.	I need an attractive partner in order to feel good about myself or about being gay.		I need to feel good about myself and love myself fully as a gay person, regardless of the partner I am with.
I soon get bored with	Sex is the most		What really

a partner sexually and want to move on to someone else.	important part of a relationship. Unless the sex is dazzling, it isn't worth doing it.	counts in a relationship is connecting and loving the other person.
I tend to keep issues to myself instead of sharing them with a partner, or once disclosed, I have trouble negotiating a solution.	I must not upset my partner by always telling the truth. If we have a problem, it will go away on its own. Working out a solution is too difficult.	I need to be honest with myself and other people, especially my partner. It is better to be hurt and real than to be placated by lies and deceit.
I have a hard time being totally honest, sincere, and respectful toward a partner.	I don't know how to have a successful relationship.	I will learn everything there is to know about maintaining a relationship with someone I want to be with.
I have trouble creating sustainable relationships.	I don't deserve to be loved and to love someone else fully.	I deserve to be loved and to give love freely to another person.
(Write any additional thoughts and beliefs you have.)		

2. Visualization Exercises

REMINDER: Complete the following exercises by using the How to Visualize pullout sheet found in the Introduction.

(a) General Visualizations—if you suffer from either the Adonis Syndrome or Chasing the Dragon Syndrome, visualize yourself after getting cured. Otherwise, picture being in a long-term relationship. What do you like about it? What do you dislike? Then imagine being single. What are its advantages and disadvantages?

(b) Specific Visualizations—Think of specific times when you had problems in a relationship. Imagine what you could have done differently that would have been more respectful, honest, or assertive. Do this for each example you can think of.

B. Changing Your Behaviour

1. General Activities
These general activities will help you create sustainable relationships:

• Until you meet someone, be visible. There is no point staying home alone if you want a relationship. Plan a strategy for meeting more gay people (e.g., attend more gay events, use a telepersonal service)
• Use your friendship circle. An excellent way to meet potential partners is through friends because their friends usually have positive qualities, and if you are unsure about the individual, you can ask your friend for advice
• Establish what your potential partner is looking for. Everybody is not in the same place: some are currently looking for a relationship, and others want nothing more than something casual. Talk to the person directly about what he or she wants right now. There is no point wasting your time on someone who is unavailable or inaccessible
• Maintain open, honest communication at all times. Every relationship needs to establish rules that are negotiated. The only way you can do this is by talking freely about what the two of you want
• If you begin experiencing relationship problems, go back to the list of 10 suggestions made in the What Needs to Change section of this chapter

2. Specific Activities
Goal-setting

Decide upon a specific behaviour that you will target for change. Your best choice is a behaviour that you have already found is causing you trouble. Here are some examples:

• Learning to speak your mind freely
• Learning to argue or disagree in a respectful and constructive manner (be specific: what would effective "fighting" look like?)
• Developing effective anger-management skills
• Accepting or tolerating a specific habit that you dislike in your partner

Shaping
Write your goal in the chart below, and then list the steps you will take to begin working on it.

GOAL:			
#	STEPS NEEDED TO HELP ME ACHIEVE THIS GOAL	DONE	REWARD
1			
2			
3			

Rewards

In the chart above, decide which of your steps should have an accompanying reward for its successful completion. Write what the specific reward will be. After completing the step, place a checkmark in the Done column and be sure to give yourself the assigned reward.

Environment Control

You probably find that some of your friends encourage you when you are in a relationship, and others want you to remain single. Decide if you need to associate with different people when you are in a relationship. In the chart below, write the environmental changes you need to make until you have established a sustainable relationship:

#	PERSON OR GROUP THAT AFFECTS YOU	+ OR - EFFECT	PLANNED ACTION (Range: complete avoidance to frequent contact—be specific)
1			
2			
3			
4			

C. Changing the Way You Feel About It

When you experience a negative feeling complete the following chart (REMINDER: instructions for using this chart are found in the Introduction):

NAME THE FEELING(S)	DESCRIBE THE TRIGGER	UNDERLYING BELIEF(S)	QUESTIONING IT	HEALTHIER BELIEF

Where I'm At After Working On It

Periodically re-test yourself to chart your progress in this area.

1=very slightly; 2=slightly; 3=moderately; 4=highly; 5=severely	NO	YES				
		1	2	3	4	5
1 I must have a partner who is extremely attractive and almost perfect physically.						
2 I soon get bored with a partner sexually and want to move on to someone else.						
3 I tend to keep issues to myself instead of sharing them with a partner, or once disclosed, I have trouble negotiating a solution.						
4 I have a hard time being totally honest, sincere and respectful toward a partner.						
5 I have trouble creating sustainable relationships.						

If you are still responding "YES" to any of these questions, continue working on change in this area. If all of your responses are "NO," you have made significant progress! Continue to monitor any remaining problems in this area, and work on these as suggested in this chapter.

Summary

Robin is plagued with two significant relationship problems: the externalized Adonis Syndrome, which means Robin is only satisfied if he is dating someone with a near perfect body; and Chasing the Dragon Syndrome, which is about his constant search to experience intense sexual highs. Until he addresses these problems, he will likely remain single for most of his life. If you are suffering from either syndrome, this chapter has provided some methods of remediation.

The most common relationship problems and types of relationships are described in this chapter. The bulk of this chapter has guided you through activities and exercises aimed at first improving your ability to find an appropriate partner before focusing on helping you create a sustainable relationship. On the next page is the Positive Affirmations pullout sheet, which can be kept by your bed or in some other highly visible place. Spend a few minutes each day reflecting on what each affirmation means to you personally.

POSITIVE AFFIRMATIONS

[Also add your own from the Healthier Belief *columns in this chapter]*

I need to feel good about myself and love myself fully as a gay person, regardless of the partner I am with.

What really counts in a relationship is connecting and loving the other person.

I need to be honest with myself and other people, especially my partner. It is better to be hurt and real than to be placated by lies and deceit.

I will learn everything there is know to about maintaining a relationship with someone I want to be with.

I deserve to be loved and to give love freely to another person.

SECTION TWO
Reconnecting with the Straight World

CHAPTER 13
Breaking the Silence

"Feelings of alienation are greatest for those gay men and lesbians who hide their sexual orientation from others by avoiding activities that would expose their homosexuality or by engaging in activities that project a false image of heterosexuality."

(Walsh, 1998, 564)

"Acknowledging publicly that I was gay was the second best decision I have ever made in my life, and in fact, it was the prerequisite to the best decision I ever made— that being to commit to spending my life in a domestic partnership with Herb Moses."

(Barney Frank, quoted in Vargo, 1998, ix)

"What does it say about my lesbian/gay/bisexual identity that I deny it in order to make myself and others comfortable in heterosexist society? How much energy am I spending protecting myself that might be more fruitfully used elsewhere? How will mainstream attitudes change if the average person never knows an LGB [lesbian, gay, bisexual] individual because we all hide?"

(Bohan, 1996, 96)

Candice doesn't see herself as any different from most of her lesbian friends. Like them, she has not disclosed her lesbian identity to anyone outside of her intimate friendship circle. She came out to herself five years ago, and decided soon after to keep this a secret from most people to avoid the potential for discrimination. Candice works as an accountant in a downtown oil and gas company and has perceived that most of her colleagues are homophobic.

Lately, however, Candice has been getting tired of the charade. Although she generally has positive self-esteem, she wonders why she holds back telling people if she really is proud of her lesbian identity. She is finding it increasingly difficult to keep telling lies. Two of her colleagues, Jeannette and Netty, have become her friends, and the three of them often have lunches together. Mondays are the hardest—each wants to know what the others did on the weekend. Her two friends especially like talking about their boyfriends. Yes, Candice has a girlfriend, but it's like she doesn't exist. When Candice shares her weekend experiences, she talks as though she does everything alone or with other friends. Consequently, Jeannette and Netty assume that Candice is looking for a boyfriend herself.

As their friendship develops, the two of them begin trying to set Candice up on dates. Through their boyfriend's friendship circle, Jeannette and Netty have now met several eligible bachelors who would be an ideal fit for Candice. Funny, they think, how Candice always has an excuse for not getting together with any of these terrific guys. Eventually they stop suggesting names and trying to set up double dates. Over time, the friendship between Jeannette and Netty becomes closer and Candice moves further to the fringe. That's okay with Candice—in fact she prefers it that way. She doesn't want any of her heterosexual friends to get too close. Same with her family. She needs to keep them at bay to protect her identity.

Without question, Candice has become accomplished at lying. No one suspects she is gay because she has become convincing after years of practice. Candice finds it easy to lie to her partner, Alexia, for the same reason. Whenever it is easier to lie than to tell the truth, she lies.

Whenever Candice hears a homophobic remark or joke in the office, she pretends it doesn't bother her. Somehow she succeeds. When she tells Alexia about the comments she hears, Alexia wonders whether these remarks are affecting Candice adversely. Alexia believes that Candice has created some emotional distance between them. Is Candice really proud of herself? If she were, wouldn't she also be proud of her partner? It bothers Alexia that so many people in Candice's life don't know that she exists. Although Candice has worked for six years in the same company, Alexia has never met any of her co-workers. She has never been to one of their house parties. She has never been invited to the company Christmas party. Although the company has same-sex benefits available through their insurance carrier, Candice would be horrified to ask about them. She would have to out herself. Instead, Alexia pays for her own prescriptions and dental bills. Sometimes Alexia feels like a nobody.

A few months later their relationship ends because Alexia doesn't see it going anywhere. She is tired of being Candice's dirty little secret. Candice grieves intensely over the loss. The pain seems almost more than she can bear, and she cannot ask for support from anyone at work or tell anyone the real reason for her saddened heart. Nor can she call her mom or dad, the ones who brought her into this world and raised her. Would they turn their back on their daughter if they knew she was hurting so badly? Candice will never know that because she won't let her parents get to know her.

The Problem

Empirical studies suggest that as many as two-thirds of lesbian women (Fassinger, 1995) and most gay men as well (Nauta, Saucier, & Woodard, 2001) do not disclose their identity to employers, which is not surprising because workplace discrimination is pervasive (Croteau, Anderson, Distefano, & Kampa-Kokesch, 2000). What is disturbing, however, is the finding that more than a third of lesbian women "have not disclosed their identity to anyone" (Fassinger, 161).

Disclosing one's sexual identity is an important part of psychological health for both women and men (Ellis & Riggle, 1995) and is related to having a positive gay identity (Frable, Wortman, & Joseph, 1997; Leserman, DiSantostefano, Perkins, & Evans, 1994). However, indiscriminate disclosure is not recommended. Fassinger and Miller (1996) suggest that gay people need to look at the holistic picture before deciding if disclosure is possible in any given environment. For example, the individual's "race/ethnicity, class, age, geographic location, religion, occupation, community support" (55) are important considerations. If you're working as a lumberjack with a contingent of rednecks, for example, you would probably do better to keep your sexual identity to yourself. Also, people from the upper socio-economic classes (Herdt, 1997) do not tend to disclose their identity (Badget, 1995), presumably because they have "the most to lose and the least to gain" (Herdt, 159).

However, the workplace is changing for many gay men and lesbian women. Some companies have formal anti-discrimination policies regarding sexual orientation, and others go further by providing same-sex benefits, training for employees regarding diversity and other gay-affirmative actions (Chojnacki & Gelberg, 1994). Regardless of the setting, gay people can be out to greater or lesser degrees at work. Passing involves pretending that one is heterosexual; covering involves trying to prevent others from finding out without feigning heterosexuality; being implicitly out involves being honest about one's life but not actually using the label of gay or lesbian; and being explicitly out involves actually disclosing one's gay or lesbian identity (Griffin, 1992, cited in Croteau, Anderson, Distefano, & Kampa-Kokesch, 2000).

Those who are explicitly out have often "found surprising acceptance and support" at work (Violette, 2001, 98). Staying closeted means denying yourself to other people. At a certain point, you have to wonder what price you are willing to pay to keep others at a distance.

Candice has paid dearly by remaining closeted. Her self-esteem has been affected by living a life of lies and deceit. Her friends at work eventually began pulling away because at some level they could sense that Candice wasn't being truthful with them. By keeping Alexia in the closet, she denied her the chance to have same-sex benefits and be treated with love and respect. Over time this eroded the fabric of their relationship, and Alexia pulled away by ending it.

By staying closeted, Candice continues to rehearse the skill of dishonesty. She is so good at it, in fact, that it is easy for her to lie even in contexts that don't require it. The lies came to a shattering pause when Candice had to grieve over her lost relationship. The double tragedy was not having the support of co-workers or family to help her through this difficult time. Sadly, she never gave these people a chance.

What Needs to Change?

You need to decide when it is time for you to break the silence. Obviously, your personal safety has to come first. Beyond this, though, you need to ask yourself if you are living in fear needlessly. What is the worst consequence of telling the people you are holding back on? Is this consequence likely or remotely possible?

Let me share with you a personal example. Before disclosing to my family, I assumed my aging mother would have the hardest time with it and that my brother would have the easiest time, given that he has known many gay men in his life. I wondered if it was worth telling my mother. Perhaps it was better to let her enjoy her remaining years without knowing. But I decided if I did that, I was denying her the chance to know me as I am, and then when she died, I would carry this as a lifetime regret.

So I told her. She replied, "You know, I saw a program on Oprah about that last week." It was her way of saying she was okay with it. My brother, on the other hand, retreated from me for a few months. After he awoke from his hibernation, we resumed our relationship. It is now better than it has ever been.

Is your fear based on fact or fiction? Fear can take on a life of its own, preventing people from living their life with integrity and courage. It is unfair to assume, as I did, that everyone will freak at finding out you are gay. If the people in your life really care about you, they aren't going to leave you out in the cold. They will need time to get used to your disclosure, but why should you deny them the chance to grow in this important area? We are upwards of 10 % of the population—that's a lot of people to deny and disregard.

Perhaps you are ready to disclose but don't know how. You may want to reread Chapter 6, which was about being assertive. The best way to come out to others is to be direct about it. Before doing so, however, make sure that you are coming from a place of being unapologetic. You are not telling them that you have cancer: you are telling them that you are a beautiful person who is proud of your gay heritage. It should be told to people with an expectation that they will love you more for it, as you have learned to do with yourself. Consequently, a better analogy than having cancer is telling them that you have been promoted at work.

Disclosing to parents will be covered in the next chapter. Disclosing to people at work can be done either individually or in a group. Both have their advantages and disadvantages. The individual approach works best if you want to test out the waters before diving in head-first. The individual you disclose to will likely tell others in the office, which is not necessarily a bad thing. That way, even before you meet with the others individually, they already have been given a "heads up." The group approach is expeditious—they all find out together, and they can affiliate with each other afterwards to process the news.

Breaking the silence is not just about doing this for yourself, but about teaching the heterosexual world that we exist. The only reason 10 % of the population has been kept in silence is because we have allowed ourselves to be invisible. After all, who can teach the world about who we are if we aren't willing to be the teachers? Can we reasonably expect heterosexual people to know us if we are constantly hiding from them?

Women were given the right to vote only after they fought for it. Aboriginals get their voices heard only when they speak up so others can hear them. African-Americans only realized equal rights after a long fight against racist discrimination. Gay people are not any different.

Where I'm At Now

Place a checkmark in the column that corresponds to your answer.

If your answer is "yes," use the following rating scale: 1=very slightly; 2=slightly; 3=moderately; 4=highly; 5=severely.

1=very slightly; 2=slightly; 3=moderately; 4=highly; 5=severely	NO	YES 1	2	3	4	5
1 I don't tell people I am gay even if they ask.						
2 I am afraid to tell people I'm gay.						
3 I never attend social events with a same-sex partner.						
4 I assume people will think less of me if I tell them I am gay.						
5 I find that I lie even when I can tell the truth, generally to avoid recrimination.						

If you respond "YES" to any of these questions, you would benefit from doing some work in this area. If all of your responses are "NO," you may want to skip this chapter.

The Solution

Since Candice's employer offers same-sex benefits through its insurance carrier, she has likely overestimated the risk of disclosing her identity to her co-workers. She has also excluded her parents from knowing her sexual identity. This means that in two important areas of life (work and family), Candice cannot be herself. Rarely a day goes by that heterosexual individuals don't talk about their partners in some capacity. Imagine how Candice does herself and her partner a disservice by never talking about the one she loves so deeply.

Candice is living in a self-created prison and needs to break the silence because it is slowly eroding her self-esteem and self-respect. The lies need to stop if she is to become authentic. It is time for her to develop the courage needed to come out.

You can probably relate to what Candice has experienced. If so, it is time for you to break out as well. The remainder of this chapter will help get you there.

A. Changing Your Thoughts

1. Beliefs Chart

REMINDER: Complete the following exercise by using the How to Question Your Beliefs pullout sheet found in the Introduction.

SAMPLE THOUGHT	UNDERLYING BELIEF	QUESTIONING IT (you complete this column)	HEALTHIER BELIEF
I don't tell people I am gay even if they ask.	I will suffer consequences if I am truthful.		"Better to be hated for what I am, than to be loved for what I am not." (André Gide, quoted in Tremblay, 1994, 18)
I am afraid to tell people I'm gay.	I'm not completely proud of being gay.		I will overcome my fear of disclosing to others by becoming increasingly proud of my gay identity.
I never attend social events with a same-sex partner.	It is better to keep my partner in the closet than risk exposure.		My partner deserves the highest amount of love and respect that I can show her (or him). There is no space in my closet for her (or him).
I assume people will think less of me if I tell them I am gay.	I need to be accepted by everybody. My truth is not as valid as their truth.		My truth is the only truth worth knowing. Everything else is to some extent irrelevant.
I find that I lie even when I can tell the truth, generally to avoid recrimination.	It is easier to lie than to tell the truth.		Although lying is sometimes easier, it does both me and all others an injustice. My truth is a reflection of my character, and it deserves my fullest respect.

(Write any additional thoughts and beliefs you have.)

2. Visualization Exercises

REMINDER: Complete the following exercises by using the How to Visualize pullout sheet found in the Introduction.

(a) General Visualizations—Mentally rehearse what you will say to the people you choose to come out to. Practice in your mind both the verbal (voice tone, intonation, rate of speech) and non-verbal (posture, facial expressions) components. Spend time practicing this each day until you have the confidence to do it.

(b) Specific Visualizations—Think of specific instances where you lied to people to keep them from knowing that you are gay. Now rehearse what you would have said to them if they already knew you were gay. Think about how much easier it is to be yourself.

B. Changing Your Behaviour

1. General Activities

These general activities will help you become ready to disclose to more people:

• Carefully assess the likely impact of your disclosure. For each person you would like to tell, think through the likely response (remember you may still be wrong, but at least you won't be going in completely blind). Then decide if it is worth it to you. If your parents are rich and you think they will write you out of their will if they find out you're gay, you may decide disclosure is not worth it. Some would still take the chance. You may be underestimating how much your parents love you.
• Decide on when and where you will make the disclosure. Set up the situation to make it as comfortable for yourself as you want.
• Mentally rehearse what you will say. This kind of practice is helpful in preparing people for all kinds of situations in life.
• Just do it. You will find it gets easier as you tell more people. Know that ultimately, you will have created a life for yourself where you no longer need to fear that someone will find out unintentionally. In fact, the fear you have felt in your life will greatly diminish within a short time. You have not only become yourself; you are also not afraid to show it!

2. Specific Activities

Goal-setting

Decide upon a specific behaviour that you will target for change. Your best choice is a behaviour that you have already found is causing you trouble. Here are some examples:

- Feeling afraid to tell people when they ask
- Finding that when I do disclose, I come across as unconvincing or disparaging about my gay identity
- Assuming that others will automatically think less of me if I tell them
- Lying about things that have nothing to do with my sexual identity

Shaping
Write your goal in the chart below, and then list the steps you will take to begin working on it.

GOAL:			
#	STEPS NEEDED TO HELP ME ACHIEVE THIS GOAL	DONE	REWARD
1			
2			
3			

Rewards
In the chart above, decide which of your steps should have an accompanying reward for its successful completion. Write what the specific reward will be. After completing the step, place a checkmark in the Done column and be sure to give yourself the assigned reward.

Environment Control
You may find it helpful to spend more time with gay people who are already out to most people in their lives. They will act as role models to you, and you may learn better techniques from them about disclosing successfully. In the chart below, write the environmental changes you need to make until your goal is successfully achieved:

#	PERSON OR GROUP THAT AFFECTS YOU	+ OR - EFFECT	PLANNED ACTION (Range: complete avoidance to frequent contact —be specific)
1			
2			
3			
4			

C. Changing the Way You Feel About It

When you experience a negative feeling complete the following chart (REMINDER: instructions for using this chart are found in the Introduction):

NAME THE FEELING(S)	DESCRIBE THE TRIGGER	UNDERLYING BELIEF(S)	QUESTIONING IT	HEALTHIER BELIEF

Where I'm At After Working On It

Periodically re-test yourself to chart your progress in this area.

		NO	YES				
1=very slightly; 2=slightly; 3=moderately; 4=highly; 5=severely		NO	1	2	3	4	5
1	I don't tell people I am gay, even if they ask.						
2	I am afraid to tell people I'm gay.						
3	I never attend social events with a same-sex partner.						
4	I assume people will think less of me if I tell them I am gay.						
5	I find that I lie even when I can tell the truth, generally to avoid recrimination.						

If you are still responding "YES" to any of these questions, continue working on change in this area. If all of your responses are "NO," you have made significant progress! Continue to monitor any remaining problems in this area, and work on these as suggested in this chapter.

Summary

Candice is not out to her co-workers or family, and this forces her to lie to people who could otherwise become emotionally supportive of her. By staying closeted, she does herself and her partner a disservice by making both of them invisible to other people. Candice is tired of the charade, and it is time for her to break the silence that has cost her so much already.

If you examine your own life carefully, you will see where you have also paid dearly for living a lie. The bulk of this chapter has guided you through activities and exercises that will help you break out of your own closet. On the next page is the Positive Affirmations pullout sheet, which can be kept by your bed or in some other highly visible place. Spend a few minutes each day reflecting on what each affirmation means to you personally.

Positive Affirmations

[Also add your own from the Healthier Belief *columns in this chapter]*

"Better to be hated for what I am, than to be loved for what I am not."

I will overcome my fear of disclosing to others by becoming increasingly proud of my gay identity.

My partner deserves the highest amount of love and respect that I can show her (or him). There is no space in my closet for her (or him).

My truth is the only truth worth knowing. Everything else is to some extent irrelevant.

Although lying is sometimes easier, it does both me and all others an injustice. My truth is a reflection of my character, and it deserves my fullest respect.

CHAPTER 14
Breaking Out of the Family Closet

"Although parents often react in a less than ideal fashion after learning of their child's same-sex attractions, limited research indicates that most eventually arrive at tolerance or acceptance of their son's or daughter's sexual orientation."

(Savin-Williams & Dube, 1998, 7)

"It is not surprising that difficulty with parents is among the most significant problems in the lives of many homosexuals"

(Weinberg, 1972, cited in Savin-Williams, 1989, 3)

"If you're not wanted by your family or are uncomfortable with them, create your own extended family and traditions. There's no rule that says you must go home. Stay with a friend, sibling, or other relative if a full-time visit home is just too much."

(Petrow & Steele, 1995, 36)

Heather began self-identifying as a lesbian when she was 22 years old. She had had a number of heterosexual partners before this but nothing seemed to click. Then she met Jessica, and the fireworks were almost immediate. Heather thought the timing of this was good as she had recently completed a bachelors degree in microbiology, was employed and living in her own apartment.

After two months of dating, Heather asked Jessica to move in with her and was thrilled that Jessica agreed. They were living together within three weeks. Heather told her parents that she had taken in a roommate to share expenses. After meeting Jessica, they thought she was an excellent roommate choice. It seemed that she and Heather shared many interests in common.

By December, Heather and Jessica had been living together for nearly eight months. Neither of their parents knew that they were a couple, so each decided it was better to spend Christmas with their own families. They missed each other a great deal and agreed that that would be the last Christmas they would spend apart.

By their second year of being a couple, Heather decided it was time to come out to her parents and her two siblings. She knew it was unfair to Jessica to keep their relationship a secret any longer. Heather told them she had something important to share with them and they arranged a get-together for the next night.

Heather was a bit surprised by how happy and full of themselves her parents seemed when she arrived. Her mom immediately asked, "You've finally met a young man, haven't you?" Heather replied, her voice trembling now, "No, that's not it. Um, I think you had better sit down." Their facial expressions changed immediately—

deep concern replaced their initial lighthearted look. "Please tell us you're not sick, Heather," her father said anxiously. "No, that's not it either," Heather said, "Jessica and I are more than roommates. We are lovers, and we have been from the very beginning."

"You are telling us you're sick," her father interjected, "in the head. What on earth has possessed you?" "I love her, Dad," replied Heather. "Impossible!," screamed her mother. "You were raised to be a decent person, and no daughter of mine is going to blaspheme our family. You must end this nonsense right away, Heather!" Heather stood her ground and told her parents that they had no right to tell her how to live her life. The argument soon escalated, and now even her sister and brother were in on it. Peter screamed, "Heather is a dyke, Heather is a dyke!" Heather had had enough. She stormed out, swearing at the top of her lungs that she would never speak to any of them again. "You can all just fuck yourselves!"

Heather had never told her parents to fuck off before, but then she had never heard such garbage from their mouths before either. The next few weeks were tense. Neither side had much to say to the other. Even trying to be civil became an unspeakable burden. Mostly they didn't talk. Heather didn't think she would ever forgive her parents for treating her like they did. Her brother she could forgive more easily—he had always been a pain in the ass. Her sister's silence on the issue was difficult to read.

Her parents didn't know how to deal with Heather's disclosure because their religious faith was intolerant of homosexuality. They could never tell their friends about this or they would become the talk of the church. They prayed that Heather would once more find God and give up this demon that now possessed her. They kept praying for years.

The Problem

Heather's parents reacted as most parents do in a similar situation. Negative reactions are the norm when hearing that one's daughter or son is gay (Goldfried & Goldfried, 2001). Given their religious background, Heather could have predicted this in advance. If Heather had planned her disclosure more carefully she would not have lost her cool. After all, they reacted the way she had expected. She also could have provided them with some reading materials after telling them, so that they could begin to learn about what it means to be gay. This would also have acknowledged that Heather understood it would take time for them to accept her new revelation.

Telling all of them at once in a nonchalant fashion was not the best approach either. If one anticipates a negative reaction from family members, it is usually better to tell them individually. The nonchalant approach is also best reserved for disclosures that do not have such an emotional impact.

Nonetheless, Heather is to be commended for telling them. Coming out to parents is often accompanied by intense fear (Ben-Ari, 1995) and for the majority of gay men and lesbian women, it is the most difficult step (Ellis & Mitchell, 2000). It takes tremendous courage to face the fear and act despite it.

Few parents actually overreact to their daughter's or son's disclosure (Savin-Williams & Dube, 1998). Examples of overreacting would be rage, physical abuse or kicking her or him out of the house. Instead, typical reactions include "shock, displays of anger, and denial: others, with knowing inevitability, acceptance, and unconditional love" (Savin-Williams & Dube, 9). Some research suggests that a significant percentage of parents already suspect that their child is lesbian or gay (Robinson et al., 1989, cited in Savin-Williams & Dube).

Thankfully, most parents do adjust to having a gay son or lesbian daughter. Four different parental responses were demonstrated in one study which examined lesbians, gay men, and their parents (Muller, 1987, cited in Goldfried & Goldfried, 2001). Loving denial is the most frequent relationship, which is characterized as a positive between parent and child, despite the parent not telling others about having a gay son or daughter. The next most common outcome is called resentful denial, which causes problems in the relationship because of the parent's resentment. A small percentage of the relationships are called loving open, meaning that these parents are accepting of their daughter/son and partner and are open and positive to others about it. The least common relationship is called hostile recognition, which results in total estrangement due to the parent's inability or unwillingness to accept or tolerate their child as gay.

Ben-Ari (1995) sampled 32 gay and lesbian young adults and 27 parents. Most of the young adults reported an improved relationship with their parents after disclosing to them. Most impressive was that an even higher percentage of mothers and fathers reported an improved relationship with their child. "While gay and lesbian participants maintained that at best their parents acknowledged that they were gay, but had not reached full acceptance, many parents at various stages of the process claim actual acceptance" (Ben-Ari, 107-108).

Obviously, the way a parent will react depends on many factors including their "religion, educational level, and political beliefs" (Goldfried & Goldfried, 2001, 685). But we also know that having personal contact with lesbian or gay individuals is related to having more positive attitudes toward them (Waldo & Kemp, 1997). Consequently, coming out to parents is also a way to help them grow to become more loving people.

The next worst thing to denying your own growth by not coming out is to deny other people the opportunity to grow by not disclosing. It is presumptuous and disrespectful for us to think they can't handle it. Our parents, after all, have lived more years on this planet than we have.

What Needs to Change?

Disclosing to parents is a difficult step. As described in Chapter 13, you need to carefully consider the consequences before deciding. In most cases, the advantages will outweigh the disadvantages. Being real with people who are important to you is fundamental to living your life with integrity. However, if you are an adolescent living at home with your parents and you know that they would react harshly to your disclosure, you might want to wait at least until you move away from home before you tell them. Sadly, about 50 % of the physical abuse levied against gay youth is at the hands of family members (Bohan, 1996).

Let's assume you are not at risk of being abused or seriously harmed if you come out to your family, and that other potential consequences are insignificant. This means it is time to disclose, and the sooner the better. Your parent(s) and other family members will probably take time to see that being gay is a blessing, just as being heterosexual is for them. The sooner they know, the sooner they can get used to it.

Disclosing to parents is not much different than disclosing to anyone else, so read Chapter 13 for suggestions on how to do this. What is different is that our family of origin is what provided roots for most of us. Therefore, the fear factor is greater because we want to continue having the support of family.

If you have a supportive family, they will help you through the trials and tribulations you face. It should go without saying that most parents truly love their children—they have a vested interest in them. Supportive parents do not reject their children for long, particularly once they know that what they need to accept is something that won't go away.

Unsupportive and critical parents or siblings, on the other hand, are this way regardless of the issue. I often tell clients to expect that angry people will get angry and that abusive spouses will abuse. Don't expect people to behave differently toward you in the present than they have toward you in the past. They will only change if they make concerted efforts to change.

After your disclosure, there will likely be some fallout. Even the most supportive parents and siblings will need time to adjust. Do what you can to help them through this. For example, you might want to provide them with gay-affirming reading materials (an excellent resource is Borhek, 1993). Give them plenty of time to ask you questions, and do your best to give them honest, frank answers. Most importantly, respect that it will take them time, just as it took you time, to accept yourself as a gay person.

It is painful if family members reject you for a period of time, or indefinitely. Family members who reject people according to one criterion often reject on many others as well.

It is also painful if they go into denial, meaning that they never talk to you about any aspect of your gay life, carrying on as though they never heard you say you are gay. Another form of denial is if they never tell anyone outside the family that you are gay. Perhaps you want them to keep it secret. If so, that defeats much of the purpose. The reason you come out to parents and family is because you have a positive gay identity, which partly means you are no longer willing to accept being gay as a devalued identity status.

Another type of breaking out of the family closet is if you have been a gay person in a relationship with a heterosexual spouse, and then decide to end the relationship to live fully as a gay individual. This often creates a crisis beyond the scope of this book, particularly if children are involved. An excellent resource to help you through this event is Buxton (1994).

Where I'm At Now

Place a checkmark in the column that corresponds to your answer.

If your answer is "yes," use the following rating scale: 1=very slightly; 2=slightly; 3=moderately; 4=highly; 5=severely.

			YES				
1=very slightly; 2=slightly; 3=moderately; 4=highly; 5=severely	NO	1	2	3	4	5	
1 I am afraid to disclose to my family, even though the consequences would not be highly disadvantageous.							
2 There is really no point telling my family that I am gay.							
3 I don't know how to deal with certain members of my family now that I am out to them.							
4 I don't know how to cope with a family member who completely rejects me because I am gay.							
5 I have trouble dealing with my family's denial of my homosexuality.							

If you respond "YES" to any of these questions, you would benefit from doing some work in this area. If all of your responses are "NO," you may want to skip this chapter.

The Solution

As mentioned earlier, if Heather had given greater thought to how she would disclose to her family, she could have created a somewhat better reception and aftermath. Now that it's done, however, she needs to make the best of it.

Heather needs to become more understanding of her family's reaction. Given her parent's religious background, it will be difficult for them to accept her homosexuality. This is one instance where Heather needs to set an example for her parents. She can make efforts to help them understand what it means to be gay, both through talking to them and by providing them with appropriate reading materials. Regarding her siblings, it doesn't appear that Heather is close to either of them. Regardless, they will always be family, and she would do well to sit with each of them individually and help them adjust as well.

Maybe you can relate to some of Heather's experience. If so, you are in the right place.

A. Changing Your Thoughts

1. Beliefs Chart

REMINDER: Complete the following exercise by using the How to Question Your Beliefs pull-out sheet found in the Introduction.

SAMPLE THOUGHT	UNDERLYING BELIEF	QUESTIONING IT (you complete this column)	HEALTHIER BELIEF
I am afraid to disclose to my family even though the consequences would not be highly disadvantageous.	I will not be able to live with varying degrees of rejection from family members.		It's time for me to become courageous and relinquish my fear of speaking my truth.
There is really no point telling my family that I by am gay.	It's none of their business do why rock the boat?		I respect myself too much to live lies. That means my family will need to know if I am to live authentically.
I don't know how to deal with certain members of my family now that I am out to them.	I have trouble dealing assertively with people who are close to me.		I will treat people the way I want to be treated. If they can't handle who I am, that's their problem.
I don't know how to cope with a family member who completely rejects me because I am gay.	I am deeply hurt by rejection.		I am my own person, and that means there will always be some people who have trouble accepting me the way that I am.
I have trouble dealing with my family's denial of my homosexuality.	My family should be as proud of me as I am for coming out.		Although I wish everyone in my family were proud of who I am, I can't make them respect me. Ultimately that is their choice.

(Write any additional thoughts and beliefs you have.)

2. Visualization Exercises

REMINDER: Complete the following exercises by using the How to Visualize pullout sheet found in the Introduction.

(a) General Visualizations—Mentally rehearse how you are going to tell your family. Think through whether telling them in a group or individually would likely create the best atmosphere. Visualize yourself staying calm, honest, direct and respectful of their reaction. If you are already out to them, imagine how you can help them expand their knowledge of gay people and increase their acceptance of your gayness.

(b) Specific Visualizations—Once you are out to your family, think of specific instances where you found yourself not responding well to a family member's reaction. Mentally rehearse how you would like to have responded. This becomes practice for future occurrences that are similar. Do this for each example you can think of.

B. Changing Your Behaviour

1. General Activities

These general activities will help you break out of the family closet:

• Decide if there will be highly disadvantageous repercussions to coming out to your family
• If disclosing to them is appropriate, decide when and where. Also decide if it will be better to disclose to them individually or as a group
• Get ready for the disclosure. Have some reading materials with you to leave for them after the disclosure
• If you are living with your parent(s), create a contingency plan in case you need to stay with someone for a few days or months
• Remember to stay calm, honest, direct and respectful when you tell them
• Give them space. If the disclosure doesn't go well, give them some time to think about what you have told them. After a few days, ask to find out how they are doing with it. If they are angry or don't wish to speak to you right now, respect their wishes and give them space. Let them talk to you when they are ready to discuss it further
• If you have ongoing problems with a family member, hold your ground. Do your best to not let unsupportive family members depress or stress you. This is one time you will need to be assertive, yet respectful of their values. They don't need to agree with you. You have told them so that you can have an honest relationship with them, whatever the quality of it, not so that you can placate them.

• Get support from friends. This may be the time you need your friends the most. Coming out to family may be the most difficult challenge you ever face with them.

• Be patient. Don't forget that most parents will come to accept their gay daughter or son. It may take far longer than you had hoped, but that is not your problem. It was your problem before you told them.

2. Specific Activities

Goal-setting

Decide upon a specific behaviour that you will target for change. Your best choice is a behaviour that you have already found is causing you trouble. Here are some examples:

- Getting enough courage to tell my father
- Dealing with my brother's homophobic attitude
- Reducing my fear of rejection
- Bringing my partner to a family function and dealing with the possible fallout

Shaping

Write your goal in the chart below, and then list the steps you will take to begin working on it.

GOAL:		
# STEPS NEEDED TO HELP ME ACHIEVE THIS GOAL	DONE	REWARD
1		
2		
3		

Rewards

In the chart above, decide which of your steps should have an accompanying reward for its successful completion. Write what the specific reward will be. After completing the step, place a checkmark in the Done column and be sure to give yourself the assigned reward.

Environment Control

If you have made all the efforts you can to help a family member at least tolerate your sexuality and are unsuccessful, you may need to avoid contact with that person until he or she begins to come around. Alternatively, you will find it helpful to spend more time with supportive family members. In the chart below, write the environmental changes you need to make right now:

#	PERSON OR GROUP THAT AFFECTS YOU	+ OR - EFFECT	PLANNED ACTION (Range: complete avoidance to frequent contact—be specific)
1			
2			
3			
4			

C. Changing the Way You Feel About It

When you experience a negative feeling complete the following chart (REMINDER: instructions for using this chart are found in the Introduction):

NAME THE FEELING(S)	DESCRIBE THE TRIGGER	UNDERLYING BELIEF(S)	QUESTIONING IT	HEALTHIER BELIEF

Where I'm At After Working On It

Periodically re-test yourself to chart your progress in this area.

1=very slightly; 2=slightly; 3=moderately; 4=highly; 5=severely	NO	YES 1 2 3 4 5
1 I am afraid to disclose to my family even though the consequences would not be highly disadvantageous.		
2 There is really no point telling my family that I am gay.		
3 I don't know how to deal with certain members of my family now that I am out to them.		
4 I don't know how to cope with a family member who completely rejects me because I am gay.		
5 I have trouble dealing with my family's denial of my homosexuality.		

If you are still responding "YES" to any of these questions, continue working on change in this area. If all of your responses are "NO," you have made significant progress! Continue to monitor any remaining problems in this area, and work on these as suggested in this chapter.

Summary

After living together for nearly two years, Heather decided it was time to come out to her family. Without giving it much thought, she arranged a family meeting that did not go well. Her religious parents were in shock and a heated argument ensued, leaving hurt feelings on both sides. Heather needed to be more sensitive and respectful of her parent's reaction, and she now has significant work to do to help them learn to understand and accept her.

The bulk of this chapter has guided you through activities and exercises that will help you deal with coming out to your family and the possible aftermath. On the next page is the Positive Affirmations pullout sheet, which can be kept by your bed or in some other highly visible place. Spend a few minutes each day reflecting on what each affirmation means to you personally.

Positive Affirmations

[Also add your own from the Healthier Belief *columns in this chapter]*

It's time for me to become courageous and relinquish my fear of speaking my truth.

I respect myself too much to live by lies. That means my family will need to know if I am to live authentically.

I will treat people the way I want to be treated. If they can't handle who I am, that's their problem.

I am my own person, and that means there will always be some people who have trouble accepting me the way that I am.

Although I wish everyone in my family were proud of who I am, I can't make them respect me. Ultimately that is their choice.

PART III
SPECIAL CONCERNS OF
ADOLESCENTS

CHAPTER 15
The Inside of Being a Gay Adolescent

"My journey would have been much less painful if, in those earlier years, I had received some sense that my feelings were not horrible and deviant, some hint that there were others like me, or some examples of healthy adults with a homosexual orientation. Perhaps a teacher or counselor could have provided that assistance, but they did not, and so for a long time I struggled alone."

(A lesbian educator, quoted in Marinoble, 1998, 6-7)

"In most respects, youths with same-sex attractions are similar to all youths, independent of sexual desires. That is, an adolescent is an adolescent is an adolescent."

(Savin-Williams, 2001, 6)

"Every day, I'd ask myself, am I gay? and I would answer, nooo! I couldn't be gay. There's no way! Those are the messages coming from society... When you're in middle school, you don't really know anything, and my friends would say, "that's bad; look at that gay person; that's gross." ..."...It doesn't bother me anymore cause I think, like last night, I was sitting in my shower and I thought, God, I'm glad that I'm gay and not straight. I'm happy to be gay, even with the stuff that I face."

(17-year-old lesbian teenager, quoted in Ginsberg, 1998, 5-6, 9)

She never thought she would be in a psychologist's office this early in life. But she was used to feeling different from her peers, so the fact that she was here and they weren't wasn't that much of a surprise. It all started three years ago.

Now that she was 15, Rhonda knew she felt the strongest desire for other teens... teenage girls, that is. She couldn't wait to see some of them nude when getting ready for gym class, especially Barbara. Barbara was a blonde, blue-eyed 16-year-old who knew how hot she was. Rhonda thought she seductively flaunted every bit of it too. Her navel was pierced and her erect nipples always protruded from beneath her bra-less undersized crop top. Her sexy look was complete with tight hip-riding blue jeans and sandals. Barbara intentionally drove the boys crazy. Unintentionally, Rhonda was being driven crazy too, but she was completely alone with her feelings. It seemed like she was the only teenage girl who felt like this. Rhonda knew of a few boys who were gay, but she didn't know of a single lesbian.

One day after gym class, Barbara noticed in the mirror that Rhonda was checking her out while showering. Her intuition immediately told her that Rhonda was hot for her, and she freaked—she had never had a girl look at her like that before. Over the ensuing days, Barbara told all of her friends about Rhonda, the "lesbo chick." Soon, practically everyone in the school knew, and her peers began ostracizing her. No one wanted to hang out with her anymore, including girls who used to be her closest friends.

Rhonda fell into depression and despair. Her mom set up an appointment with Dr. Jones, the psychologist, after Rhonda swallowed more than 30 sleeping pills. Having her stomach pumped was not as painful as the isolation she was feeling at school. Dr. Jones helped her get into a different school, and although that ended some of her problems she was still feeling alone in her thoughts, fantasies and desires. And if her parents ever found out she was a lesbian, she would end up having to leave home as well.

Dr. Jones was understanding, but she couldn't really help. She could neither take away the feeling of deep loneliness nor of being left out. Rhonda's depression lifted, but the aching continued unabated. She wanted a girlfriend so bad, and despite what Barbara had done, she couldn't stop thinking about her. Where does a 15-year-old go to meet other lesbian teens?

Her counselling lasted for a year. By the end of it, Dr. Jones had convinced her that dating guys would be okay until she finished high school. Unbeknownst to Rhonda, Dr. Jones thought that her same-sex desire was just a phase, and if she gave guys a chance she would probably give up her interest in girls.

Rhonda felt desperate for intimacy and was willing to try anything. Guys were okay, Rhonda thought, and they were better than nothing. Sex was passionless and meaningless, but at least she was next to a warm body. After they had had their way with her, they soon moved on. Again, unbeknownst to Rhonda, these guys could tell that Rhonda was distant when having sex, as though a part of her was detached. This was unsettling to guys because they didn't know whether the disconnection was within them or her. Either way, they were happy to end it. Rhonda was thinking she would be happy to end it as well—her life, that is.

The Problem

Suicide is the third leading cause of death among adolescents (Cooley, 1998). Many published articles suggest that gay youth are two to six times more likely to attempt suicide compared to heterosexual youth (McFarland, 1993; Morrison & L'Heureux, 2001), although a recent study sheds doubt as to both the frequency and seriousness of these attempts (Savin-Williams, 2001). Regardless, gay youth generally suffer more than any other segment of the gay community (Marino, 1995, cited in Fontaine, 1998). The list of potential problems seems endless. Compared to their heterosexual counterparts, gay youth are more likely to:

- abuse drugs and alcohol (Telljohann, Price, Poureslami, & Easton, 1995)
- suffer rejection (Telljohann et al.), victimization (Russell, Seif, & Truong, 2001; Sapp, 2001) and physical abuse (Goldfried & Goldfried, 2001) from their peers. Gay youth often have trouble interacting and relating to their peers for several reasons (Marinoble, 1998), resulting in social isolation (Kottman,

Lingg, & Tisdell, 1995).
• have problems with social anxiety and depression (Hart & Heimberg, 2001)
• have school-related problems (Barber & Mobley, 1999)
• have conflicts with the law (Bohan, 1996)
• run away from home (Bayes, 1985; Russell, 1989). (Some researchers suggest that between 40 to 60 % of street youth are gay). (Kunreuther, 1991, cited in Radkowsky & Siegel, 1997)
• become HIV positive if they are male (Rotheram-Borus, Murphy, Kennedy, Stanton, & Kuklinski, 2001)
• lack positive role models (Gonsiorek, 1993; Kottman, Lingg, & Tisdell, 1995)

Enough for the bad news. It's actually not as bleak as it sounds. Despite their increased propensity to experience problems, "the vast majority of gay male, bisexual, and lesbian youths cope with their daily, chronic stressors to become healthy individuals who make significant contributions to their culture." (Savin-Williams, 1994, 262) They also have self-esteem that is just as positive as heterosexual youth (Savin-Williams, 2001). In a study of 15-to 21-year-old gay, lesbian and bisexual youth, the single best predictor of mental health was self-acceptance (Hershberger & D'Augelli, 1995). If gay youth can grow up in a supportive and informed environment, they have just as good mental health when compared to the general adolescent population (Gonsiorek, 1993). There is no substitute for developing a positive gay identity if you are gay or lesbian, regardless of your age.

Rhonda was experiencing the most common problem faced by younger gay youth: isolation (Hetrick & Martin, 1987). Once the age of majority is reached, the gay bar becomes the primary social outlet for many gay individuals (Shannon & Woods, 1991).

Rhonda's problems are not atypical for gay teens, and unlike the anecdotes found in the previous chapters, Rhonda is not doing anything wrong. The problem is not with her—it is with a society that fails to support gay youth in their development. In the next section, I will focus on what you can do to stay healthy psychologically. In Chapter 16, I will look at some ways you can insulate yourself from the effects of homophobia and heterosexism, regardless of its source.

Rhonda can become a well-functioning lesbian, and it is frightening to read that she is again considering suicide. Suicide is never an option—please, please remember that. If you are going through a really difficult period, you need to speak with a gay-affirmative therapist. I will offer some suggestions for finding one in Appendix B at the end of this book.

What Needs to Change?

Ultimately, society needs to change, but in the meantime let's look at what you can do to help you deal with the inside of being a gay adolescent, including your psychological health and mental well-being. You need to develop a positive gay identity like every other gay person, which means this entire book will be helpful to you, not just this chapter and the next one. However, some of the recommendations contained in previous chapters might not be applicable to you due to your age (e.g., going to gay bars).

Recall from reading in the previous section that the major problem facing gay youth is isolation. Major cities have a gay and lesbian information line or resource centre that know about or offer a gay youth group. That is an excellent place to start. We all have a need to belong, and a gay youth group will accept you the way you are. If this is unavailable where you live you can make friends with people over the World Wide Web if you have a computer with an Internet connection. One caution here: many of the people that represent themselves as gay teens on the Internet are not teens at all. Lamb (1998) did a study of this phenomenon and found that many people are dishonest when they communicate over Internet chat lines. After extensive research, he found that there were three types of people who used chat lines: (1) the browsers, who were genuinely curious and were not out to deceive others; (2) the cruisers, who wanted sex and often created false personas; and (3) the pornographers, who wanted to gather and trade pornography over the Internet. The honest ones, the browsers, were the smallest group, representing less than 10 % of the chat-line users, whereas the cruisers composed about 65 % of the users.

If you are planning to meet someone you have met off the Internet, be sure to keep your full identity a secret (use only your first name) and decide to meet somewhere public. Also, for your own protection, do not provide your address or telephone number. You are young and vulnerable. If after meeting the person, he or she is genuine and has not misrepresented herself or himself to you, then consider exchanging telephone numbers.

Being gay forces you to build strength of character, which is covered in Chapter 6. Becoming a strong person psychologically and learning to be assertive are your best defenses against the recrimination you may occasionally face from others. You have a right to be you—in fact, there isn't really any choice, is there? You're the only one you'll ever be, so you need to love yourself with all your heart and soul. Only then will you be able to live a life of integrity and be fully able to love others.

If you are having problems with family, which is the second most common problem that gay youth experience, read Chapter 14. Depending on your age and circumstances, it might not be advisable to come out to your family yet, or at your school. These are not easy decisions and cannot be taken lightly. Once you tell people you're gay, it's hard to take it back.

Drug and alcohol abuse is common within the overall gay community, not just with gay adolescents. Some people can enjoy the occasional joint and leave it at that, while others are constantly looking to get high. Many illegal drugs are potentially dangerous and can cost you your life. If you are tempted to use drugs, learn as much as you can about the drug you are thinking of trying before you try it. If you want to play with fire, be sure you know which end is burning. Ignorance will only lead you down an undesirable path.

Having sound mental health and a positive gay identity are not the same thing (Alderson, 2000). You might have a positive gay identity, but that doesn't mean you aren't subject to the same mental-health issues that heterosexual individuals face. Some otherwise healthy people are vulnerable to major depression or anxiety problems, and unfortunately some have more serious conditions such as schizophrenia.

However, if you have a negative gay identity, you are more likely to have mental-health problems like anxiety, depression and personality disturbances, compared to heterosexual individuals. You are also more likely to abuse alcohol, drugs and yourself in countless ways. Do the work necessary to develop a positive gay identity. If needed, consult with a gay-affirmative counsellor or psychologist. You won't be sorry you did.

Where I'm At Now
Place a checkmark in the column that corresponds to your answer.

If your answer is "yes," use the following rating scale: 1=very slightly; 2=slightly; 3=moderately; 4=highly; 5=severely.

			YES				
1=very slightly; 2=slightly; 3=moderately; 4=highly; 5=severely	NO	1	2	3	4	5
1	I don't feel anyone understands me.						
2	I don't have enough gay friends or I don't know where to meet other gay people.						
3	I am having family problems.						
4	I am either anxious or depressed right now because of problems resulting from being gay.						
5	I am unsure if I am gay.						

If you respond "YES" to any of these questions, you would benefit from doing some work in this area. If all of your responses are "NO," you may want to skip this chapter.

The Solution
Rhonda needs to meet some lesbian adolescents and women. This may be easy or difficult, depending on where she lives. If she is in a small town or desolate area, she may need to simply befriend people who are open-minded and accepting of her sexuality. Having sex with guys is not doing it for either her or the guys she beds. In fact, it may be hurting more than it is helping because it leaves her detached from her passion toward other teenage girls. Her suicidal thoughts are a real concern—she has attempted once before. Rhonda should share these thoughts with her psychologist, who will help her as best she can. If there is a gay-affirmative psychologist where

Rhonda lives, she would do better to continue counselling sessions with that person.

You might be able to relate to some of what Rhonda has experienced and is experiencing. Don't be alone with your thoughts—share them with someone you trust. If you don't know of someone, see your school counsellor and ask for a referral to someone who can help.

A. Changing Your Thoughts

1. Beliefs Chart

REMINDER: Complete the following exercise by using the How to Question Your Beliefs pullout sheet found in the Introduction.

SPECIAL NOTE: In this chapter, be aware that the Underlying Beliefs column below may be the reality for you as a gay adolescent. In the Questioning It column, you need to ask yourself on what basis you believe what you believe. If your reasons for believing it are grounded in reality, there is no need to write anything in the Questioning It column other than it is true for you right now. Remember that it won't always be the case.

SAMPLE THOUGHT	UNDERLYING BELIEF	QUESTIONING IT (you complete this column)	HEALTHIER BELIEF
I don't feel anyone understands me.	No one could understand what it means to be gay where I live.		The most important thing is that I learn to understand myself. Secondly, I will find someone who at least tries to understand me.
I don't have enough gay friends or I don't know where to meet other gay people.	I am isolated and alone as a gay person.		I will plan a strategy for how and where to meet gay people, even if I am limited to only having Internet contact with them right now.
I am having family problems.	My family doesn't understand me.		I will do what I can to improve my

		family situation. If this is not possible, I will seek help from a professional counsellor.
I am either anxious or depressed right now because of problems resulting from being gay.	The people around me are not supportive of who I am.	If I cannot overcome my negative feelings by myself over the next week, I will seek help from a professional counsellor.
I am unsure if I am gay.	I am conflicted about my sexual orientation.	It is common for young people to be confused about their sexuality. I will learn more about myself through experience or with the help of a professional counsellor.

(Write any additional thoughts and beliefs you have.)

2. Visualization Exercises

REMINDER: Complete the following exercises by using the How to Visualize pullout sheet found in the Introduction.

(a) General Visualizations—Visualize how things are going to get better for you when you are a little older. Picture yourself succeeding in life, with a good job, many caring friends and a loving partner. Also imagine that your relationship with your parents and siblings has improved (chances are it will).

(b) Specific Visualizations—Think of specific instances where you felt badly because you are gay. Then imagine how you could have better managed the situation or problem. Brainstorm in your imagination as many possible solutions as you can think of. Although this may be difficult, know that there are always steps you could have taken to improve a situation, but also appreciate that solutions are not perfect. A solution may simply be the best alternative of several possible actions.

B. Changing Your Behaviour

1. General Activities

These general activities will help you improve your psychological health and mental well- being:

- Establish a support group. This is important when you are young. In a major city you can get involved in the gay youth group run by your city's gay and lesbian information or referral service. Look in the white pages of your telephone book under Gay. If you don't find anything, contact your school counsellor for advice.
- Realize that friends come in many sexual orientations and ages. Your best friend doesn't need to be a gay or lesbian teenager. He or she might be heterosexual or older than yourself. Friendship is about having people you can be yourself around who like and respect you the way you are. Don't throw away gold in your search for a sapphire.
- Overcome anxiety and depression. Whether the problem is gay-related or not, don't succumb indefinitely to these negative mood states. Do something to correct the problem if you can. If you can't or don't know how, seek out help from a professional counsellor.
- Make responsible decisions about alcohol and drug use. This is your body, and you are the only one who can take good care of it. If the peer pressure encouraging you to use alcohol or drugs confuses you, get a second opinion. Learn what you can about alcohol and drugs, and don't be afraid to ask for advice from a physician or mental-health professional (like a professional counsellor).
- Always practice safer sex. If you are sexually active, read Chapter 11 and Appendix E. Proper use of condoms is your best protection from HIV transmission and many other venereal diseases.
- If you feel suicidal, get help now. Don't wait until your life becomes an intolerable crisis. If it is already a crisis, seek out professional help immediately. Trust me when I tell you that suicidal thoughts will soon end after you get help.

2. Specific Activities

Goal-setting

Decide upon a specific behaviour that you will target for change. Your best choice is a behaviour that you have already found is causing you trouble. Here are some examples:

- Making at least one gay friend
- Becoming aware of the gay resources where I live
- Plan a strategy for controlling, reducing or eliminating my anxiety
- Begin to focus less on negative thoughts and more on positive ones

Shaping

Write your goal in the chart below, and then list the steps you will take to begin working on it.

GOAL:			
#	STEPS NEEDED TO HELP ME ACHIEVE THIS GOAL	DONE	REWARD
1			
2			
3			

Rewards

In the chart above, decide which of your steps should have an accompanying reward for its successful completion. Write what the specific reward will be. After completing the step, place a checkmark in the Done column and be sure to give yourself the assigned reward.

Environment Control

Peers have a lot of influence in your life when you are young. Spending time with accepting friends is vital to your mental health and sense of well-being. Likewise, being with people whom you feel you have to be dishonest with to find acceptance are not really friends at all. In the chart below, write the environmental changes you need to make until your goal is successfully achieved:

#	PERSON OR GROUP THAT AFFECTS YOU	+ OR - EFFECT	PLANNED ACTION (Range: complete avoidance to frequent contact—be specific)
1			
2			
3			
4			

C. Changing the Way You Feel About It

When you experience a negative feeling complete the following chart (REMINDER: instructions for using this chart are found in the Introduction):

NAME THE FEELING(S)	DESCRIBE THE TRIGGER	UNDERLYING BELIEF(S)	QUESTIONING IT	HEALTHIER BELIEF

Where I'm At After Working On It

Periodically re-test yourself to chart your progress in this area.

		YES				
1=very slightly; 2=slightly; 3=moderately; 4=highly; 5=severely	NO	1	2	3	4	5
1 I don't feel anyone understands me.						
2 I don't have enough gay friends or I don't know where to meet other gay people.						
3 I am having family problems.						
4 I am either anxious or depressed right now because of problems resulting from being gay.						
5 I am unsure if I am gay.						

If you are still responding "YES" to any of these questions, continue working on change in this area. If all of your responses are "NO," you have made significant progress! Continue to monitor any remaining problems in this area, and work on these as suggested in this chapter.

Summary

Rhonda has experienced recurring bouts of unhappiness and depression because she is a lesbian who feels alone and isolated from others like her. After being caught cruising a heterosexual girl in the shower, she was outed to her peers at school. Even her friends began ostracizing her, which led to deeper feelings of despair. In response, Rhonda attempted suicide, and this led her mother to schedule a session for her with a psychologist. More than anything, Rhonda wants to have someone love her, especially a girlfriend. Her psychologist encourages her to date boys, which she does, and this leads to deeper feelings of unhappiness and desperation.

Perhaps you can relate to some of Rhonda's experience. If so, this chapter has guided you through activities and exercises that will help you stay psychologically healthy and well- adjusted. On the next page is the Positive Affirmations pullout sheet, which can be kept by your bed or in some other highly visible place. Spend a few minutes each day reflecting on what each affirmation means to you personally.

Positive Affirmations

[Also add your own from the Healthier Belief *columns in this chapter]*

The most important thing is that I learn to understand myself. Secondly, I will find someone who at least tries to understand me.

I will plan a strategy for how and where to meet gay people, even if I am limited to only having Internet contact with them right now.

I will do what I can to improve my family situation. If this is not possible, I will seek help from a professional counsellor.

If I cannot overcome my negative feelings by myself over the next week, I will seek help from a professional counsellor.

It is common for young people to be confused about their sexuality. I will learn more about myself through experience or with the help of a professional counsellor.

CHAPTER 16
The Outside of Being a Gay Adolescent

"Many of those rites of passage through which other teens pass are not open to the gay and lesbian adolescent. The glances and shy smiles exchanged across a classroom, the sending of a valentine, the agony of the first telephone call asking for a date, the shared bag of popcorn in a movie theater and the walk home on a moonlit night with arms about one another, the first kiss and touch— all of these are simply not realities for most gay and lesbian teens or are experienced heterosexually with a sense of falseness and confusion."

(Bidwell, 1988, quoted in Radkowsky & Siegel, 1997, 196)

"The symbolic annihilation of gay and lesbian youth exhibited by television and textbooks contributes to a dysfunctional isolation that is supported by the mutually-reinforcing invisibility of homosexual adolescents on the television screen, in the curriculum, and throughout the "real world.""

(Kielwasser & Wolf, 1993-94, 75)

"The stigmatization of homosexuality makes it difficult for gay youth to achieve the tasks of adolescence. Peer acceptance, exploration of intimate relationships, individuation, and formation of a positive identity are all hindered because these youths are generally taught to despise a vital part of themselves. And because gay adolescents must hide their sexuality, they are denied the pleasurable and maturing experiences of adolescent love relationships. Research indicates that the stigmatization and unhappiness these youth experience greatly increase the risk of suicide."

(Radkowsky & Siegel, 1997, 212)

Lawrence had known since he was six that he was strongly attracted to guys. He used to stare at their penises in the locker rooms after his swimming lessons, and in the summer, he could hardly get enough glances at sweaty shirtless guys playing outdoor sports. By age 14 his hormones were in overdrive, and he started looking for his first sexual experiences. He knew, however, that most people would disapprove of the direction his pulsing hard-on wanted to take. Where would he find an eligible partner?

Lawrence started having sleepovers, hoping to catch a feel at least, but his friends were straight, and he didn't dare make the first move. Trouble was, neither did they. A year of sleepovers and nothing happened. Now it was the end of school and beginning of summer. Once again, hot guys were everywhere.

Now that Lawrence was 15 and looking sexy and buff himself, he decided it was time to be more aggressive in his pursuit of sex. The aching in his groin on this exceptionally hot humid day was almost more than he could bear. He had heard that sex occurred in Heaven's Park near downtown, and filled with fear and excitement, he headed there. Most of the guys weren't his type, but out of the bushes soon appeared a young, shirtless stud in his late teens or early twenties. "Wow," Lawrence thought, as the guy began cruising his own half-naked body. The guy asked him if he wanted to go home with him to use some drugs. Lawrence had never taken drugs before, but in his excitement he was willing to do anything to be with this guy. They soon took off to this guy's apartment, whose name he later found out was Steve.

Steve pulls out some white powder that he spreads as a thin line on his tabletop. The next thing Lawrence feels is more euphoria, peace and confidence than he has ever felt before. Steve immediately grabs him, strips off his shorts, and gives him head. Minutes seem like hours, orgasm feels like an eternity. They go at it four times over the next three hours. Lawrence is getting exposed to every sex act imaginable between two guys—and line after line of the white drug.

The next day, Lawrence feels not only exhausted and mildly depressed—he is also having deep cravings for the drug. He calls Steve, who absolutely understands. Steve picks him up and they repeat yesterday's stellar performance. More sex, more drugs, and Lawrence is in his glory.

Until the next day. Lawrence feels tired, depressed and has mad cravings. Only one thing has changed. Steve is not prepared to give him drugs unless Lawrence sucks off his "friend," Roger, who is sitting beside him. Lawrence already feels like he is in love with Steve and will do anything to please him. After giving Roger head, the lines are again laid out on the table, and the three of them partake. Once high, sex between the three of them occurs, until it abruptly ends when Roger readies to leave. Before he does, however, he gives Steve a hundred dollars and thanks him for a great time.

Over the next few weeks, Steve becomes Lawrence's best friend, providing him all the drugs and sex with other guys that he could ever want. Lawrence, however, does not want sex with these "tricks," as Steve calls them. He wants Steve.

When Lawrence finally becomes aware that Steve has about five young guys on the beat, he is devastated. Yet he can't resist going back to Steve, and not for the sex either. That white drug—he doesn't seem happy or confident without it. He lives for the next fix. Steve is kind enough to give it to him.

The Problem

It is a cruel and insensitive world for gay youth. Our society has done a pathetic job of assisting them in developing a positive gay identity. Perhaps many adults assume there are few of them because they are more invisible than any other contingent within the gay community (Kottman, Lingg, & Tisdell, 1995). Adolescence is a time of identity development (Morrow, 1997), and because of the emotional turmoil experienced by most teenagers in acquiring a gay identity (McFarland, 1993), the vast majority of gay youth will not adopt this identity label (Savin-Williams, 1994).

More likely, however, is that many adults don't want to know that gay youth exist. The code of silence toward gay people of all ages has been pervasive (Sapp, 2001). The media has ignored them (Kielwasser & Wolf, 1993-94) and grade schools, particularly those that are religious-based, are reluctant if not unwilling to allow speakers in who can educate young people about gay individuals.

Besides invisibility, it is difficult for gay youth to find support and feel a sense of belonging. Heterosexual peers are often rejecting of their gay counterparts. For example, only 12 % of male youths between the ages of 15 and 19 felt confident that they could befriend a gay person (Massiglo, 1993, cited in Telljohann, Price, Poureslami, & Easton, 1995). Gay adults themselves are often reluctant to act as role models to gay youth because of fear that others will think they are "recruiting" these youth into homosexuality (Gonsiorek, 1993).

Society's efforts to keep homosexuality in the closet results in the ongoing mental abuse and spiritual raping of gay people, and there are consequences to forcing people to remain isolated for long periods of time. Children raised in complete isolation, for example, rarely develop "age-appropriate levels of physical and mental development" (Blumenfeld & Raymond, 1993, 37). Validation of gay youth helps to normalize their experience and provides a buffer from psychological distress (Radkowsky & Siegel, 1997). Who is going to provide this validation?

Because Lawrence was unable to date anyone he knew, he went on the street looking for validation through the physical contact that sex provides. This led him unintentionally into cocaine addiction and prostitution. Gay youth are vulnerable to exploitation, especially if they feel unsupported and alone. There are many "Steves" out there looking for young people like Lawrence.

The problem is that Lawrence doesn't know other gay youth in his age cohort. Furthermore, he doesn't have anyone who can act as a positive gay role model to him. Most heterosexual youth can rely on their parents for support, whereas most gay youth don't know this yet about their parents. Lawrence needs someone who will give to him through love, not take from him through manipulation. Once innocence is lost, there is no coming back. Fifteen-year-old Lawrence is headed down a painful and twisted path, and there is no one to save him.

What Needs to Change?

Society is changing, as you will learn in Chapter 17, but progress is still slow. Until gay people are truly treated with equal respect and dignity as compared to their heterosexual cousins, you will need to insulate and protect yourself from the effects of homophobia, heterosexism, isolation, alienation, exploitation and physical assault. Does it sound like a difficult challenge? It is, but you are up for it. If you have worked through the previous chapters you now have a positive gay identity. Congratulations! There are still many who never achieve this (McDonald, 1980, cited in Coleman 1981-1982), and the average length of time before self-identifying as gay and developing a positive gay identity is 16 years (Obear & Reynolds, 1986, cited in Pope, Prince, & Mitchell, 2000).

Having a positive gay identity doesn't protect you from those who are externalizing their homophobia. Your personal safety has to be your top consideration wherever you are and whatever you are doing. Gay bashings are not uncommon (Wills & Crawford, 2000). Homophobia is not over, and the fight has not been won. Violence against gay individuals occurs everywhere and at any time of day.

It is hard to be gay in a vacuum. If you are alone as a gay person, you need to find support from people who accept you. If you don't have any idea what to do, seek help from a professional counsellor, such as your school counsellor. This person may not be ideal if he or she is personally homophobic or heterosexist, but at least a professional will try to help you and be supportive. Make contacts with gay people through the Internet, but remember the caveats to this discussed in the last chapter.

You would be wise to not come out in most grade schools as they remain institutes of narrow-mindedness. Sex is still a taboo subject in North American culture, and many people still think that being gay merely equates to having sex with the same gender. You know differently, but that doesn't help you much right now. My advice is that unless you are in a gay-friendly school, don't disclose your sexuality until you are finished high school. Furthermore, if your family will be impossible to live with if they find out you're gay, delay telling them until you move out. If you believe people's reaction to your disclosure will be negative, but you feel the need to tell them anyway, be sure you already have the strength of character and wherewithal to cope with the fallout.

If you are headed down a destructive path toward alcohol abuse, drug abuse or prostitution, you need professional help that is beyond the scope of this book. Every city and town provides services for people struggling with alcohol and drug abuse, and a listing is provided at the beginning of the white pages in your telephone book. Services to help sex-trade workers are available in cities. If you live in a small community, consider talking to a professional counsellor or psychologist about your predicament.

Many gay men and lesbian women move from smaller communities to larger cities when they can do so (Bagley & Tremblay, 1998) to find greater levels of tolerance and acceptance. Moving may be important for you down the road as well. Many gay people find that their friends become closer to them than their family (Bohan, 1996), particularly in cases where the family remains unsupportive.

You are struggling to be yourself and an authentic human being. There is nothing nobler than the pursuit of integrity. You may not hear it enough at first, so let me say it: I am proud of you, of who you are, and of what you represent. You are a loving soul in search of self. Don't believe anyone who tells you otherwise.

Where I'm At Now

Place a checkmark in the column that corresponds to your answer.

If your answer is "yes," use the following rating scale: 1=very slightly; 2=slightly; 3=moderately; 4=highly; 5=severely.

1=very slightly; 2=slightly; 3=moderately; 4=highly; 5=severely	NO	YES 1	2	3	4	5
1 I don't know how to deal with homophobic people.						
2 I am having trouble coping with isolation.						
3 I have become dependent on alcohol or drugs to cope with the negativity I face because I am gay.						
4 I am having trouble not telling certain people I am gay, despite knowing it is the best thing right now.						
5 I don't feel that anyone provides me any validation for being gay, or I don't have any positive gay role models.						

If you respond "YES" to any of these questions, you would benefit from doing some work in this area. If all of your responses are "NO," you may want to skip this chapter.

The Solution

Lawrence, like most 15-year-olds, wants sex as hormones rage inside his body. But he has gone about it in an unsafe manner. Picking someone up in a park or from some other public place is risky business—you don't know this person. He or she might be a homophobe looking to beat or rape you. Lawrence doesn't know if he will be taken to Steve's home, where a number of other guys could be waiting, or down a deserted country road.

If Lawrence needed to have sex with a guy, he would be better off connecting with someone over the Internet close to his age and then arranging to first meet the guy to check him out. Instructions for keeping yourself safe and anonymous (at least initially) were provided in Chapter 15.

Now that Lawrence is connected to Steve, a solution will require that Lawrence realize how Steve has manipulated him for purposes of prostitution. He may then need to check into a rehabilitation program for drug addicts because cocaine is known to be the most psychologically addictive drug available. It is unlikely that Lawrence will be able to stop his drug addiction alone. If you are having trouble dealing with your environment, the outside of being a gay adolescent, this chapter will provide you with some coping tips.

A. Changing Your Thoughts

1. Beliefs Chart

REMINDER: Complete the following exercise by using the How to Question Your Beliefs pull-out sheet found in the Introduction.

SAMPLE THOUGHT	UNDERLYING BELIEF	QUESTIONING IT (you complete this column)	HEALTHIER BELIEF
I don't know how to deal with homophobic people.	I don't know how to be appropriately assertive with homophobes.		Assertiveness is a skill I need to learn to deal with the homophobic people I will encounter periodically.
I am having trouble coping with isolation.	Being alone as a gay person is too hard for me.		I don't need to be alone—I will find either gay or straight friends who accept me. If I can't find any, I will seek out the help of a professional counsellor for some suggestions.
I have become dependent on alcohol or drugs to cope with the negativity I face because I am gay.	I need to anesthetize myself in order to cope with being gay or to cope with other people's reaction to my being gay.		I will not live my life dependent on alcohol and/or drugs. Therefore, I will seek help from someone who works with addiction problems.
I am having trouble not telling certain people I am gay, despite knowing it is the best thing right now.	I want everyone to like me for who I am, not for who they want me to be.		The most important thing is that I love myself for being who I am. I need to be patient and tell

		people when it is an appropriate time in my life.
I don't feel that anyone provides me any validation for being gay, or I don't have any positive gay role models.	No one I know accepts me as gay, or else I have no one to look up to who is gay. Either way, it leaves me feeling invalidated and undervalued.	I will continue my search to find friends who validate me. If I am unsuccessful, I will seek out the help of a professional counsellor for some suggestions.

(Write any additional thoughts and beliefs you have.)

2. Visualization Exercises

REMINDER: Complete the following exercises by using the How to Visualize pullout sheet found in the Introduction.

(a) General Visualizations—Imagine yourself coping better with your environment. What are you thinking, feeling and doing differently compared to now? Focus on these three elements of change. By doing so, you are practicing at becoming a more effective individual with a more positive gay identity.

(b) Specific Visualizations—Think of a specific instance where you found yourself not handling another person's homophobic remark or prejudicial treatment of you very well. Visualize how you wish you would have handled the situation. Also do this for any other negative environmental influence that has affected you in the past.

B. Changing Your Behaviour

1. General Activities

These general activities will help you deal with the outside of being a gay adolescent:

• Even if you are not out to someone, you can still make an assertive response if they talk in a heterosexist or homophobic way. Gay people are largely to blame for heterosexual individuals not understanding us better. Because so many gay adults have remained in the closet, many who know them have no idea they are gay. When asked, these same heterosexual individuals will tell you they don't know anyone who is gay, and so then it becomes easy for them to develop heterosexist attitudes and homophobic feelings toward the gay people they supposedly don't know. When you hear remarks that are derogatory toward gays, you can tell the person that you are offended by such comments as they put down a lot of people out there approximately 10% of the population. Most people change their behaviour when they realize it is no longer appropriate

• Be aware of your personal safety at all times. For example, in most locales, it is not safe to walk hand-in-hand with a same-sex partner. I suspect this will change eventually, but trying to effect change by being the sole martyr is not a good idea, particularly when you are young and have a lot to lose

• Establish a support system. Enough has already been said about this, but because it is so important, remember to do it. Don't wait for people to come knocking on your door—knock on theirs instead

• If you are heading down a destructive path, carefully reflect on what you are doing and why you are doing it. And then do something about it. Once habits are entrenched, they are hard to break. Some drugs cause more than just a bad habit. Some are physically and/or psychologically addictive. If you abuse either drugs or alcohol, you are more prone to making bad decisions, such as saying things you later regret, doing something inappropriate, not protecting yourself with proper condom use and taking chances that could lead to a fatal accident. Get help if you can't moderate and control your alcohol and drug use.

2. Specific Activities

Goal-setting

Decide upon a specific behaviour that you will target for change. Your best choice is a behaviour that you have already found is causing you trouble. Here are some examples:

- Becoming assertive with older guys trying to pick me up for sex
- Learning to deal effectively with homophobic individuals
- Saying no to drugs
- Working on improving my relationship with my mother and/or father

Shaping

Write your goal in the chart below, and then list the steps you will take to begin working on it.

GOAL:			
# STEPS NEEDED TO HELP ME ACHIEVE THIS GOAL		DONE	REWARD
1			
2			
3			

Rewards

In the chart above, decide which of your steps should have an accompanying reward for its successful completion. Write what the specific reward will be. After completing the step, place a checkmark in the Done column and be sure to give yourself the assigned reward.

Environment Control

Who you associate with is going to have a significant impact on your life. If your peer group is into drugs and excessive drinking, it will be hard for you to resist the temptation to do the same. Similarly, if you have a positive gay role model to hang out with, this person will have a positive effect on your life. In the chart below, write the environmental changes you need to make until your goal is successfully achieved:

# PERSON OR GROUP THAT AFFECTS YOU	+ OR - EFFECT	PLANNED ACTION (Range: complete avoidance to frequent contact—be specific)
1		
2		
3		
4		

C. Changing the Way You Feel About It

When you experience a negative feeling complete the following chart (REMINDER: instructions for using this chart are found in the Introduction):

NAME THE FEELING(S)	DESCRIBE THE TRIGGER	UNDERLYING BELIEF(S)	QUESTIONING IT	HEALTHIER BELIEF

Where I'm At After Working On It
Periodically re-test yourself to chart your progress in this area.

1=very slightly; 2=slightly; 3=moderately; 4=highly; 5=severely	NO	YES 1	2	3	4	5
1 I don't know how to deal with homophobic people.						
2 I am having trouble coping with isolation.						
3 I have become dependent on alcohol or drugs to cope with the negativity I face because I am gay.						
4 I am having trouble not telling certain people I am gay, despite knowing it is the best thing right now.						
5 I don't feel that anyone provides me any validation for being gay, or I don't have any positive gay role models.						

If you are still responding "YES" to any of these questions, continue working on change in this area. If all of your responses are "NO," you have made significant progress! Continue to monitor any remaining problems in this area, and work on these as suggested in this chapter.

Summary
Lawrence feels isolated from gay peers. In his search for sex and possibly intimacy, he ends up being manipulated into drugs and seduced into prostitution. Because the drug is cocaine, he soon becomes addicted to it. He begins a spiral down into the depths of depression if he is unable to get another fix.

Lawrence needs to get control of his life, which he will not be able to do on his own now that he is an addict. Perhaps getting control of your life and managing your environment better is a problem for you right now. If so, this chapter has guided you through activities and exercises that will help you better cope with the outside of being a gay adolescent. On the next page is the Positive Affirmations pullout sheet, which can be kept by your bed or in some other highly visible place. Spend a few minutes each day reflecting on what each affirmation means to you personally.

Positive Affirmations

[Also add your own from the Healthier Belief *columns in this chapter]*

Assertiveness is a skill I need to learn to deal with the homophobic people I will encounter periodically.

I don't need to be alone—I will find either gay or straight friends who accept me. If I can't find any, I will seek out the help of a professional counsellor for some suggestions.

I will not live my life dependent on alcohol and/or drugs. Therefore, I will seek help from someone who works with addiction problems.

The most important thing is that I love myself for being who I am. I need to be patient and tell people when it is an appropriate time in my life.

I will continue my search to find friends who validate me. If I am unsuccessful, I will seek out the help of a professional counsellor for some suggestions.

PART IV
TODAY AND TOMORROW

CHAPTER 17
Breaking Out Around the World

"Whether homosexuality is innate, acquired, consciously chosen, or any combination of these, the highest ethical imperative in a humanistic society mandates that gays and lesbians be treated no differently than any other religious, ethnic, or racial group, or indeed, than heterosexuals in general. The only reasonable ethical consideration is whether or not the overt behavior of any individual is harmful or destructive to others."

(Marmor, 1998, quoted in Ellis & Mitchell, 2000, 206)

"That point is that most Americans are less homophobic than they think they are supposed to be."

(Barney Frank, in the forward to Vargo, 1998, x)

Canada and the United States

For the first time in history, gay men and lesbian women are experiencing ever increasing amounts of tolerance and acceptance in many countries throughout the world. We don't have to look far—two such countries are Canada and the United States.

In Canada, incredible changes have occurred during the past four years. The Canadian Senate passed Bill C-23 on 14 June 2000, an act providing same-sex couples with the same legal standing as unmarried heterosexual couples ("Senate OKs omnibus DP," 2000). A report released by the Law Commission of Canada on 29 January 2002 suggested that restrictions against legal same-sex marriages are discriminatory (Bueckert, 2002).

The fight has begun in the courts of some provinces for legal gay marriages (Egale, 2002). Same-sex couples can now adopt children in Nova Scotia (Auld, 2001) and Newfoundland and Labrador (Equal Marriage for Same-Sex Couples, 2002), and proposed legislation would provide the same in Manitoba (Canadian Press, 2002b). In Quebec, full parental rights are provided to homosexual couples in addition to legal civil unions (Seguin, 2002). In 1999, the Government of Ontario amended 67 Ontario laws to become more inclusive of same-sex partners (Equal Marriage for Same-Sex Couples, 2002), and in Saskatchewan in 2001, legislation was advanced extending marital rights and responsibilities to same-sex couples (Equal Marriage for Same-Sex Couples).

There are openly gay aldermen in Toronto, Vancouver, Ottawa and Edmonton (Canadian Press Newswire, 2000a), and the eighth largest city in the nation, Winnipeg, has had an openly gay mayor since 28 October 1998 ("Contemporary Canadian Biographies," 2001). The Canadian Census began asking in 2001 for the first time ever if people were living in a same-sex common-law relationship, respecting the requests made by gay activists to include this question (Bunner, 2000).

Most provinces now have or will soon have employment benefits for gay and lesbian employees (Lloyd, 2002). Furthermore, gay couples who have lived together for at least one year have the same entitlements to old age security and the Canada Pension Plan as do common-law heterosexual couples (Human Resources Development Canada, 2002).

Canada now has a cable television station dedicated to the gay, lesbian, bisexual and transgendered community (PrideVisionTV, 2002), and the United States is about to get one as well (Vilanch, 2002). *Queer as Folk* is a gay sitcom that is shown by the television channel Showcase. The channel reports that *Queer as Folk* is their second-highest-rated show, next to the soft-core *Red Shoe Diaries* (Underwood, 2002). *Queer as Folk* is also watched by large numbers of heterosexual viewers

The Anglican Church has not supported gay marriages in Canada, but New Westminster, British Columbia, may soon be the first diocese/parish to bless homosexual unions (Canadian Press, 2002a). Also in British Columbia, a high school student was recently awarded $4,000 in damages because he was victimized by frequent harassment at school for being gay (O'Neill, 2002). A message from the Human Rights Commission re-emphasized that homophobia needs to be stopped throughout British Columbia's schools.

Even conservative Alberta has been forced to submit to change on the gay front. Sexual orientation was written into the province's Human Rights Legislation in 1998 (Laghi, 1998). In 2001, the province rewrote its laws to allow people in same-sex relationships inheritance rights, and in 2002, the government amended its laws to provide gays and lesbians working in the public sector the same pension rights as heterosexuals (Equal Marriage for Same-Sex Couples, 2002). Bill 30, introduced in 2002 by the Alberta government, will provide gay couples some of the same legal rights as married couples if passed (Cotter, 2002).

The Canadian military allows openly gay personnel to join the forces (Canadian Press Newswire, 2000b). Openly gay and lesbian people are also welcome to join the Scouts in Canada (Brooke, 2000).

Significant changes have occurred simultaneously in the United States. In 2001, George W. Bush nominated an openly gay party member to head a national AIDS program ("Gay man to lead," 2001). There are now about 150 out of 3,300 post-secondary institutions, including some religious schools, that offer medical benefits to the same-sex partners of employees (Nelson, 2001).

On 1 July 2000, Vermont became the first state to recognize civil unions between gay individuals (Wood, n.d.), although these unions are not recognized in other states. In October 2001, a domestic-partnership bill was signed in California, making it second only to Vermont in providing rights and protections to same-sex couples (Allen, 2002). Hawaii currently allows gay couples to register as domestic partners (Wood, n.d.), and they are provided some conjugal rights as well.

Western Europe & Australia

Some countries in Western Europe lead the world in terms of gay rights. On 1 October 1989, Denmark became the first country in the world to legally recognize same-sex partnerships, and by 2001, this had extended to Norway, Sweden, Iceland and the Netherlands (Wood, n.d.). Italy, Spain and Israel are looking at bringing in similar legislation (Wood). Today, the Netherlands offers "the world's most comprehensive legal recognition of gay rights" (Wood, 2, para. 4). That country's laws provide same-sex couples the same rights as heterosexuals to marry and adopt children, even those not belonging to their partner. Nearly 2,000 gay marriages occurred in the Netherlands within six months after they were legalized ("London to recognize," 2001), and there are now 50,000 gay couples living together in the Netherlands, an increase of 25 % over the past five years ("Dutch statistic bureau," 2002).

Finland, Portugal and Germany also permit registered same-sex unions, each offering a variety of conjugal rights to accompany this status (Allen, 2002). Belgium may also become a frontrunner in the movement toward gay rights. It may soon become the second country in the world to recognize gay marriages that have identical legal status to heterosexual marriages ("Belgian government," 2001). Sweden has recently approved same-sex adoption ("Sweden's parliament approves," 2002) and has outlawed antigay hate speech (Associated Press, 2002). Same-sex marriages are also offered in some parts of Australia (Mellgren, 2002).

Other Developments

In 2001, the United Kingdom lowered its age of consent for those engaging in homosexual acts from 21 down to 16 ("Gay age of consent," 2001), and also in the same year, London's city government began recognizing same-sex unions (Associated Press, 2001). The first gay games (similar to the Olympic Games) began in San Francisco in 1982 (Gallagher, 1998). They now occur every four years. Montreal, Canada will host the 2006 gay games, after having won the bid over Los Angeles, Chicago and Atlanta (Canadian Press, 2001). Every year, a huge gay Mardi Gras also occurs in Sydney, Australia.

The Future

Gay people are finally securing the basic rights that heterosexual individuals have always enjoyed in many parts of the world. The leader in the gay rights movement is Western Europe, with significant changes also occurring in Canada, the United States and Australia.

Beyond the Western world, however, it is a different story. Just as women are still struggling for equal rights in many countries, so are gay people continuing to struggle. A change in global attitudes that respects diversity and the equality for all has only just begun.

EPILOGUE
Final Thoughts and Reflections

"In general, to undertake to convert a fully developed homosexual into a heterosexual does not offer much more prospect of success than the reverse, except that for good practical reasons the latter is never attempted."

(Freud, 1920/1955, cited in Murphy, 1992a, 27)

"The importance of establishing a positive gay identity cannot be overstated."

(Shannon & Woods, 1991, 198)

"What is most remarkable is that the vast majority of LGB individuals successfully negotiate the passage to homophilic identity, emerging with exemplary mental health and personal well-being."

(Bohan, 1996, 100)

". . . there is nothing second-class about homosexuality."

(quoted from a lesbian in a research project, Schafer, 1976, 60)

"Today is the beginning of my life. It is for you as well. Do you like what you see in the mirror today? You are God's creation. Be thankful for what he has created. You are exactly as God wants you to be."

(Kevin Alderson)

Positive gay identity. A few years ago I didn't know what it meant to be gay, let alone what it would mean someday to beam radiantly with self-realization and self-acceptance. One of the definitions of the word gay in Webster's dictionary is "keenly alive and exuberant." Are you beginning to see why the definition fits so well for you?

The concept of acquiring a positive gay identity would have been considered an oxymoron by mental-health professionals and most other Canadians just over 30 years ago. Homosexual behaviour was considered a criminal offense in Canada until 1969 (Lee, 1977). The American Psychiatric Association considered homosexuality a mental disorder until removing "it" from their classification system in 1973. In 1975, The American Psychological Association responded accordingly with its declaration that:

homosexuality, per se, implies no impairment in judgment, stability, reliability, or general social or vocational capabilities; further, the American

Psychological Association urges all mental-health professionals to take the lead in removing the stigma of mental illness that has long been associated with homosexual orientation. (Conger, 1975, 633)

We live in exciting times as we witness the fast-paced changes occurring throughout many parts of the world. Gay rights have never been more strongly acknowledged than today. Many heterosexual people have woken up—they finally appreciate that we are decent people who have been given a bum rap since the beginning of modern history. We are at the beginning of what will someday be the end of the mental and spiritual abuse of gay people. I am so pleased to witness this in my lifetime.

This book has helped walk you through practical exercises and activities to help you build a positive gay identity. As you have seen through the anecdotes in Chapters 1 through 16, and through your own life, there is no substitute for developing a positive gay identity. Each of us is unique and builds an identity that fits who we are. Consequently, no two gay people are exactly alike. What is important is that you can fully appreciate and love the person you are becoming. When you love yourself, you will become more loving of everyone around you.

I hope you have enjoyed reading this book, and more importantly, I hope you have gained something useful from it. If you haven't noticed, there is no other book on the market like this one. This is the book I needed to read after I came out. E-mail me at alderson@ucalgary.ca if you have suggestions for how the second edition of this book might be improved. I would love to hear from you.

I am still learning what it means to have a positive gay identity because new challenges face me everyday, as they do you. We never arrive—we just keep moving closer to a destination off in the mirage. Our growth must never end.

REFERENCES

Alderson, K. (2000). *Beyond Coming Out: Experiences of Positive Gay Identity.* Toronto, ON: Insomniac Press.

Allen, D. (2002, January 22). "Gay Marriage Worldwide: 2001 Was a Year of Small But Numerous Victories for Same-Sex Partner Rights." *The Advocate.* 22.

Allen, D. J., & Oleson, T. (1999). "Shame and Internalized Homophobia in Gay Men." *Journal of Homosexuality*, 37(3), 33-43.

Associated Press. (2001, June 28). "London to Recognize Same-Sex Unions." Associated Press Online.

Associated Press (2002, May 17). "Sweden to Outlaw Anti-Gay Hate Speech." http://www.gay.com/news/article.html?2002/05/17/3

Auld, A. (2001, July 10). "Ruling Approves Same-Sex Adoptions." *St. Johns Telegram* (Final ed.).

Badget, M. V. L. (1995). "The Wage Effects of Sexual Orientation Discrimination." *Industrial and Labor Relations Review*, 48, 726-739.

Bagley, C., & Tremblay, P. (1998). "On the Prevalence of Homosexuality and Bisexuality, in a Random Community Survey of 750 Men Aged 18 to 27." *Journal of Homosexuality*, 36(2), 1-18.

Barber, J. S., & Mobley, M. (1999). "Counselling Gay Adolescents." A. M. Horne, M. S. Kiselica, et al. (Eds.), *Handbook of Counselling Boys and Adolescent Males: A Practitioner's Guide*. Thousand Oaks, CA: Sage Publications, 161-178.

Bartlett, J. (1992). *Familiar Quotations.* Toronto: Little-Brown.

Beane, J. (1981). "'I'd rather be dead than gay'": Counselling Gay Men Who Are Coming Out." *The Personnel and Guidance Journal*, 60, 222-226.

Beard, J., & Glickauf-Hughes, C. (1994). "Gay Identity and Sense of Self: Rethinking Male Homosexuality." *Journal of Gay & Lesbian Psychotherapy*, 2(2), 21-37.

"Belgian Government Approves Gay Marriage Bill. (2001, June 23). AP Worldstream.

Bell, A. P., and Weinberg, M. S. (1978). *Homosexualities: A Study of Diversity Among Men and Women*. New York: Simon and Schuster.

Ben-Ari, A. (1995). "The Discovery That an Offspring Is Gay: Parents', Gay Men's, and Lesbians' Perspectives." *Journal of Homosexuality*, 30(1), 89-112.

Ben-Ari, A. T. (1998). "An Experiential Attitude Change: Social Work Students and Homosexuality." *Journal of Homosexuality*, 36(2), 59-71.

Blumenfeld, W. J., & Raymond, D. (1993). *Looking at Gay and Lesbian Life* (updated and expanded.) Boston: Beacon Press.

Bohan, J. S. (1996). *Psychology and Sexual Orientation: Coming to Terms*. New York: Routledge.

Borhek, M. V. (1993). *Coming Out to Parents: A Two-Way Survival Guide for*

Lesbians and Gay Men and Their Parents. Cleveland: Pilgrim Press.

Boxer, A. M., Cook, J. A., & Herdt, G. (1991). "Double Jeopardy: Identity Transitions and Parent-Child Relations Among Gay and Lesbian Youth." In K. Pillemer & K. McCartney (Eds.), *Parent-Child Relations Throughout Life*. New Jersey: Lawrence Erlbaum Associates, 59-92.

Brooke, J. (2000, July 3). "Gay and Lesbian Scouts Received With Open Arms in Tolerant Canada." *San Francisco Chronicle*. www.commondreams.org/headlines/070300-02.htm

Bryant, S., & Demian (1994). "Relationship Characteristics of American Gay and Lesbian Couples: Findings From a National Survey." *Journal of Gay and Lesbian Social Services*, 1, 101-117.

Bueckert, D. (2002, January 29). "Government Should Remove Restrictions on Same-Sex Marriage, Says Study." Canadian Press Newswire.

Bunner, P. (2000). "'Are You, Er, Married?'" New Year, For the First Time Anywhere, the Canadian Census Will Count Homosexual Households." *Report Newsmagazine*, 27(9), 16-17.

Buxton, A. P. (1994). *The Other Side of the Closet: The Coming-Out Crisis for Straight Spouses and Families* (revised and expanded). Toronto: John Wiley & Sons.

Canadian Press. (2001, October 25). "Montreal's Gay Community Says 2006 Gay Games to Bring Dollars, Exposure."

Canadian Press. (2002a, June 12). "Blessing Gay Unions Back on the Table."

Canadian Press. (2002b, June 7). "Manitoba Bill Allows Gay Couples to Adopt." Globe and Mail

Canadian Press Newswire. (2000a, March 26). "Bulletproof Vest Protects Winnipeg's Gay Mayor Against Threats.

Canadian Press Newswire. (2000b, June 4). "Gays and Lesbians in the Military Coming Out to Form Social Clubs."

Centers for Disease Control and Prevention. (2001, January 31). "HIV and its Transmission." www.cdc.gov/hiv/pubs/facts/transmission.htm.

Chaplin, J. P. (1975). *Dictionary of Psychology* (Rev. ed.). New York: Dell.

Chojnacki, J. T., & Gelberg, S. (1995). "The Facilitation of a Gay/Lesbian/Bisexual Support-Therapy Group by Heterosexual Counselors." *Journal of Counseling & Development*, 73, 352-354.

Chuang, K. (1999). "Using Chopsticks to Eat Steak." *Journal of Homosexuality*, 36(3-4), 29-41.

Cochran, S. D. (2001). "Emerging Issues in Research on Lesbians' and Gay Men's Mental Health: Does Sexual Orientation Really Matter?" *American Psychologist*, 56, 931-947.

Cody, P. J., & Welch, P. L. (1997). "Rural Gay Men in Northern New England: Life Experiences and Coping Styles." *Journal of Homosexuality*, 33(1), 51-67

Coleman, E. (1981-82). "Developmental Stages of the Coming Out Process." *Journal of Homosexuality*, 7(2-3), 31-43.

Colgan, P. (1987). "Treatment of Identity and Intimacy Issues in Gay Males." *Journal of Homosexuality*, 14, 101-123.

Conger, J. J. (1975). "Proceedings of the American Psychological Association for the Year 1974: Minutes of the Annual Meeting of the Council of Representatives." *American Psychologist*, 30, 620-651.

Contemporary Canadian Biographies. (2001, November). "Glen Murray: Mayor of Winnipeg, Manitoba."

Cooley, J. J. (1998). "Gay and Lesbian Adolescents: Presenting Problems and the Counselor's Role." *Professional School Counseling*, 1(3), 30-34.

Cotter, J. (2002, May 8). "Alberta to Give Same-Sex Couples Similar Rights as Married Couples." *St. Johns Telegram* (Final ed.), A7.

Croteau, J. M., Anderson, M. Z., Distefano, T. M., & Kampa-Kokesch, S. (2000). "Lesbian, Gay, and Bisexual Vocational Psychology: Reviewing Foundations and Planning Construction." R. M. Perez, K. A. Debord, & K. J. Bieschke (Eds.), *Handbook of Counseling and Psychotherapy With Lesbian, Gay, and Bisexual Clients*. Washington: American Psychological Association, 383-403.

D'Augelli, A. R. (1991). "Gay Men in College: Identity Processes and Adaptations." *Journal of College Student Development*, 32, 140-146.

Drescher, J. (1998). "I'm Your Handyman: A History of Reparative Therapies." *Journal of Homosexuality*, 36(1), 19-42.

DuBay, W. H. (1987). *Gay Identity: The Self Under Ban*. Jefferson, NC: McFarland.

Dunkle, J. H., & Francis, P. L. (1996). "'Physical attractiveness stereotype'" and the Attribution of Homosexuality Revisited." *Journal of Homosexuality*, 30(3), 13-29.

"Dutch Statistic Bureau Reports 50,000 Gay Couples Living Together." (2002, June 4). AP Worldstream.

Dworkin, S. H. (2000). "Individual Therapy with Lesbian, Gay, and Bisexual Clients." R. M. Perez, K. A. Debord, & K. J. Bieschke (Eds.), *Handbook of Counseling and Psychotherapy with Lesbian, Gay, and Bisexual Clients*. Washington, DC: American Psychological Association, 157-182.

Dworkin, S. H., & Gutierrez, F. (1989). Introduction to special issue. "Counselors be Aware: Clients Come in Every Size, Shape, Color, and Sexual Orientation." *Journal of Counseling and Development*, 68, 6-8.

Egale. (2002). Home page (web site). www.egale.ca.

Elliott, J. E. (1993). "Career Development with Lesbian and Gay Clients." *Career Development Quarterly*, 41, 210-226.

Ellis, A. L., & Mitchell, R. W. (2000). "Sexual Orientation." L. T. Szuchman & F. Muscarella (Eds.), *Psychological Perspectives on Human Sexuality*. New York: John Wiley & Sons, 196-231.

Ellis, A. L., & Riggle, E. D. B. (1995). "The Relation of Job Satisfaction and Degree of Openness About One's Sexual Orientation for Lesbians and Gay Men. *Journal of Homosexuality*, 30(2), 75-85.

"Equal Marriage for Same Sex Couples." (2002). Equality & Marriage: In Canada. www.samesexmarriage.ca/equality/incanada.html

Falk, P. J. (1993). "Lesbian Mothers: Psychosocial Assumptions in Family Law." L. D. Garnets & D. C. Kimmel (Eds.), *Psychological Perspectives on Lesbian and Gay Male Experiences* . New York: Columbia University Press, 420-436.

Fassinger, R. E. (1995). "From Invisibility to Integration: Lesbian Identity in the Workplace." *Career Development Quarterly*, 44, 148-167.

Fassinger, R. E., & Miller, B. A. (1996). "Validation of an Inclusive Model of Sexual Minority Identity Formation on a Sample of Gay Men." *Journal of Homosexuality*, 32(2), 53-78.

Fontaine, J. H. (1998). "Evidencing a Need: School Counselors' Experiences with Gay and Lesbian Students." *Professional School Counseling*, 1(3), 8-14.

Frable, D. E. S., Wortman, C., & Joseph, J. (1997). "Predicting Self-Esteem, Well-Being, and Distress in a Cohort of Gay Men: The Importance of Cultural Stigma, Personal Visibility, Community Networks, and Positive Identity." *Journal of Personality*, 65(3), 599-624.

Friedman, R. C., & Downey, J. I. (1999). "Internalized Homophobia and Gender-Valued Self-Esteem in the Psychoanalysis of Gay Patients." *Psychoanalytic Review*, 86(3), 325-347.

Gallagher, J. (1998, August 18). "Gay Athletes Through History." *The Advocate*.

Gamson, J. (1995). "Must Identity Movements Self-Destruct? A Queer Dilemma." *Social Problems*, 42, 390-407.

Garnets, L., Herek, G.M., & Levy, B. (1990). "Violence and Victimization of Lesbians and Gay Men: Mental Health Consequences." *Journal of Interpersonal Violence*, 5, 366-383.

Garnets, L. D., & Kimmel, D. C. (1993). "Introduction: Lesbian and Gay Male Dimensions in the Psychological Study of Human Diversity." L. D. Garnets & D. C. Kimmel (Eds.), *Psychological Perspectives on Lesbian and Gay Male Experiences*. New York: Columbia University Press, 1-51.

"Gay Age of Consent to Fall to 16." (2001, August 3). *The Australian*.

"Gay Man to Lead Bush AIDS Fight." (2001, April 11). *The Australian*.

Ginsberg, R. W. (1998). "Silenced Voices Inside our Schools." *Initiatives*, 58(3), 1-15.

Golden, C. (1987). "Diversity and Variability in Women's Sexual Identities." The Boston Lesbian Psychologies Collective (Eds.), *Lesbian psychologies: Explorations and Challenges* . Urbana, IL: University of Illinois Press, 18-34.

Goldfried, M. R., & Goldfried, A. P. (2001). "The Importance of Parental Support in the Lives of Gay, Lesbian, and Bisexual Individuals." *In Session: Psychotherapy in Practice*, 57, 681-693.

Gonsiorek, J. C. (1982). "Results of Psychological Testing on Homosexual Populations." *American Behavioral Scientist*, 25, 385-396.

Gonsiorek, J. C. (1993). "Mental Health Issues of Gay and Lesbian Adolescents." L. D. Garnets & D. C. Kimmel (Eds.), *Psychological Perspectives on Lesbian and*

Gay Male Experiences . New York: Columbia University Press, 469-485.

Grodi, R. H. (1995). "The Experience of Personal Freedom." (Doctoral dissertation, Union Institute, 1995). Dissertation Abstracts International, 56(02), 1089B.

Haldeman, D. C. (1994). "The Practice and Ethics of Sexual Orientation Conversion Therapy." *Journal of Consulting and Clinical Psychology*, 62, 221-227.

Harmon, L. W., Hansen, J. C., Borgen, F. H., & Hammer, A. L. (1994). *Strong Interest Inventory: Applications and Technical Guide*. Stanford, CA: Stanford University Press.

Hart, J. (1981). "Self and Professional Help." J. Hart & D. Richardson (Eds.), *The Theory and Practice of Homosexuality* . Boston, MA: Routledge & Kegan Paul, 128-138.

Hart, T. A., & Heimberg, R. G. (2001). "Presenting Problems Among Treatment-Seeking Gay, Lesbian, and Bisexual Youth." *In Session: Psychotherapy in Practice*, 57, 615-627.

Hekma, G. (1998). "'As Long as They Don't Make an Issue of It...': Gay Men and Lesbians in Organized Sports in the Netherlands." *Journal of Homosexuality*, 35(1), 1-23.

Helminiak, D. A. (1994). *What the Bible Really Says about Homosexuality*. San Francisco: Alamo Square Press.

Herdt, G. (1997). *Same Sex, Different Cultures*. Boulder, CO: Westview Press.

Herring, R. D. (1998). *Career Counseling in Schools: Multicultural and Developmental Perspectives*. Alexandria, VA: American Counseling Association.

Herrman, B. (1990). *Being—being happy—Being Gay*. San Francisco: Alamo Square Press.

Hershberger, S. L., & D'Augelli, A. R. (1995). "The Impact of Victimization on the Mental Health and Suicidality of Lesbian, Gay, and Bisexual Youths." *Developmental Psychology*, 31, 65-74.

Hetrick, E. S., & Martin, A. D. (1987). "Developmental Issues and their Resolution for Gay and Lesbian Adolescents." *Journal of Homosexuality*, 14(1-2), 25-43.

Human Resources Development Canada. (2002). "Are you living in a same-sex or opposite-sex common-law relationship?" www.hrdc-drhc.gc.ca/isp/common/inpay_e.shtml

Isay, R. A. (1996). *Becoming Gay: The Journey to Self-Acceptance*. New York: Pantheon Books.

Jacobs, J. A., & Tedford, W. H. (1980). "Factors Affecting the Self-Esteem of the Homosexual Individual." *Journal of Homosexuality*, 5, 373-381.

Jones, A. J. (1997). "Truth and Deception in AIDS Information Brochures." *Journal of Homosexuality*, 32(3-4), 37-75.

Jourard, S. M. (1968). *Disclosing Man to Himself*. New York: Van Nostrad.

Kalat, J. W. (1990). *Introduction to Psychology* (2nd. ed.). Belmont, CA: Wadsworth Publishing.

Karlen, A. (1980). "Homosexuality in History." J. Marmor (Ed.), *Homosexual*

Behavior. New York: Basic Books, 75-99.

Katz, J. N. (1990). "The Invention of Heterosexuality." *Socialist Review*, 20(1), 7-34.

Kielwasser, A. P., & Wolf, M. A. (1993-94). "Silence, Difference, and Annihilation: Understanding the Impact of Mediated Heterosexism on High School Students." *High School Journal*, 77(1-2), 58-79.

Kitzinger, C., & Wilkinson, S. (1995). "Transitions from Heterosexuality to Lesbianism: The Discursive Production of Lesbian Identities." *Developmental Psychology*, 31, 95-104.

Klamen, D. L., Grossman, L. S., & Kopacz, D. R. (1999). "Medical Student Homophobia." *Journal of Homosexuality*, 37(1), 53-63.

Klein, F., Sepekoff, B., & Wolf, T. J. (1985). "Sexual Orientation: A Multi-Variable Dynamic Process." *Journal of Homosexuality*, 11(1-2), 35-49.

Kottman, T., Lingg, M., & Tisdell, T. (1995). "Gay and Lesbian Adolescents: Implications for Adlerian Therapists." *Individual Psychology*, 51, 115-128.

Kroger, J. (1996). *Identity in Adolescence: The Balance Between Self and Other* (2nd ed.). New York: Routledge.

Laghi, B. (1998, April 11). "Rage Finds its Voice in Alberta. *Globe and Mail*, A1, A4.

Lamb, M. (1998). "Cybersex: Research Notes on the Characteristics of the Visitors to OnlineChat Rooms." *Deviant Behavior*, 19(2), 121-135.

Lee, J. A. (1977). "Going Public: A Study in the Sociology of Homosexual Liberation." *Journal of Homosexuality*, 3, 49-78.

Leserman, J., DiSantostefano, R., Perkins, D. O., & Evans, D. L. (1994). "Gay Identification and Psychological Health in HIV-positive and HIV-negative Gay Men." *Journal of Applied Social Psychology*, 24, 2193-2208.

Lloyd, J. (2002). "Employment Benefits for Gay and Lesbian Employees." *Law Now*, 26(4), 29-32.

"London to Recognize Same-Sex Unions." (2001, June 28). Associated Press Online.

Malyon, A. K. (1982a). "Biphasic Aspects of Homosexual Identity Formation." *Psychotherapy: Theory, Research, and Practice*, 19, 335-340.

Malyon, A. K. (1982b). "Psychotherapeutic Implications of Internalized Homophobia in Gay Men." *Journal of Homosexuality*, 7(2-3), 59-69.

Marinoble, R. M. (1998). "Homosexuality: A Blind Spot in the School Mirror." *Professional School Counseling*, 1(3), 4-7.

Martin, A. D. (1982). "Learning to Hide: The Socialization of the Gay Adolescent." *Adolescent Psychiatry*, 10, 52-65.

Martin, April. (1982). "Some Issues in the Treatment of Gay and Lesbian Patients." *Psychotherapy: Theory, Research and Practice*, 19, 341-348.

Mays, V. M., & Cochran, S. D. (2001). "Mental Health Correlates of Perceived Discrimination Among Lesbian, Gay, and Bisexual Adults in the United States." *American Journal of Public Health*, 91, 1869-1876.

McFarland, W. P. (1993). "A Developmental Approach to Gay and Lesbian Youth." *Journal of Humanistic Education and Development*, 32, 17-29.

Mellgren, D. (2002). "Norway's Finance Minister Marries his Gay Partner. AP Worldstream.

Merriam-Webster's Collegiate Dictionary (10th ed.). (1996). Springfield, MA: Merriam-Webster.

Money, J. (1988). *Gay, Straight, and In-between: The Sexology of Erotic Orientation.* New York: Oxford University Press.

Morin, S. F. (1977). "Heterosexual Bias in Psychological Research on Lesbianism and Male Homosexuality." *American Psychologist*, 32, 629-637.

Morin, S. F., & Rothblum, E. D. (1991). "Removing the Stigma: Fifteen Years of Progress." *American Psychologist*, 9, 947-949.

Morrison, L. L., & L'Heureux, J. (2001). "Suicide and Gay/Lesbian/Bisexual Youth: Implications for Clinicians." *Journal of Adolescence*, 24, 39-49.

Morrow, S. L. (1997). "Career Development of Lesbian and Gay Youth: Effects of Sexual Orientation, Coming Out, and Homophobia." *Journal of Gay and Lesbian Social Services*, 7(4), 1-15.

Murphy, T. F. (1992a). "Freud and Sexual Reorientation Therapy." *Journal of Homosexuality*, 23(3), 21-38.

Murphy, T. (1992b). "Redirecting Sexual Orientation: Techniques and Justifications." *Journal of Sex Research*, 29, 501-523.

Nauta, M. M., Saucier, A. M., & Woodard, L. E. (2001). "Interpersonal Influences on Students' Academic and Career Decisions: The Impact of Sexual Orientation." *Career Development Quarterly*, 49, 352-362.

Nelson, C. M. (2001, March 1). "Southern Methodist University to Extend Benefits to Gay Workers' Partners. *Dallas Morning News*.

New American Standard Master Study Bible. (1981). Nashville, TN: Holman Bible Publishers.

Nicolosi, J., Byrd, A. D., & Potts, R. W. (2000b). "Retrospective Self-Reports of Changes in Homosexual Orientation: A Consumer Survey of Conversion Therapy Clients." *Psychological Reports*, 86, 1071-1088.

Norton, J. L. (1995). "The Gay, Lesbian, Bisexual Populations." N. A. Vacc & S. B. DeVaney (Eds.), *Experiencing and Counseling Multicultural and Diverse Populations* (3rd ed.). Philadelphia, PA: Accelerated Development, 147-177.

O'Neill, T. (2002, May 13). "Gays Win, Christians Lose." *Newsmagazine* (Alberta ed.), 29(10), 43.

Olson, E. D., & King, C. A. (1995). "Gay and Lesbian Self-Identification: A Response to Rotheram-Borus and Fernandez." *Suicide and Life-Threatening Behavior*, 25, supplement 95, 35-39.

Otis, M. D., & Skinner, W. F. (1996). "The Prevalence of Victimization and its Effects on Mental Well-Being Among Lesbian and Gay People." *Journal of Homosexuality*, 30(3), 93-121.

Peplau, L. A. (1993). "Lesbian and Gay Relationships." L. D. Garnets & D. C. Kimmel (Eds.), *Psychological Perspectives on Lesbian and Gay Male Experiences.*

New York: Columbia University Press, 395-419.

Percy, W. A., III (1996). *Pederasty and Pedagogy in Archaic Greece*. Chicago: University of Illinois Press.

Petrow, S., & Steele, N. (1995). *The Essential Book of Gay Manners and Etiquette*. New York: HarperCollins.

Philipp, S. F. (1999). "Gay and Lesbian Tourists at a Southern U.S.A. Beach Event." *Journal of Homosexuality*, 37(3), 69-86.

Pope, M. S., Prince, J. P., & Mitchell, K. (2000). "Responsible Career Counseling with Lesbian and Gay Students." D. A. Luzzo (Ed.), *Career Counseling of College Students: An Empirical Guide to Strategies That Work*. Washington, DC: American Psychological Association, 262-282.

PrideVisionTV. (2002). Home page. www.pridevisiontv.com

Prochaska, J. O., Norcross, J. C., & Diclemente, C. C. (1994). *Changing for Good: Revolutionary Six-Stage Program for Overcoming Bad Habits and Moving Your Life Positively Forward*. New York: Avon.

Radkowsky, M., & Siegel, L. J. (1997). "The Gay Adolescent: Stressors, Adaptations, and Psychosocial Interventions." *Clinical Psychology Review*, 17(2), 191-216.

Richardson, D. (1993). "Recent Challenges to Traditional Assumptions About Homosexuality: Some Implications for Practice." L. D. Garnets & D. C. Kimmel (Eds.), *Psychological Perspectives on Lesbian and Gay Male Experiences*. New York: Columbia University Press, 117-129.

Risdon, C., Cook, D., & Willmns, D. (2000). "Gay and Lesbian Physicians in Training: A Qualitative Study." *Canadian Medical Association* Journal, 162, 331-334.

Risman, B., & Schwartz, P. (1988). "Sociological Research on Male and Female Homosexuality." *Annual Review of Sociology*, 14, 125-147.

Rogers, C. R. (1961). *On Becoming a Person: A Therapist's View of Psychotherapy*. Cambridge, MA: Riverside Press.

Rothblum, E. D. (1994). "'I Only Read About Myself on Bathroom Walls: The Need for Research on the Mental Health of Lesbians and Gay Men." *Journal of Consulting and Clinical Psychology*, 62, 213-220.

Rothblum, E. D., & Factor, R. (2001). "Lesbians and Their Sisters as a Control Group: Demographic and Mental Health Factors." *Psychological Science*, 12, 63-69.

Rotheram-Borus, M. J., Murphy, D. A., Kennedy, M., Stanton, A., & Kuklinski, M. (2001). "Health and Risk Behaviors Over Time Among Youth Living with HIV." *Journal of Adolescence*, 24, 791-802.

Russell, S. T., Seif, H., & Truong, N. L. (2001). "School Outcomes of Sexual Minority Youth in the United States: Evidence from a National Study." *Journal of Adolescence*, 24, 111-127.

Russell, T. G. (1989). "AIDS Education, Homsexuality, and the Counselor's Role. *The School Counsellor*, 36, 333-337.

Rutledge, L. W. 1987). *The Gay Book of Lists*. Boston, MA: Alyson.

Sapp, J. (2001). "Self-Knowing as Social Justice: The Impact of a Gay Professor on Ending Homophobia in Education." *Encounter: Education forMeaning and Social Justice*, 14(4), 17-28.

Savin-Williams, R. C. (1989). "Coming Out to Parents and Self-Esteem Among Gay and Lesbian Youth." *Journal of Homosexuality*, 18(1-2), 1-35.

Savin-Williams, R. C. (1994). "Verbal and Physical Abuse as Stressors in the Lives of Lesbian, Gay Male, and Bisexual Youths: Associations with School Problems, Running Away, Substance Abuse, Prostitution, and Suicide." *Journal of Consulting and Clinical Psychology*, 62, 261-269.

Savin-Williams, R. C. (2001). "A Critique of Research on Sexual-Minority Youth." *Journal of Adolescence*, 24, 5-13.

Savin-Williams, R. C., & Dube, E. M. (1998). "Parental Reactions to their Child's Disclosure of a Gay/Lesbian Identity." *Family Relations*, 47(1), 7-13.

Schafer, S. (1976). "Sexual and Social Problems of Lesbians." *The Journal of Sex Research*, 12, 50-69.

Seguin, R. (2002, June 8). "Gay Couples in Quebec Get Full Parental Rights." *Globe and Mail* (Print ed.), A1.

Sell, R. L. (1996). "The Sell Assessment of Sexual Orientation: Background and scoring." *Journal of Gay, Lesbian, and Bisexual Identity*, 1, 295-309.

Senate OKs omnibus DP. (2000, June 22). www.groovyannies.com/news/2000/press45.html

SF AIDS Foundation. (1998, December 15). How HIV is spread. www.sfaf.org/aids101/transmission.html.

Shannon, J. W., & Woods, W. J. (1991). "Affirmative Psychotherapy for Gay Men." *The Counseling Psychologist*, 19(2), 197-215.

Shively, M., & De Cecco, J. P. (1977). "Components of Sexual Identity." *Journal of Homosexuality*, 3, 41-48.

Siegel, S., & Lowe, E. (1994). *Uncharted Lives: Understanding the Life Passages of Gay Men*. New York: Plume.

Silverstein, C., & Picano, F. (1992). *The New Joy of Gay Sex*. New York: HarperCollins.

Simonsen, G., Blazina, C., & Watkins, C. E. (2000). "Gender Role Conflict and Psychological Well-Being Among Gay Men." *Journal of Counseling Psychology*, 47, 85-89.

Slater, B. R. (1988). "Essential Issues in Working with Lesbian and Gay Male Youths." *Professional Psychology: Research and Practice*, 19(2), 226-235.

Smith, R. B., & Brown, R. A. (1997). "The Impact of Social Support on Gay Male Couples." *Journal of Homosexuality*, 33(2), 39-61.

Sternberg, R. J. (1986). "A Triangular Theory of Love." *Psychological Review*, 93, 119-135.

Strang, J., Griffiths, P., & Gossop, M. (1997). "Heroin Smoking by 'Chasing the Dragon': Origins and History." *Addiction*, 92, 673-683.

Strickland, B. R. (1995). "Research on Sexual Orientation and Human Development: A Commentary." *Developmental Psychology,* 31, 137-140.

"Sweden's Parliament Approves Proposal Letting Same-Sex Couples Adopt Children." (2002, June 5). AP Worldstream.

Telljohann, S., Price, J., Poureslami, M., & Easton, A. (1995). "Teaching About Sexual Orientation by Secondary Health Teachers." *Journal of School Health,* 65(1), 18-22.

Tremblay, P. J. (1994, November). *The Gay, Lesbian and Bisexual Factor in the Youth Suicide Problem.* Unpublished manuscript.

Troiden, R. R. (1984-85). "Self, Self-Concept, Identity, and Homosexual Identity: Constructs in Need of Definition and Differentiation." *Journal of Homosexuality,* 10(3-4), 97-109.

Underwood, N. (2002, January 21). "Queer as Mainstream: Returning for Season Two, *Queer as Folk* has a Long Heterosexual Following." *Macleans,* 115(3), pp. 42, 44.

Unks, G. (Ed.). (1995). *The Gay Teen: Educational Practice and Theory for Lesbian, Gay and Bisexual Adolescents.* New York: Routledge.

Valocchi, S. (1999). "The Class Inflected Nature of Gay Identity." *Social Problems,* 46(2), 207-224.

Vargo, M. E. (1998). *Acts of Disclosure: The Coming-Out Process of Contemporary Gay Men.* Binghamton, NY: Harrington Park Press.

Vilanch, B. (2002, March 19). "Gay Enough for You?" *The Advocate,* p. 49.

Violette, R. J. (2001, October 15). "Gay Men, Straight Jobs." [Review of the book *Gay Men, Straight Jobs*]. *Library Journal,* 126(17), 98.

Waldo, C. R., & Kemp, J. L. (1997). "Should I Come Out to my Students? An empirical Investigation." *Journal of Homosexuality,* 34(2), 79-94.

Walsh, A. L. (1998). "'My secret life': The Emergence of One Gay Man's Authentic Identity." The American Journal of Occupational Therapy, 52, 563-569.

Weiten, W., & Lloyd, M. (2000). *Psychology Applied to Modern Life: Adjustment at the Turn of the Century.* Stamford, CT: Wadsworth.

Wills, G., & Crawford, R. (2000). "Attitudes Toward Homosexuality in Shreveport-Bossier City, Louisiana." *Journal of Homosexuality,* 38(3), 97-116.

Wood, O. (n.d.). "The Fight for Gay Rights: World Timeline." www.cbc.ca/news/indepth/background/gayrights2.html

Yip, A. K. T. (1997). "Attacking the Attacker: Gay Christians Talk Back." *The British Journal of Sociology,* 48, 113-127.

Appendix A
How Do I Know If I Am Gay?

Sexual orientation is an ill-defined term, and it often means different things to different people. The majority of researchers define it as a combination of sexual behaviour and sexual fantasies (Sell, 1996), but it is probably more complex than this (Klein, Sepekoff, & Wolf, 1985).

The key to sexual orientation is who you have the propensity (or predisposition) to fall in love with. If you can only fall in love romantically with people of the same gender, you have a homosexual orientation, and it makes sense for you to adopt a gay identity to go with it. If you can fall in love romantically with members of either gender, you have a bisexual orientation. Finally, if you can only fall in love with the opposite gender, you have a heterosexual orientation. Obviously, it takes time to know who you can fall in love with. However, most gay men typically report knowing about their same-sex affections during early adolescence. (D'Augelli, 1991). In at least in one sample of 202 gay and lesbian young people attending a youth group, aged 14 to 21, the majority were not confused about their sexual orientation (Boxer, Cook, & Herdt, 1991), suggesting that many young people are able to accurately define their sexual orientation during adolescence.

Especially when you are young, you don't want to attribute too much importance to having sex with either gender, unless you feel passionate feelings of love toward that person. Then, depending on the gender of the individual, you will gain a sense of whether you have a homosexual, heterosexual or bisexual orientation. Knowing that you have a bisexual orientation probably takes the most time because it requires you to have fallen in love romantically with both genders.

The fact is, we can have sex with anybody and practically anything, so the sex act per se says little about our sexual orientation. If you find yourself in a situation where you end up having sex with someone you didn't think you would have sex with, don't be hard on yourself. Instead, listen to your heart—it is the guide that leads you to knowing your sexual orientation.

Below are some questions to ask yourself which may help you determine your sexual orientation. If you can't answer them yet, it means you aren't ready to make a decision. In this case, don't define your sexuality. When people ask, tell them you don't know yet, or call yourself queer, or bi-curious. Neither of these terms puts a lasting label on you.

1. "If I lived on an uninhabited island by myself and one other person, would I want to have a male or a female with me?"
2. "When I fantasize about having sex, which gender do I fantasize having sex

with?"

3. "Who turns me on?"
4. "Do I feel sexually attracted to both good-looking men and women?"
5. "Who would I like to have sex with?"
6. "Do I enjoy having sex with women as much as having sex with men?"
7. "With which gender is sex more exciting?"
8. "When I am masturbating, what proportion of my sexual fantasies include males, and what proportion include females?"
9. "Do most of my sexual dreams have homosexual content or heterosexual content?"
10. "What proportion of my crushes have been with males compared to females?"
11. "Do I believe I have ever fallen in love romantically with someone?"
    (a) If YES, "With which gender or genders have I fallen in love romantically? Do I believe I have control over who I have fallen in love with romantically?"
    (b) If NO, "With which gender or genders do I envision falling in love romantically in the future?" Also ask this question if you believe you have fallen in love romantically before.

If your answers to the questions above are pointed exclusively toward the same gender, and you are at least 21 years old, you are likely gay. Although choosing the age of 21 is somewhat arbitrary, research indicates that sexual orientation develops early for most gay men (Strickland, 1995), and that once established is relatively fixed and unchanging (Friedman & Downey, 1999; Herring, 1998).

Identity development is the most important task of adolescence (Kroger, 1996). By age 18, most people develop stable career interests (Harmon, Hansen, Borgen, & Hammer, 1994), which is another aspect of identity development. By late adolescence, the conditions are right for a person to develop a stable sense of identity (Weiten & Lloyd, 2000).

Appendix B
Choosing a Therapist

If you are gay, you need to find a therapist who is gay or gay-positive. Because we were all raised in a culture that has traditionally been unsupportive and judgmental of gay men and lesbian women, everyone needs to do inner work to overcome the influence of this negative conditioning. You cannot assume that most therapists have done this work. In fact, "heterosexist and homophobic attitudes continue to be prevalent in psychologists" (Morrison & L'Heureux, 2001, 43), and school counsellors do not fare any better (Russell, Seif, & Truong, 2001). Ideally, you would do best with a gay-affirmative therapist, someone who is gay-positive and who believes that gay status is equal to heterosexual status.

You also want to find a therapist who is well trained in his or her field of counselling. Below is a step-by-step guide to finding a gay-affirmative therapist who is competent.

1. Be aware of the proper credentials for a professional therapist. In most parts of theworld, anyone can call themselves a counsellor or therapist. It is up to the consumer to ensure that the person is properly qualified. Look for a therapist who has one of the following credentials:
   (a) Licensed psychiatrist—Psychiatrists are medical doctors who specialize in treating mental disorders. They have hospital admitting privileges (if you are really messed up, this may be occasionally needed) and they can prescribe psychotropic medication.
   (b) Licensed psychologist—Psychologists are not medical doctors, and therefore they do not have hospital privileges. With additional training, however, some jurisdictions do allow them to prescribe psychotropic medication. Their training requires attending graduate school for anywhere from two to six years following a baccalaureate degree. Becoming licensed requires that they complete an internship and successfully pass required exams.
   (c) Registered social worker—Social workers often have different levels of training. Ensure that the one you are thinking of seeing has at least a masters degree in clinical social work. Also be sure he or she is registered with the provincial or state social work association.
   (d) Certified counsellor—There are also certified counsellors in Canada and the United States. These individuals have a master's degree or doctorate in a counselling field, and become licensed by a national or federal certifying organization, such as the Canadian Counselling Association or the National Board for Certified Counselors in the US.

2. Get a recommendation if possible. If your city has a gay and lesbian information and referral service, it will likely be your best referral source to a gay-
affirmative therapist. You might also want to check with gay or lesbian friends
for a recommendation. Another source of referral is through the certifying
board or association for the particular type of professional you want to see.
For example, the provincial or state medical association could suggest a gay-
affirmative psychiatrist, just as the provincial or state psychological association could suggest a gay-affirmative psychologist.

3. Have some questions prepared and get them answered first. Regardless of how
you made contact with the professional counsellor, ask some questions before
you book your first appointment. Here are some sample questions:

   (a) Do you believe that a person's sexual orientation can be changed through
   therapy? If the answer is yes, then ask: "Do you provide conversion therapy to clients (or patients) who request it?"

   (b) Are you a gay-affirmative therapist? If the answer is yes, then ask: "What
   does being a gay-affirmative therapist mean to you?"

   (c) "What training or experience have you had in counselling gay men and/or
   lesbian women?"

The answer to these questions should help you decide if this therapist is right for
you. Finding the right therapist is like finding the right hairstylist. You need to shop
around until you find someone that you're compatible with. Be sure you feel some
connection with the person who is going to learn more about you than you have perhaps told anyone in your life. You're worth it.

Appendix C
Internet Resources

There are many Internet resources for gay men and lesbian women. Here are some that provide highly useful and accurate information:

1. www.gaycanada.com. This is the most comprehensive resource for Canadian gays and lesbians. It provides information about most of the resources available across the nation.
2. www.egale.ca. Provides a wealth of good information, including legal actions happening across Canada in the fight for equal rights for gays and lesbians.
3. www.gay.com. This American resource is outstanding. If you are travelling anywhere, the Ferrari guide available on this Web site will help you decide what to do, where to go, and where to stay.
4. www.pflag.ca/index2.htm. This is the official Web site for the Canadian division of Parents, Families, and Friends of Lesbians and Gays (P-FLAG), an organization dedicated to helping the other side of the closet (i.e., everyone you know who isn't gay or lesbian).
5. www.pflag.org. This is the American Web site for P-FLAG.
6. www.apa.org/about/division/div44.html. This is the division of the American Psychological Association (division 44) focused on the psychology of gays and lesbians. A great source of well-referenced, up-to-date information about us.

APPENDIX D
Recommended Readings

Alderson, K. (2000). *Beyond Coming Out: Experiences of Positive Gay Identity*. Toronto: Insomniac Press. Truly an outstanding book—if I do say so myself! This book is about 16 gay men and one gay male adolescent who have developed positive gay identities. It is ideal for gay men and gay male adolescents who want to understand what it means to have a positive gay identity through the experience of others. Each section also provides a careful look at what comprises the elements of a positive gay identity. I also tout Beyond Coming Out as the best book for heterosexual individuals who want to understand gay males better.

American Psychological Association. (2002). "Answers to Your Questions about Sexual Orientation and Homosexuality." www.apa.org/pubinfo/orient.html. This is an excellent brochure describing what we know about sexual orientation.

Blumenfeld, W. J., & Raymond, D. (1993). *Looking at Gay and Lesbian Life* (updated and expanded ed.). Boston: Beacon Press. This academic book reviews many aspects of gay and lesbian life based on what we know through actual research on the topic.

Bohan, J. S. (1996). *Psychology and Sexual Orientation: Coming to Terms*. New York: Routledge. The most comprehensive academic book I have seen on the topic of sexual orientation.

Clark, D. (1997). *Loving Someone Gay* (Rev. ed.). Berkeley, CA: Celestial Arts. The first edition of Clark's classic is the first book I ever read about gay people. It will help you love yourself more, and help others understand and appreciate you more.

Garnets, L. D., & Kimmel, D. C. (Eds.) (1993). *Psychological Perspectives on Lesbian and Gay Male Experiences*. New York: Columbia University Press. Another excellent academic book for those of you who want to study this further.

Helminiak, D. A. (1994). *What the Bible Really Says About Homosexuality*. San Francisco, CA: Alamo Square Press. If you are from a Christian background, this book will help open your eyes on this subject.

Herdt, G. (1997). *Same Sex, Different Cultures*. Boulder, CO: Westview Press. A wonderful book looking at the cross-cultural study of homosexuality.

Isay, R. A. (1996). *Becoming Gay: The Journey to Self-acceptance*. New York: Pantheon Books. Dr. Isay is a gay psychiatrist with plenty of experience in counselling gay people. An easy, interesting and informative read.

Kinsey, A. C., Pomeroy, W. B., & Martin, C. E. (1948). *Sexual Behavior in the Human Male*. Philadelphia: W. B. Saunders. This was the classic work that shocked the United States when it was released. More Americans were having sex, both heterosexual and otherwise, than people at the time wanted to believe.

Miller, N. (1995). *Out of the Past: Gay and Lesbian History From 1869 to the Present*. New York: Vintage. A good book if you want to know more about the history of gays and lesbians.

Money, J. (1988). *Gay, Straight, and In-between: The Sexology of Erotic Orientation*. New York: Oxford University Press. I couldn't put this book down once I started reading it. If you are interested in psychology, you'll love Money's work.

Townsend, J. M. (1998). *What Women Want—What Men Want: Why the Sexes Still See Love and Commitment So Differently*. New York: Oxford University Press. This book is not specifically about gays and lesbians, although they are included in Townsend's careful analysis of the research looking at sex differences between men and women.

Appendix E
Preventing HIV/AIDS Update

All sexual behaviour between two people that involves physical contact with contaminated semen, blood, vaginal secretions and breast milk carries some risk of HIV transmission (Centers for Disease Control and Prevention, 2001). That is why receptive anal sex is considered the highest risk sexual activity. The rigorousness of anal sex leaves the bowels open to minor hemorrhaging (bleeding), and the efficient absorption ability of the intestinal lining provides still more opportunity for contraction of the virus into the bloodstream. The penetrator is also at risk because of having contact with the receiver's blood.

Blood contains the highest concentration of the virus, followed by semen, followed by vaginal fluids. Breast milk can also contain a high concentration of the virus, but in this situation, transmissibility depends on WHO and HOW. An adult can ingest a small amount of breast milk at no probably risk. But an infant, with its very small body and newly forming immune system, consumes vast quantities of breast milk relative to its body weight. Therefore an infant is at risk from breast milk, whereas an adult may not be. (SF AIDS Foundation, 1998, 4)

Three conditions must be met for HIV transmission to occur:
1. HIV must be present—Infection can only happen if one of the persons involved is infected with HIV. Some people assume that certain behaviors (such as anal sex) cause AIDS, even if HIV is not present. This is not true.
2. In sufficient quantity—The concentration of HIV determines whether infection may happen. In blood, for example, the virus is very concentrated. A small amount of blood is enough to infect someone. A much larger amount of other fluids would be needed for HIV transmission.
3. It must get into the bloodstream—It is not enough to be in contact with an infected fluid to become infected. Healthy, unbroken skin does not allow HIV to get into the body; it is an excellent barrier to HIV infection. HIV can only enter through an open cut or sore, or through contact with the mucous membranes in the anus and rectum, the genitals, the mouth, and the eyes. (SF AIDS Foundation, 1998, 1-2)

Sexual Routes of Transmission
1. Sexual intercourse (vaginal and anal)—In the genitals and the rectum, HIV may infect the mucous membranes directly or enter through cuts and sores caused during intercourse (many of which would be unnoticed).
2. Oral sex (mouth-penis, mouth-vagina)—The mouth is an inhospitable environ-

ment for HIV (in semen, vaginal fluid or blood), meaning the risk of HIV transmission through the throat, gums, and oral membranes is lower than through vaginal or anal membranes. There are however documented cases where HIV was transmitted orally, so we can't say that getting HIV-infected semen, vaginal fluid or blood in the mouth is without risk.

3. Heterosexual transmission studies—It is evident, from epidemiological studies as well as common sense, that AIDS can be transmitted sexually between men and women. Several studies, usually with the female partners of hemophiliacs who have been infected, show that male to female sexual transmission does occur. This conclusion is supported by the statistics of women who have AIDS, whose only risk factor was sex with a man with AIDS or a man at risk for AIDS. Female to male transmission seems to be less efficient, but it certainly does occur. (SF AIDS Foundation, 1998, 5)

According to Jones (1997, 40), nearly all researchers in the U.S. subscribe to a model of AIDS that includes the following four propositions:

1. The continuity of HIV infection and AIDS. AIDS is the terminal stage of a single, slowly-unfolding disease process which begins with HIV infection.
2. The near certainty that HIV infection will result in AIDS. While the incubation period is highly variable, the probability is extremely high that HIV infection will eventually cause AIDS, unless medical treatments not yet discovered or death from other causes should intervene.
3. The lethality of AIDS. Although the life expectancy of individuals diagnosed with AIDS is highly variable, the probability is extremely high that AIDS will eventually cause death, unless medical treatments not yet discovered or death from other causes should intervene.
4. The importance of behavior rather than group membership in determining the risk of HIV infection. The sexual transmission of HIV is not determined by sexual orientation, but by sexual behavior. Unprotected sexual activity increases the risk of HIV infection for heterosexuals and homosexuals alike.

To date, there is no cure for HIV/AIDS. Do not deceive yourself into thinking that today's drug cocktails will save you. They prolong life, but they do not kill the virus that eventually causes AIDS.

If you are not thoroughly familiar with HIV/AIDS and how to prevent it, detailed information is available from the U.S. National Center for HIV, STD and TB Prevention at www.cdc.gov/hiv/dhap.htm. Another excellent Web site is www.sfaf.org/aids101/transmission.html.